THE SCOTS AFRIKANERS

Scottish Religious Cultures *Historical Perspectives*

Series Editors: Scott R. Spurlock and Crawford Gribben

Religion has played a key formational role in the development of Scottish society shaping cultural norms, defining individual and corporate identities, and underpinning legal and political institutions. This series presents the very best scholarship on the role of religion as a formative and yet divisive force in Scottish society and highlights its positive and negative functions in the development of the nation's culture. The impact of the Scots diaspora on the wider world means that the subject has major significance far outwith Scotland.

Available titles

George Mackay Brown and the Scottish Catholic Imagination
Linden Bicket

Poor Relief and the Church in Scotland, 1560–1650
John McCallum

Jewish Orthodoxy in Scotland: Rabbi Dr Salis Daiches and Religious Leadership
Hannah Holtschneider

Miracles of Healing: Psychotherapy and Religion in Twentieth-century Scotland
Gavin Miller

George Strachan of the Mearns: Seventeenth-century Orientalist
Tom McInally

Scottish Liturgical Traditions and Religious Politics: From Reformers to Jacobites, 1560–1764
Edited by Allan I. Macinnes, Patricia Barton and Kieran German

Dissent After Disruption: Church and State in Scotland, 1843–63
Ryan Mallon

Scottish Presbyterianism: The Case of Dunblane and Stirling, 1690–1710
Andrew Muirhead

The Scots Afrikaners: Identity Politics and Intertwined Religious Cultures in Southern and Central Africa
Retief Müller

Forthcoming titles

Dugald Semple and the Life Reform Movement
Steven Sutcliffe

The Dynamics of Dissent: Politics, Religion and the Law in Restoration Scotland
Neil McIntyre

The Catholic Church in Scotland: Financial Development 1772–1930
Darren Tierney

William Guild and Moderate Divinity in Early Modern Scotland
Russell Newton

Protestantism, Revolution and Scottish Political Thought: The European Context, 1637–1651
Karie Schultz

edinburghuniversitypress.com/series/src

THE SCOTS AFRIKANERS

Identity Politics and Intertwined Religious Cultures
in Southern and Central Africa

RETIEF MÜLLER

EDINBURGH
University Press

Edinburgh University Press is one of the leading university presses in the UK. We publish academic books and journals in our selected subject areas across the humanities and social sciences, combining cutting-edge scholarship with high editorial and production values to produce academic works of lasting importance. For more information visit our website: edinburghuniversitypress.com

© Retief Müller, 2022

Edinburgh University Press Ltd
The Tun – Holyrood Road
12 (2f) Jackson's Entry
Edinburgh EH8 8PJ

Typeset in 10/12 ITC New Baskerville by
Servis Filmsetting Ltd, Stockport, Cheshire

A CIP record for this book is available from the British Library

ISBN 978 1 4744 6295 2 (hardback)
ISBN 978 1 4744 6297 6 (webready PDF)
ISBN 978 1 4744 6298 3 (epub)

The right of Retief Müller to be identified as author of this work has been asserted in accordance with the Copyright, Designs and Patents Act 1988 and the Copyright and Related Rights Regulations 2003 (SI No. 2498).

Contents

Abbreviations	vi
Acknowledgements	vii
1 Introduction: Scots Influence on the Dutch Reformed People of South Africa	1
2 Scots in South African Dutch Pulpits in the Early to Middle Nineteenth Century	23
3 Scottish Ministers, Evangelical Revival and Church-based 'Apartheid'?	53
4 The Scottish (and American) Foundations of a Trans-frontier Afrikaner Missionary Enterprise	81
5 The South African War (1899–1902) and the Scots Afrikaners	108
6 Other(ing) Identity Formations: From Mission Field Ecumenism to Home Church Controversy	127
7 Afrikaner *Volkskerk* Ideologues and the Scots Afrikaners	154
8 Conclusion: The Scottish Legacy in Afrikaner Religiosity Reassessed	188
References	204
Index	216

Abbreviations

CCAP	Church of Central Africa Presbyterian
CSV	*Christelijke Strevers-Vereeniging*; also the student organisation and publisher *Christelijke Studentenvereniging*
DEIC	Dutch East India Company
DRC	Dutch Reformed Church
GMC	general mission commission
GK	Gereformeerde Kerke
GKSA	Gereformeerde Kerke in Suid Afrika
LMS	London Missionary Society
MMU	Ministers' Missionary Union
OFS	Orange Free State
PEMS	Paris Evangelical Missionary Society
SRP	Abbreviation for Strictly Reformed Patriot, a translation of a pseudonym for an author who wrote anonymously as *Streng Gereformeerde Patriot*
UMCA	Universities' Mission to Central Africa

Acknowledgements

Early in 2012, when I arrived in Stellenbosch to start a period of postdoctoral research, my fellowship's stipulations were sufficiently vague to allow for some creative interpretation. It mandated an exploration of connections between religion and human dignity in one way or another, but I could decide on the exact angle. Christian mission and missionaries had always fascinated me. I grew up hearing stories of Malawi and specifically Nkhoma, where my maternal grandfather was born and raised as a child of Dutch Reformed Church (DRC) missionaries. Academically, the history of mission was central to the PhD programme from which I graduated at Princeton Theological Seminary. So at Stellenbosch, where I not only had access to family collections relating to the DRC's missionary enterprise in wider Africa, but moreover to the extraordinarily well-managed and carefully preserved records of the DRC Archive, it seemed almost self-evident that I would focus my research on this very topic of the DRC's 'foreign' missionary enterprise and missionary interactions with Africans.

I give credit then in the first instance to an ancestral connection. The missionary parents of my grandfather, who was born at Nkhoma, were part of the Murray family, among the central cast of characters in this book. Secondly, I am thankful for the different academic studies and connections which enabled me to consider the Protestant missionary movement from a wide angle. I am especially indebted to the Hope Fellowship at Stellenbosch University, which through the above-mentioned postdoctoral appointment helped me to make initial inroads into a field of research that eventually led to this book, among other things.

When I was eventually appointed to teach church history at Stellenbosch, I found myself with an immediate incentive to make a connection between my already established interest in missionary narratives and the wider history of Christianity in southern Africa, which was my main teaching area. Conversations I had with several colleagues both at Stellenbosch and beyond, for example through interactions at the Church Historical Society of Southern Africa, shaped this general research trajectory in decisive ways. Connections between mission, nationalism and politics increasingly occupied my interest.

A key catalyst was my meeting and subsequent academic collaborations with Dr Scott Spurlock at the University of Glasgow. It was he who first suggested that my research on Scottish diasporic missionaries in southern and central Africa might be a good fit for the Scottish Religious Cultures book series at Edinburgh University Press. He also invited me to spend three months' worth of research leave at the University of Glasgow in 2017, which proved immeasurably helpful for research and writing the earlier drafts of a couple of the chapters that finally made it into this book.

I am extremely grateful to Pascal Pienaar, who as postgraduate student under my supervision also served for a time as my research assistant. With much skill and patience, she assisted various aspects of the research, writing and editing process, and she contributed significantly to the fourth chapter of this book, which partly overlaps with her own research topic.

Several family members read and commented upon drafts of my writing, which proved very helpful indeed.

Finally, although I have mentioned the DRC Archive in Stellenbosch above, I should reiterate that this book, and indeed much of my research over the past decade, would have been impossible without the meticulous and impeccable assistance I have received from that fine institution's staff. I should especially emphasise the help I received there from Dr Isabel Murray, whose enthusiasm for this research topic brought forth many valuable perspectives that I would not have pursued of my own accord. It is my humble hope that this book might in turn help to inspire further research by younger scholars into the rich resources housed at the DRC Archive.

CHAPTER ONE

Introduction: Scots Influence on the Dutch Reformed People of South Africa

This book, generally, is a mid-nineteenth- to mid-twentieth-century narrative of Scots influence on the Dutch/Afrikaner[1] people of South Africa, particularly in the Dutch Reformed Church (DRC) and its missionary movement. I keep the dating somewhat open-ended because there is important background to take note of prior to the arrival of the first Scottish ministers in the DRC in the early 1820s. The narrative draws to a close with Afrikaner nationalist opposition to the Scots legacy in the church, which is a discourse that reached a crescendo during the height of apartheid, but which continued to be influential through much of the twentieth century. I pay close attention to what I see as the missionary identity of the Scots in the DRC. Then I consider this identity and the evangelical missionary tradition inspired by it within their relationship to themes like Afrikaner nationalism, segregation and apartheid. On the one hand, this tradition has been implicated in the early construction of apartheid as a form of ecclesiastical segregation.[2] On the other hand, this book will show the strong and mounting opposition against this tradition within nationalistic segments of the Dutch/Afrikaner population as history unfolds. This means that an underlying question addressed here concerns the extent to which the Scots-inspired missionary tradition also became a counter-narrative to the reigning discourse of Afrikaner nationalist apartheid theology in the twentieth century.

It is perhaps surprising that the missionary tradition proved quite strong and influential far beyond what might be expected given the general inertia, even anti-missionary sentiment, among DRC members until deep into the nineteenth century. Although Scots in the DRC of South Africa did not have exclusive ownership of the missionary tradition in that church, after their virtual takeover of the DRC in the 1820s, to be discussed in Chapter 2, they provided a massive impetus to missionary enthusiasm, thereby kindling a flame that sputtered and burned quite warmly at times for more than a century. A central argument in this book is that the Scottish influence in the DRC was primarily the influence of a missionary identity. The fact that this missionary identity superseded ethnicity proved on the one hand challenging to a developing sense of Afrikaner ethnic identity. On the other hand, it smoothed the way for the relatively calm, if not problem-free, assimilation of Scots ministers into the bosom of a Dutch Afrikaner church.

There were layers of underlying tension inherent to this situation, much of it germane to a more general Scottish diasporic context in South Africa. John Mackenzie's work, *The Scots in South Africa*, is particularly helpful for laying out this general context, and so what follows in this chapter draws liberally on Mackenzie's work,[3] among other sources.

The Dutch Reformed Church and the Dutch East India Company

The DRC arrived at the Cape via the *Vereenigde Oostindische Compagnie* (Dutch East India Company: DEIC) in 1652 when members of that company established a supply post for the benefit of its ships travelling between the Netherlands and the Dutch East Indies. Initially the church was only unofficially present and occasionally serviced by company chaplains (*sieketroosters*). A fort at Cape Town served as the original venue for the local congregation, which was only officially constituted with the arrival of the first minister, Ds Joannes van Arckel, who was inducted on 23 August 1665.[4] For the next century and a half the DRC in South Africa resorted under the classis of Amsterdam, until the constitution of its own synod occurred for the first time in 1824.

The DEIC and subsequent colonial authorities considered the DRC an established or public church. Baptisms were liberally conducted, including on the children of 'freeburghers', company servants, 'free blacks, in later years also Khoi, Basterds and *Griekwa*'.[5] Nevertheless, church membership was hardly ubiquitous. Schutte mentions that by 1700 membership in the three existing congregations numbered 50 per cent of the freeburgher population of Drakenstein, 25 per cent in Stellenbosch and only 8 per cent of the entire 'European' population in Cape Town.[6] Although all company slaves were baptised, as were many of the slaves in private so-called ownership, the membership details of slaves and free blacks were much more sparsely recorded.[7]

Schutte stresses that during the course of the nineteenth century the Reformed church in the Netherlands became more active, recognising that its role as a public church translated into responsibility for education and the discipline of society. It even developed aspirations to be a national church during this period. Towards the end of the eighteenth century the welfare and discipline of the 'lowest classes' became more of a concern, and similar although slower movements were afoot in the Cape, which saw a substantial increase in church membership from around 1770 onwards.[8]

Authors like Duff, Elphick and Giliomee[9] have similarly pointed to the marginal role played by the DRC at the Cape for much of the eighteenth century, functioning primarily as a cultural and societal 'gatekeeper' for the DEIC.[10] Promotion and social mobility in the Cape society seemed to be predicated on church membership, so that was an obvious attraction. Yet, if one were to search for an inspiring religious centre to a budding sense of Afrikaner identity and popular theology, then it seems one should look beyond the eighteenth century. This was despite, or perhaps because of, the fact that the DRC was the only officially recognised church at the Cape.

Calvinism and the Dutch-controlled Cape Colony?

In the twentieth-century apartheid era there was a widely accepted narrative in South Africa and beyond that the early Cape society was a Calvinist society, and that especially the French Huguenots who settled in the area of Drakenstein by the end of the seventeenth century were brave Calvinist refugees, who exercised a marked religious influence on the Cape Dutch community to which they assimilated.[11] What has become known as the 'primitive Calvinism'[12] paradigm pointed to migrating farmers (*trekboere*) setting out into the wilderness in search of land and pasture with only the Bible as guide and educator to accompany them. Such Boer families, influenced by the Calvinist notion of predestination, would divide the populace of the land between the elect and the reprobate. They identified themselves as firmly belonging to the first category. Moreover, being readily attracted to the Old Testament, it was supposedly a short step for such a community in an unfamiliar and dangerous landscape to identify themselves with the biblical Israel existing in a covenantal relationship with a possessive and vengeful God who gave them licence to smite the encountered heathens along the way. This type of narrative was for example popularised by the historical novelist James A. Michener in his 1980 classic, *The Covenant*.[13]

Although the Calvinist paradigm in the early Cape Dutch colony had some scholarly currency, as seen for example in Willem de Klerk's work,[14] another perspective considered it a flawed narrative, even a 'myth', as chiefly indicated by André du Toit.[15] Subsequent to du Toit's forceful challenge to the notion of strong Calvinist sensibilities among early Dutch Afrikaners, other historians generally followed suit, although some, like Giliomee, argued that du Toit might have gone a bit too far in his denunciation of the notion of 'primitive Calvinism' as a factor among the early colonists.[16]

The heroic notion of the French Huguenots in South Africa, a group of people that in the late nineteenth century began to have monuments erected in their honour due to their supposedly strong influence on Afrikaner religious and political development, has similarly been debunked as an 'invented tradition'.[17] In contrast to the invented tradition, Denis points out that a much higher percentage of German immigrants constituted the early Afrikaner population compared to the French, yet the French Huguenot legacy was the one celebrated due to the heroic Calvinism they supposedly represented.[18] 'Considering the bad relationship between the Huguenots and the Dutch East India Company in the years following their arrival in the Cape Colony and the fact that they were subjected to a policy of forced assimilation, this is rather ironic.'[19]

Perhaps the Dutch Afrikaners were 'no chosen people', then, to appropriate the title of du Toit's above-mentioned article. At least it would seem no strong cohesive religious ideology underpinned their relationships with slaves and the indigenous population. Yet the world of the DEIC at the Cape was a differentiated one, not one based on equality. No Calvinist paradise to be sure, but a place wherein everyone knew their place.[20] For the Dutch colonists, it seems, skin-colour-based prejudice was a cultural force from early on.[21] The more the time passed for them and their descendants in Africa, the more this type of hierarchy hardened. Schutte mentions several examples, including the DRC in Stellenbosch, which after having had interracial services and joint communion since its foundation in the late seventeenth century, eventually buckled under social pressure and decided in 1825 to segregate its communion services along racial lines, despite acknowledging that scripture made no such provision.[22]

Afrikaner identity formation developed throughout the nineteenth century. It steadily acquired nationalist overtones underpinned by a separatist religious ideology inspired by a form of neo-Calvinism emerging from the late nineteenth century onwards. By and large, this was a reactive phenomenon with roots in the late eighteenth century, but it was nonetheless an 'imagined or invented' nationalism.[23] Robert Ross describes a complex situation in the earlier Cape Colony with no fixed Dutch ethnic identity. One example concerns the above-mentioned community of French Huguenots in Drakenstein (later Paarl). It seems that even though they had undergone a process of forced assimilation, as Denis puts it, the community remembered their heritage and perhaps even imagined in subsequent years that they had not in fact been successfully assimilated, despite evidence to the contrary. Ross tells a story of how the first missionaries of the Paris Evangelical Mission Society paid a visit to Paarl in order to visit these descendants of Huguenots. Despite needing a letter of introduction in Dutch in order to make themselves understandable, Ross relates how they were treated as long-lost brethren by the locals. Then he comments: 'Evidently, those of Huguenot descent needed a way of differentiating themselves from the rougher trekboers of the interior. As Frenchmen and women, even if they did not speak any French, they were at least civilized.'[24] Ross also comments on a situation of specific relevance to this book, that is, the way in which the elite Cape Dutch acquiesced to a nineteenth-century British colonial policy of local anglicisation as a way of distinguishing for themselves a 'Cape colonial identity', and also to mark themselves as loyal subjects of the British Empire.[25]

The British Empire and Settlers at the Cape

Let me briefly return to the close of the eighteenth century and the arrival and eventual annexation of the Cape by Britain, first in 1795, and definitively in 1806. This British takeover of what had been a Dutch colony might be taken as a convenient root cause of the later imaginings of Afrikaner nationalism. However, Giliomee, the pre-eminent scholar of Afrikaner history, indicates that although the Cape Dutch colonists might not have been thrilled by their subjugation under the Union Jack – that they were in fact annoyed by 'English nationalism'[26] – they simply had very little by way of an answer to claims of British, and specifically English, superiority.

> By 1806 the colony could boast of no great economic advances or cultural achievements, apart from the Cape Dutch homesteads. There were no books, paintings or innovations on which Afrikaners could pride themselves. They were a rural, isolated, relatively backward people, with only a few who received more than a rudimentary education. The lack of military resistance to the British conquests in 1795 and 1806 contributed to the sense of social impotence.[27]

Giliomee indicates that it was the underwhelming colonial administration of the Dutch East India Company, which supported slavery, neglected education and allowed the expansion of *trekboers* to go unchecked, among other things, that became the main target of British critique and self-justification for the area to be under British rule instead. In this discourse the Dutch colonists themselves were of course also negatively implicated, as the above quote suggests.[28]

The irony of this is that the situation in Britain in the aftermath of the Napoleonic Wars was no paradise either. Economic stagnation and conditions of destitution among the working classes drew massive protests. Analogies based on abolitionist rhetoric drawing links between systemic white working-class poverty at home and overseas black slavery were appropriated by some among the white working class.[29] One solution to this problem of working-class unemployment and strife was a resettlement scheme in South Africa, which ultimately occurred in 1820. It so happens that the new colonial authorities in South Africa preferred to have a buffer zone between the amaXhosa and amaThembu on the Eastern frontier and the more colonially settled areas in the West. Several wars had already been waged between colonial troops and these African groups, which meant much hardship for the latter. Johns writes that the newly arrived Brits would be settled in an area that had undergone 'ethnic cleansing'.[30] Moreover, the settlers originated for the most part from artisanal backgrounds, and in the Cape Colony they were to be settled as farmers on plots of land not entirely suited for agrarian cultivation. The result was that many settlers could not make an agricultural living and moved to the nearby towns of Grahamstown and Port Elizabeth to take up more familiar trades.[31]

Others found fertile soil for creative growth. The most influential narrator of the British settler experience was the Scottish poet, Thomas Pringle (1789–1834). His work *The Emigrant's Cabin*, inspired by life on his farm in the Eastern Cape, served as an advertisement for a life of honest, fulfilling and profitable work that might be had in the Colony by the industrious immigrant. Although Pringle returned to Britain after a six-year sojourn, his literary work left a lasting impression: 'For in this wilderness there's work to do . . .'[32]

There developed an ambiguous relationship between the British settlers and the existing inhabitants. While the settlers tended to adhere to abolitionist sentiments, even if misappropriating such sentiments to a degree, as indicated above, they also landed firmly and not always uncomfortably in the developing imperial discourse of British superiority. One aspect of this concerns the very issue of work as highlighted in the above-quoted line from Pringle's poem. What constitutes work, how it is defined and who does it, seemed to be cardinal questions of the time. Despite, or perhaps because of, the unemployment and unfavourable labour conditions in Britain from which the settlers escaped, African and Afrikaner approaches to work were cast in a critical light when viewed through lenses crafted in the industrial society from whence these immigrants had come. Giliomee, interestingly, interprets the assessment of the Dutch Afrikaner by Pringle as not entirely negative: '[Pringle], while finding his Afrikaner neighbors uncultivated and highly prejudiced against the Khoikhoi, considered them as a people civil, good-natured, and "exceedingly shrewd" at bargain making.'[33]

Timothy Johns argues that South Africa's reputation for 'indolence', much decried by British critics, was in fact, at least partly, a creation of Romantic French philosophers and travel writers such as Jean-Jacques Rousseau (1712–78) and one of his disciples, François Le Vaillant (1753–1824), author of *Voyage dans l'intérieur de l'Afrique* (1790), which popularised a primitivist vision of Khoi life flourishing in a pre-industrial state of bliss, in contrast to the hardships experienced by workers in Europe. This type of writing naturally occurred under the guise of the well-known myth of the 'noble savage'. For the sake of British colonial self-justification, such romanticised racial tropes might be usefully employed to construct an alternative vision against the French idealist one. In the British evangelical humanitarian version, the Khoi's state of existence appeared to abide in slothful sin rather than savage nobility. It is all a matter of perspective, of course. Johns writes in reference to J. M. Coetzee: 'In British eyes, the Khoi appeared to emblematize – through a general disinterest in private property, cultivation of no crop except *dagga* (marijuana), and apparent determination *not* to work – the "degeneration of man into brute".'[34]

However, Johns points out that the real scandal of British visions of South African laziness had less to do with the supposed indolent lifestyle of the Khoi, and more with the perceived laziness and civilisation-shunning attitudes of the Dutch Afrikaner. The primal fear in this regard seemed to be that especially the isolationist Boer frontier, slave-holding lifestyle, disconnected as it was from evangelical ideals of thriftful industriousness and removed from the European-controlled economy, represented "sinister evidence" of the possibility that 'European stock can regress after a few generations in Africa'.[35] The 'further one travelled away from Cape Town and towards the frontier, the more poverty-stricken, indolent and brutal, the more generally degraded, Dutch colonial burghers seemed to become within British official discourse'.[36]

This was the context into which the 1820 British settlers landed. Giliomee indicates that while there developed on the one hand a degree of common understanding and even some sympathy between them and the neighbouring Dutch Afrikaners, as indicated in reference to Pringle above, the British settlers' presence also spurred on a growing preoccupation with Afrikaner identity development. Dutch publications such as *Het Nederduitsch zuid-afrikaansch tydschrift* (*NZAT*) and *De Zuid-Afrikaan* ran articles on how the colonist identities should define themselves over against one another or in some other formation. Might this be in the form of a dual identity, for example, as one suggestion would have it, or should Afrikaner be an umbrella identity incorporating all loyal colonists, as was proposed in the first editorial of *De Zuid-Afrikaan* in 1830?[37]

Within the British colonial framework in South Africa it is a fact that Scots were a small minority, originally mainly constitutive of the intellectual and commercial elite. MacKenzie mentions, for example, Scottish shipbuilders and other merchants who seized the opportunity to fill a lacuna when the British took control of the Cape and supplanted the DEIC. Scots were also strongly represented in the military regiments stationed at the Cape.[38] However, compared to Scottish migration to other parts of the British Empire, MacKenzie remarks on the relatively smaller numbers of Scots who made their way to southern Africa, but whose 'influence was out of proportion to their numbers'.[39]

They were able to be so influential primarily due to the positions they occupied as members of the intellectual and mercantile classes, but also due to their ability to constitute something of a bridge between the contrasting English and Dutch worlds at the Cape. This second point will be elaborated on shortly, and the intellectual influence has already been mentioned in the example of Thomas Pringle. Although Scots constituted only about 10 per cent of the between 4,000 and 5,000 Brits comprising the 1820 settlement,[40] Pringle as influential representative of this minority group suggested that Scots were better suited to adapt to the harsh southern African environment, which was perhaps reminiscent of their own, specifically highland, landscape, than the English who were more acclimated to 'the rich tameness of ordinary English scenery...'[41] Moreover the Scots, according to Pringle's assessment, were much more adaptable agriculturists, happy to acquire seeds from the Boers, for example, which was a successful characteristic as part of a settlement of farmers.[42]

Pringle, on at least one aspect, found himself at odds with many among the settler community, Dutch and British alike: 'Above all, he was an evangelical, and argued passionately, contrary to many settlers, for the efficacy of missionaries on the frontier.'[43]

Scots 'Missionaries' and the Dutch Afrikaners

The above allusions to Pringle will serve well to set the stage for what I take to be two central and apparently contrasting themes in relation to the Scottish influence on South Africa's DRC, an influence that would trace its history also to this decade of the 1820s, although there was no direct connection to Pringle and the 1820 settlers. The two themes in question are assimilation on the one hand and missionary enthusiasm on the other.

Assimilation or attempts at assimilation feature on different levels here. First, in terms of the Scottish diaspora more generally, there is the complexity of Scots identity within the context of the general Britishness of the Empire. MacKenzie indicates that a somewhat ironic consequence of imperial reach and settlement was that British regional identities might have become exaggerated abroad over against even more local clannish patterns in their places of origin.[44] Furthermore, an emphasis on Scottish ethnicity did not stand in any conflict with a more general colonial identity. Scots were after all already a polyglot people who were used to negotiating and combining different identities. MacKenzie writes:

> As well as Gaelic and English, most of the Scottish population spoke dialects of the Scots tongue which, though linguistically related, were more or less impenetrable to the English. Burns, after all, wrote in both Scots and standard English. Many ministers were accustomed to delivering sermons in both Gaelic and English, or at times with Scots variants. Scottish culture was thus thoroughly hybrid and this was to be highly significant in its colonial manifestations.[45]

The term hybrid is indeed aptly used here, and it is furthermore interesting that this pattern of dual, multiple or hybrid identity might have facilitated the Scots' successful but also problematic transplantation not only into South African soil more generally, but also more particularly within the Dutch Afrikaner culture over time. This latter theme is primarily what this book is about, as focused within the peculiar milieu of Afrikaner religiosity and the DRC.[46]

From the local colonial government's point of view, the 1820 settlement would play an important role in the imperial policy of anglicisation at the Cape[47] by inserting a substantial English-speaking contingent into the settler culture. However, anglicisation was not simply about strengthening the 'English' presence at the Cape. It was quite a strategic and surreptitious way of exerting rulership in a foreign colony over a people of European extraction[48] – in the case of the Cape, the Dutch Afrikaners. One of the complexities of this type of colonialism was that in addition to the more typical subjection of indigenous peoples to imperial rule, it also sought to colonise the consciousness of the pre-existing colonists. Particularly since the Comaroffs' groundbreaking work in this regard,[49] the role of religion, most notably religious conversion, has been understood as a potential vehicle for the colonisation of consciousness, although it has also been a theme of some dispute.[50] It seems to me that a certain colonisation of consciousness was attempted via the vehicle of the DRC at the Cape, albeit with mixed results, as I shall explain.

The British imperial authority at the Cape quickly realised the importance and potential of the Dutch church it found there. Perhaps the DRC had underperformed as a religious institution under the DEIC, but it was undoubtedly the most important cultural bastion among the Dutch Afrikaners, providing a sense of structure, orderliness and history, among other things. Hence, after the British takeover of the colony, the DRC was recognised as the established church, but now it fulfilled that role alongside the Anglican Church. In addition to making sure that the DRC was subjected to the civil courts in matters of legal dispute, it also afforded the government the role of appointing ministers, among other regulations.[51]

Lord Charles Somerset, who was governor at the Cape from 1814 to 1826, took his role of making pastoral appointments seriously. Initially, anglicisation evidently did not factor into his strategising in this respect, because he first attempted to find Dutch ministers to fill vacancies in the Cape DRC, but without success.[52] Then, in the aftermath of the 1820 British settlement scheme, through a series of events that will be detailed in Chapter 2, Somerset determined to recruit Scottish Presbyterian ministers for the DRC from 1821 onwards. It was understood that the Church of Scotland had no theological conflict with the Dutch Reformed tradition. In fact, the Scots recruits were understood to be even more orthodox in that respect than many of their peers in Holland who had come under the spirit of rationalism, and on the understanding that the Scots would first become proficient in Dutch, they could fit the mould quite nicely.[53] The degree to which the Scots ministers became fluent in Dutch undoubtedly varied, but the fact that they took on the task falls in line with the above-made point about Scots' linguistic adaptability and long-established polyglot tendencies. Learning the vernacular is of course also a basic principle of missionary preparation and training and, as mentioned above, it is my argument in this book that the Scots tradition in the DRC might best be understood as a missionary tradition.

Somerset, soon after the successful implementation of this recruitment project, started to turn the screws on the anglicisation policy. For example, in 1825 he 'decreed that English alone should be legal for all public documents and judicial proceedings – a measure which soon became a fertile cause of misunderstanding and resentment'.[54] When measures were put in place to have English services in the DRC, Dutch Afrikaner anxiety increased exponentially. Giliomee mentions that the DRC clergy found the pressure to anglicise unacceptable, and the 1824 synod 'refused a request by the Scottish ministers to offer some of their services in English'.[55] Moreover, *De Zuid-Afrikaan* in 1834 gave the following dire warning: 'Members of the Synod consult ancient history to persuade yourselves that to change the language of your religion you would be taking the first step to betray your belief and religion.'[56]

This newspaper commentary gives an interesting glimpse into the way DRC religiosity had functioned as protector of Dutch-centredness at the Cape. In marked contrast to the openness to hybridity in Scots Presbyterianism, here an implicit link is drawn between linguistic adaptation and religious apostasy. Yet, despite these basic attempts at resistance, the Scottish coup of the DRC proceeded apace. Depending on one's perspective, what had occurred here might be interpreted in different ways, of course. MacKenzie seems to indicate that the Scots all but saved the DRC from a premature ecclesiastical demise.[57] Others might interpret it more along the lines of equivalence to an ecclesiastical annexation by a colonising power. Whatever the case, by 1835, twelve of the twenty-two ministers in the DRC were Scots.[58] Whichever way you want to look at it, it constituted a successful project.

This book will show in detail how the Scots in the DRC were able to steer the nineteenth-century course of affairs regarding this church. With their influence in the mainstream DRC waning as the twentieth century proceeded, Scots Afrikaners still maintained a central role in the DRC's 'foreign' missionary movement.

MacKenzie gives various commentaries about the greater sympathy that seemed to exist between Scots and Dutch Afrikaners versus the relationship between the latter group and the English. One example draws on the commentary of the celebrated historian W. M. Macmillan, who migrated with his family to South Africa in the final decade of the nineteenth century, where they settled in Stellenbosch, which had a strong Scots community. There he encountered easy-going relations between Scots and Dutch Afrikaners, especially at the ecclesiastical level. Scots Presbyterians for a time even used the DRC church to hold their services and they invited both Dutch and Scots ministers to preach. Of central importance seems to be that Scots in South Africa tended to accentuate their general Presbyterianism, which came at the expense of their relationship with the English, and which in turn generated a sense of religious kinship with the Dutch Afrikaners. 'Scots were powerfully aware of the Presbyterian culture shared by the majority of them, a Calvinist character which they felt (and repeatedly uttered as a propagandist device, often against the English) drew them closer to the Dutch or Afrikaners.'[59]

In sharp contrast to this description of late-nineteenth-century amicability between Scots and Afrikaners in Stellenbosch, Giliomee makes note of the generally low esteem in which rural Afrikaners were held by Victorian-era English observers. Afrikaners were seen as 'ignorant, superstitious and conservative' and uninterested in education. English writer Olive Schreiner, who had spent several years during the 1860s and '70s among Afrikaners in the Karoo, subsequently commented on the superiority of the English vis-à-vis these lowly Boers who, among other things, practised such poor personal hygiene that she could not, for example, consider sleeping 'between sheets a Dutchman had slept between'.⁶⁰ And an Afrikaans writer, M. E. Rothman, commented regarding Swellendam in the last quarter of the nineteenth century that the social relations between English and Dutch Afrikaners were decidedly skewed. Afrikaans farmers would address English traders and officials as 'mister', while they in turn would be called upon their first names. To this Giliomee comments: 'In many ways Afrikaners, ironically, were being subjected to the same rituals of subjection and degradation as those they employed to keep coloreds and black in their inferior place.'⁶¹

No doubt there were Afrikaners and then there were Afrikaners, and the more elite contingent in Stellenbosch could perhaps not be compared to the rustic types inhabiting the Karoo and beyond. There are also instances, which I shall comment upon in the following chapters, where Scots, including the Scots Afrikaner ministers I write about, commented in disparaging tones about the Boers. Yet, in the case of Scots Afrikaner ministers such as Andrew Murray Jr, always careful to present himself as 'a Dutch minister',⁶² a common designation seen in his writings to family members, for example, was to refer to the Dutch Afrikaners as 'our people' even in the midst of criticising some aspect of their behaviour.

It might be argued in retrospect that within the South African context with its complicated racial history the Scots did not do themselves any favours by aligning themselves with Afrikaner interests. This type of qualified alignment no doubt compromised them, as indeed any hybridity is a compromise of sorts. And given the general Afrikaner racial attitudes that eventually ended in apartheid, these Scots might not, had they had access to the proverbial time machine, have wanted to end up on the wrong side of history. As it were, they became entangled and complicit in the racialised history that followed, as this book will also indicate in the next chapters. Regarding the Scots' complicity in the 'programme of racial domination', MacKenzie gives the following general comment that is well worth noting:

> This was closely bound up with the manner in which the Scots positioned themselves as intermediaries between the Afrikaners and the English. By stressing their affinities with Afrikaans people and by participating in the central notion that the prime 'racial' problem was this relationship among the whites they contributed to the suppression of African interests and concerns.⁶³

The degree to which mission is a 'discourse of difference' might be debated, and I shall comment more on this shortly, but the dominant colonial discourse more generally was of course very directly invested in the othering of its subjects.⁶⁴ Had the othering of Dutch Afrikaners in a British colonial setting meant that they thereby also qualified to be plausible subjects of missionary interest? That I take to be an underlying subtext to the narrative unfolding here.

That missionary discourses were often, despite general 'proclamations about human universalism', structured 'through the marking of difference',[65] as Esme Cleall has argued, is undoubtedly true. However, although missionaries are often and rightly cast in the role of othering agents, a diachronic historical perspective would reveal that the categories of difference were not static. While race and gender have often been treated as static categories of difference for long periods of their histories, as constructed categories they were of course changeable. At least, they did and of course still do have great potential for reinvention. Cleall, for example, mentions that while early colonial racial discourses centred on difference of clothing, such cultural markers of demarcation gave way to pseudo-biological discourses of difference regarding facial structures, and so on, towards the latter part of the nineteenth century. 'What race denotes varies over time, place, context and discursive community. Part of the power of race lies in its ability to be naturalised by numerous visible signifiers.'[66]

Cleall, focusing on London Missionary Society (LMS) representatives in India and South Africa, interprets missionary expressions of shock and horror at their fellow countryfolk's brutal excesses against indigenous people as part of the missionary construction of a discourse of difference. 'Missionary outrage at European violence drew on ideas of "racial", national and religious "superiority" that suggested that fellow "Englishmen" should "rise above" behaviour fit for "savages".'[67] Cleall suggests that it was crucial for missionaries to be able to demonstrate European superiority and civility as an ideal to strive for in their attempts to convert indigenous people elsewhere. Therefore, when British soldiers in India and traders in Africa committed atrocities, Cleall argues that missionaries were primarily concerned with how such actions distorted in the eyes of Indians and Africans the models of civility that missionaries wished to portray regarding their own culture. Hence when traders and soldiers acted violently, it disturbed the ideal and created the impression that such European perpetrators 'were not only an *embarrassment* to "their race", but they were actually a *corruption* of it'.[68]

Conversely, of course, the violence of the indigenous other could be interpreted as a validation of their savagery and as a justification both for colonial rule over them and for their subjection to missionary programmes of evangelism and education. I have mentioned above some of the ways in which the Dutch Afrikaners, especially those on the rural frontier, became a topic of scandal and shame in colonial discourse. The primary problem with them seemed to be the suspicion that even though they were known to be Christian people of European descent, they had in a sense degenerated on African soil, becoming effectively like Africans even though they were supposedly of European stock. This kind of outsider construction of Boer identity severely challenged discourses of generic whiteness in colonial South Africa. Hence the Dutch Afrikaners were problematic in the general colonial identity formation process, but they also provided a useful separate identity construct, over against which British colonial expansion could be justified.

Cleall writes: 'Missionaries were important in creating, disseminating and weaving this understanding into the British interpretation of colonial relations in southern Africa, and missionary magazines and periodicals were a forum where this narrative was forged.'[69] The writings of missionaries based on specific encounters with Boers became very useful in the construction of the Boer identity as ignorant, uncivilised and violent. To further elaborate, it is best to quote Cleall at some length:

> Boer/African battles were often presented as having a 'tribal', not a 'colonial', quality, with Boer commandos constructed similarly to the Ndebele *impi*. Unlike violence inflicted by British settlers which, for the most part, was kept vague and thereby 'softened' in the missionary press, Boer violence was (like 'heathen' violence) gruesomely detailed. Violence was used to suggest Boer 'degeneracy', and particularly a degenerate masculinity, as they became simply one of the 'tribes' against whom missionaries had to contend. Such a construction was used to ridicule further what missionaries read as a Boer insistence on racial superiority.[70]

Scots certainly counted strongly among missionaries not known for their sympathetic sentiments towards the Dutch Afrikaners or Boers, with John Philip[71] and David Livingstone[72] perhaps best known for their respective critiques. I shall also give more detailed attention to the views of James Stewart regarding the Boers and the causes of the South African War. However, as indicated above in reference to MacKenzie, a different, perhaps more influential Scottish/Afrikaner perspective in South Africa was one of familiarity based on shared Reformed/Presbyterian backgrounds. In this construct, Scots and (some) Afrikaners identified more closely with one another in contradistinction to the English.

Yet the construct of the Dutch Afrikaners as degenerating into uncivility and the construct of their spiritual kinship to the Scots Presbyterians were not mutually exclusive. In some important ways they intermingled. Even Scots in the DRC who assimilated for all practical purposes to Dutch Afrikaner identity were in various ways influenced by perspectives regarding their adopted people as less than noble savages. Such variegated perspectives influenced the Scots Afrikaners' identity construction vis-à-vis (within and against) Afrikanerdom in interesting ways to be explored in the pages ahead. Perhaps the most interesting subtext to consider is the possibility that missionary-enthused Scots ministers entering the DRC understood themselves primarily as missionaries to the Dutch Afrikaners. Their ultimate assimilation and hybrid identity within this ethnic construct did not negate this suggested missionary perspective at all. Although 'discourses of difference' were certainly important for underpinning missionary identities, the fact of the matter is that this would not be the first nor the last time in history that missionaries would *go native* in their all-out attempt at communicating their message. However, this suggested perspective to which I shall return, of seeing the Scots ministers in the DRC as missionaries, is on the level of an underlying discourse that could never be openly acknowledged. There already existed a good amount of antagonism between Dutch Afrikaners and, mainly LMS, missionaries. To imagine themselves as missionary subjects would have been too much for the already challenged communal self-esteem of the rural Dutch Afrikaners among whom Scots ministers were placed. Pragmatic missionaries, including many Scottish missionaries in South Africa, were able to approach their vocation strategically, and missionary subjects were not always privy to all of the assumptions and biases of those evangelising them.

MacKenzie comments about the fact that the Scottish churches were slightly late in starting their own missionary movements. Therefore, the initial Scottish missionary engagement in South Africa occurred under the purview of the LMS and the Glasgow Missionary Society, respectively launched in 1795 and 1796. Scots missionaries of evangelical inclination were happy to join these non-denominational societies, which allowed them to pursue their vocation in Africa and elsewhere.[73] Indeed, as the next chapter will show, some of the earliest Scots to join the DRC as ministers were formerly LMS missionaries.

Despite the early radicalism of Dr John Philip, 'the highly influential superintendent of the London Missionary Society',[74] and other LMS missionaries, some other famous Scottish missionaries like Robert Moffat of Kuruman and James Stewart of Lovedale were perhaps less known for their radical egalitarianism and more for their paternalism. Moffat, though an ardent adherent of monogenism in human origins, who like most evangelical missionaries and early abolitionists subscribed to the 'one blood' doctrine,[75] also described his relationship to Africans and people of African descent in the West Indies as that of a father to a 'son or daughter'.[76] Stewart had a long career, occupying different positions during the course of it, but he tended to maintain fuzzy boundaries between missionary interests and the aims of the British Empire.[77] The history of Lovedale College, the educational institution in the Eastern Cape where Stewart spent the bulk of his career, is itself a case study in pragmatism and adaptation to the position of the civil authorities. 'By the end of the century the former radicalism of the Scottish Churches seemed to have drained away. A tradition of obedience to the civil authority was established and racially separatist tendencies emerged.'[78] MacKenzie adds that R. H. W. Shepherd, the last missionary principal of Lovedale, likely even favoured segregated education towards the end of his career, despite the original integrationist and equalist stance of the institution.[79]

General pragmatism and adaptability to the social context, sometimes to the detriment of sound principles and ideals, also characterised the more narrowly defined subject of the Scottish influence in the DRC and

Afrikanerdom more generally. On that theme, MacKenzie briefly weighs in on a theme of central importance to this book: '[T]he open question must be whether they Scotticised the DRC, or whether they were, in turn, Afrikanerised.'[80] After some discussion he provided a basic answer, which I also affirm as a general hermeneutical lens through which to read what follows in this book: 'In the end the DRC became something of a Dutch/Scots hybrid.'[81]

I believe hybridity is one overarching frame of reference to be used here. Additionally I would like to present the idea that for the Scots who became ministers in the DRC this was not an accidental hybridity, but part of a general missionary mindset of finding points of contact and inhabiting the world views of those among whom one ministers. Let me now briefly introduce the chapters to come.

Outline of Chapters

Chapter 2, 'Scots in South African Dutch Pulpits in the Early to Middle Nineteenth Century', details the inception phase of what has been described as a Scottish takeover of the DRC.[82] In so doing it highlights some of the more significant and/or controversial Scots ministers recruited by the British governor, Lord Charles Somerset, to serve the DRC in South Africa. Particular attention is given to Revds George Thom, Andrew Murray Sr, William Robertson, John Taylor and Thomas Reid. These ministers all had notable influence, and often contentious relationships with their Dutch-speaking congregants at a time when many of the latter were engaged in or contemplating emigrating away from the British-controlled Cape Colony in protest at anti-slavery legislation taking effect. Such emigrants would become known as *Voortrekkers* in the subsequent Afrikaner legendary retelling, which hailed them as conquerors of a deeper and darker African frontier. This chapter also covers the early part of Andrew Murray Jr's (second son of Andrew Sr) career as a DRC minister, as well as the early career of his slightly older brother, John, who would eventually become the first professor of the Stellenbosch Seminary. Andrew Murray Jr was perhaps the most influential character of the Scottish diaspora in South Africa, especially in so far as his cross-cultural engagement within Afrikanerdom was concerned. In the mid-nineteenth century he served a community comprised of both Dutch and English speakers in the *Voortrekker* settlement of Bloemfontein. At the time Murray had pro-imperialist leanings, which caused some tensions between him and his congregants.

Andrew Murray Jr is also a central character in Chapter 3, 'Scottish Ministers, Evangelical Revival and Church-based "Apartheid"?', which tells the story of his association with a wave of evangelical revival that hit the DRC in the 1860s. This in turn was part of an international movement of awakenings and revivals, especially in Britain and North America. At the Cape, Murray and a number of other Scots such as Revds Robert Shand

and William Robertson became central figures in fostering this movement within the DRC. It subsequently led to growing interest and enthusiasm for mission, which resulted in the recruitment of more Scottish ministers and missionaries to serve the DRC. Hence, among the first two DRC missionaries to what was at the time the foreign country of the Northern Transvaal was a Scot, Alexander McKidd. Scots were involved in movements influencing theological history in South Africa, which included the founding of the Theological Seminary at Stellenbosch, which was to train ministers for the DRC locally and thereby contribute to combating the so-called 'liberalism' that was seen as a threatening factor among Dutch-trained clergy at the Cape. The second-generation Scots immigrant brothers, Andrew and John Murray, played leading roles in this movement, with John, as already mentioned, becoming one of the first two professors at the Seminary.

A central theme to be addressed in this chapter is a controversial and somewhat ironic synodical decision of 1857 when Andrew Murray Sr, father of the above-mentioned Andrew and John, was the DRC moderator. The missionary focus of the Scots ministers, particularly, had contributed to an increase in the number of black members in the DRC. Hence the synod had come under pressure from members who were less enthusiastic about this state of affairs to allow racially segregated congregations. While the opinion of the leadership, in which Scots ministers predominated, was that such segregation would be unscriptural and wrong, they nevertheless acceded to demands to allow such segregation if this became unavoidable due to the 'weakness of some'. This step, unwillingly undertaken though it might have been, is often interpreted as the beginning of structural apartheid in South Africa.

Chapter 4, 'The Scottish (and American) Foundations of a Trans-frontier Afrikaner Missionary Enterprise', introduces the Ministers' Missionary Union (MMU), which was an independent organisation within the DRC, initiated in the late nineteenth century chiefly by Andrew Murray Jr, who by this time was a well-known author and international evangelical leader. It was through the auspices of this organisation that contact was established with representatives of the Free Church of Scotland, which then invited missionaries from the MMU to become part of its missionary enterprise in Nyasaland (Malawi). Among other things, this chapter details the adventures and misadventures of Andrew Charles Murray, a nephew of Andrew Jr, who became the first missionary of the MMU after much contact and negotiation with various representatives of both the Free Church at Livingstonia and eventually also the Church of Scotland in Blantyre, Nyasaland. This chapter also touches upon the development of DRC missionaries' thinking regarding their environment, particularly with respect to their attitudes to the natural ecology, as well as their attitudes to Africans as expressed in their own writings. Particular focus is given to the voice of A. C. Murray in this respect. All of this is discussed in relation to their contacts with Scots Presbyterian missionaries, such as Robert Laws, Donald Fraser, Alexander

Hetherwick and others, which sometimes resulted in disagreements within a wider context of mentorship as provided by the Scots to the Afrikaner missionaries.

This chapter also considers a collaborative Bible translation project involving particularly the DRC's William Hoppe Murray, another nephew of Andrew Jr, and the Blantyre mission's Dr Hetherwick. In addition to the main theme of Nyasaland, this chapter starts off by elaborating on some of the ways in which graduates from the Huguenot seminary, an educational institute for women founded in Wellington under the inspiration of Andrew and (his wife) Emma Murray and on the model of Mount Holyoke College in Massachusetts, was responsible for much of the early impetus for foreign missionary work.

At the turn of the century, 'The South African War (1899–1902) and the Scots Afrikaners' (Chapter 5) concerns increasingly complicated relationships, not only between (Scots) Afrikaners and Scots on the mission field, but also between some leading missionary statesmen in South Africa and internationally. This chapter elaborates on the widely divergent views held by James Stewart, founder of Livingstonia and long-time principal of Lovedale College, on the one hand, and Andrew Murray Jr, on the other, regarding the causes and the origins of aggression in this war. It becomes clear that by this time Andrew Murray held a much more sympathetic line regarding the Boers, whom he portrayed as victims of the conflict, compared to the pro-imperial view of Stewart that was ever distrustful of the intentions of these rustic Afrikaners. In this respect, Stewart closely followed the line espoused by his own missionary mentor, David Livingstone, who had also viewed the Boers with great suspicion. Central to this chapter are narratives relating to developments on overseas camps holding Boer prisoners of war. On these so-called islands of exile, most particularly Ceylon and St Helena, some ministers and organisations connected to the Scots Afrikaners ministered to, or perhaps more aptly evangelised, the POWs, which inculcated in many of them an enthusiasm for foreign mission. The Christian Endeavour Society was particularly important in this regard, as were the chaplaincy roles fulfilled by Revds George Murray and A. F. Louw, who were respectively a brother and a nephew of Andrew Murray Jr. Through the foundation of a missionary training institute specifically formed to accommodate returning POWs with a missionary vocation, as well as other DRC institutions, several ex-POWs ended up as DRC missionaries in various places, including Nyasaland.

'Other(ing) Identity Formations: From Mission Field Ecumenism to Home Church Controversy' (Chapter 6) follows some of these above-mentioned ex-POWs into Nyasaland, where some of them became participants in an intricate ecumenical project involving the DRC's Nkhoma Synod in the centre of the country, and the Free Church of Scotland's Livingstonia Synod to the north, as well as the Church of Scotland's Blantyre Synod in the south. From early in the twentieth century, the Scottish missions in the north and the south negotiated about the possibility of founding one unified Presbyterian church. Increasingly the DRC missionaries under the leadership of A. C. Murray, W. H. Murray and others expressed themselves as interested in joining this unified body. Eventually the mission, with the strong backing of the Cape DRC's mission commission, was able to convince their home synod to accede to the union and become part of the Church of Central Africa Presbyterian (CCAP). This in turn led to tensions with Afrikaner nationalist factions in the home DRC, particularly in the Orange Free State, where there was much opposition to the idea of cooperation with 'English' churches. Hence, this chapter is concerned with how foreign mission field conditions, in which Scottish connections played a formative role, inculcated other ideas and ideals about identity and belonging than those cultivated at the same period of time among mainstream Afrikaner religiosity in South Africa. This chapter also reflects on an apparently ironic and telling recurrence of the 'weakness of some' theme again nearly jeopardising church unity, on this occasion in the twentieth century and now with respect to the CCAP. This time around, however, the 'weak' were DRC missionaries, including Scots Afrikaners, who were ultimately accommodated in their 'weakness' by the Scots missions in Nyasaland.

Chapter 7, 'Afrikaner *Volkskerk* Ideologues and the Scots Afrikaners', focuses on the various ways in which the Scottish ministers and their legacy of irenic evangelical ecumenism became unpopular and even denounced as anathema under the developing Afrikaner nationalism that became an influential political factor as the twentieth century developed. This latter stream of thought found its religious estuary in the notion of a *volkskerk* (people's church), which also developed a theology that served its particular purposes. Over time this would become the theology of apartheid. Generally speaking, the chapter shows how a discourse that was first introduced within the theological thinking of the so-called *Doppers*, that is, the ultra-conservative Gereformeerde Kerke, which typecast the Scottish ministers as heterodox, anti-nationalist 'Methodists', over time also became quite central to the mainstream of theological opinion in the apartheid-era DRC. Conceptually, a specific reformed identity and exclusivist Afrikaner identity were tied together as an inseparable unity by ideologues of otherwise diverse background such as the anti-modernist ministers S. J and J. D. du Toit, on the one hand, but also by the theologically more liberal-minded D. F. Malan. Malan's older sister, Cinie, was married to A. A. Louw, who was the pioneer DRC missionary to Mashonaland and another Murray descendant. Malan would become the first apartheid-era prime minister in 1948. This chapter discusses among other things a letter that Andrew Murray wrote in his old age, protesting against the young Malan's earlier decision to exchange his church ministry for a life of politics.

The concluding chapter (8), 'The Scottish Legacy in Afrikaner Religiosity Reassessed', does not attempt to give a full overview of what had come before. Instead, key themes are emphasised and explained, particularly the nature of the reformed Christian nationalist opposition to the Scots Afrikaners. The missionary identity of the Scots in the DRC is assessed in reference to several situations and movements that featured in the preceding pages. Of specific interest here is the question how the Dutch Afrikaner people might have been a missionary subject for Scottish evangelism. How such an approach might have been perceived by the projected missionary subjects is discussed as possibly part of a hidden or at least under-acknowledged discourse, but perceivable in the fierce opposition against what had become denounced as Scottish 'Methodism'. The question of hybridity and its limits in this context are addressed, and finally the question regarding the extent to which the Scots Afrikaners represented a counter-tradition in Afrikaner reformed religiosity receives attention.

Notes

1. The term 'Afrikaner' is an emerging identity throughout the history described here. I variously refer to Cape Dutch, particularly in the earlier phase, or, following the cue of S. E. Duff (2018) 'The Dutch Reformed Church and the Protestant Atlantic: Revivalism and Evangelicalism in the Nineteenth-Century Cape Colony', *South African Historical Journal*, 70:2, p. 327, the term Dutch Afrikaners more generically. Terms such Hollander or more commonly Boer have been ascribed or used in self-descriptions.
2. Richard Elphick (2012) writes persuasively about this theme in a chapter entitled 'The Evangelical Invention of Apartheid', in *The Equality of Believers: Protestant Missionaries and the Racial Politics of South Africa*. Scottsville: University of KwaZulu-Natal Press.
3. John M. MacKenzie and Nigel Dalziel (2007) *The Scots in South Africa: ethnicity, identity, gender and race, 1772–1914*. Manchester: Manchester University Press.
4. See 'Oorsig van die Geskiedenis van die NG Kerk', *Gemeentegeskiedenisargief: 'n oorsig van die geskiedenis van die NG Kerk, sy gemeentes en predikante*. https://www.gemeentegeskiedenis.co.za/oorsig-van-die-geskiednis-van-die-ng-kerk/ (accessed 10 June 2020).
5. Gerrit J. Schutte (1998/1999) 'Between Amsterdam and Batavia: Cape Society and the Calvinist Church under the Dutch East India Company', *Kronos*, 25, pp. 17–49, p. 41.
6. Ibid., p. 39.
7. Ibid., pp. 40–1.
8. Ibid., pp. 44–5.
9. S. E. Duff (2018) 'The Dutch Reformed Church and the Protestant Atlantic: Revivalism and Evangelicalism in the Nineteenth-Century Cape Colony', *South African Historical Journal*, 70:2, pp. 324–47, DOI: 10.1080/02582473.2018.1468810 p. 329; R. Elphick and H. Giliomee (2014) 'The Origins and Entrenchment of European dominance at the Cape, 1652–c. 1840', in Elphick and Giliomee (eds), *The Shaping of South African Society, 1652–1840*, 2nd edition. Middletown, CT: Wesleyan University Press, pp. 521–66, p. 535.
10. Duff (2018) 'The Dutch Reformed Church and the Protestant Atlantic', p. 329.
11. See P. Coertzen (2011) 'The Huguenots of South Africa in history and religious identity', *Nederduitse Gereformeerde Teologiese Tydskrif*, 52:1–2, pp. 45–57.

12. See Schutte, 'Between Amsterdam and Batavia', p. 47.
13. James A. Michener (2015) *The Covenant: a novel*. New York: The Dial Press.
14. W. A. de Klerk (1978) *The Puritans in Africa: a Story of Afrikanerdom*. London: Rex Collings.
15. André du Toit (1983) 'No Chosen People: The Myth of the Calvinist Origins of Afrikaner Nationalism and Racial Ideology', *American Historical Review*, 88:4, pp. 920–52.
16. 'From the early days of the Cape Colony the variant of Calvinism that held sway had at its very core the idea of an omnipotent, sovereign God who intervened directly in the lives of individuals and communities. A covenant theology was reinforced by the sacrament of baptism. The doctrine underpinning baptism held that there was continuity between God's covenant with the Jews and the one He had with Christians. Accordingly, children of European parents at the Cape were considered 'born Christians' and as such deemed saved in the womb, which was symbolised by baptising the child as an infant.' Hermann Giliomee (2003) '"The Weakness of Some": The Dutch Reformed Church and White Supremacy', *Scriptura*, 83, pp. 212–44, p. 223.
17. Philippe Denis (2004) 'The Cape Huguenots and Their Legacy in Apartheid South Africa', in Bertrand Van Ruymbeke and Randy J. Sparks (eds), *Memory and Identity: The Huguenots in France and the Atlantic Diaspora (Carolina Low Country and the Atlantic World)*. Columbia: University of South Carolina Press, pp. 285–309, p. 301.
18. Ibid., pp. 300–1.
19. Ibid., p. 301.
20. See Schutte, 'Between Amsterdam and Batavia', p. 47.
21. See Elphick, *The Equality of Believers*.
22. Schutte, 'Between Amsterdam and Batavia', p. 49.
23. Robert Ross (2009) *Status and respectability in the Cape Colony, 1750–1870: a tragedy of manners*. Cambridge: Cambridge University Press, p. 47.
24. Ross, *Status and respectability*, p. 51.
25. Ibid.
26. Hermann Giliomee (2011) *The Afrikaners: biography of a people*. London: Hurst & Co., p. 194.
27. Ibid., p. 195.
28. Ibid.
29. See Timothy Johns (2013) 'The 1820 Settlement Scheme to South Africa.' *BRANCH: Britain, Representation and Nineteenth-Century History*. Ed. Dino Franco Felluga. Extension of *Romanticism and Victorianism on the Net*. Web (accessed 11 June 2020).
30. Ibid.
31. See Leonard Thompson (1995) *History of South Africa*. Revised Edition. New Haven, CT: Yale University Press, p. 55.
32. Thomas Pringle, *The Emigrant's Cabin*, quoted in Johns (2013).
33. Giliomee, *The Afrikaners*, p. 195.
34. Timothy Johns (2013); see J. M. Coetzee (1988) *White Writing: On the Culture of Letters in South Africa*. New Haven, CT: Yale University Press, p. 2.
35. See Johns (2013) in reference to Coetzee, p. 30.
36. Alan Lester (2001) *Imperial Networks: Creating Identities in Nineteenth-Century Britain and South Africa*. London: Routledge, p. 16, quoted in Johns (2013).

37. Giliomee, *The Afrikaners*, pp. 195–6.
38. John M. MacKenzie, with Nigel R. Dalziel (2007) *The Scots in South Africa: Ethnicity, Identity, Gender and Race, 1772–1914*. Johannesburg: Wits University Press, p. 9.
39. MacKenzie and Dalziel, *The Scots in South Africa*, p. 8.
40. Ibid., p. 48.
41. Thomas Pringle quoted in MacKenzie, p. 52.
42. MacKenzie and Dalziel, *The Scots in South Africa*, p. 55.
43. Ibid.
44. Ibid, p. 10.
45. Ibid., p. 13.
46. What makes this particularly interesting, and an important endeavour to pursue, is the fact that this history has been silent, even absent, in otherwise extensive recent research on Scottish–African connections. For example, I find no mention of this narrative in Afe Adogame and Andrew Lawrence (2014) *Africa in Scotland, Scotland in Africa: Historical Legacies and Contemporary Hybridities*. Leiden: Brill.
47. James Sturgis (1982) 'Anglicisation at the Cape of Good Hope in the early nineteenth century', *The Journal of Imperial and Commonwealth History*, 11:1, pp. 5–32. DOI: 10.1080/03086538208582629.
48. Kent Fedorowich (1991) 'Anglicization and the politicization of British immigration to South Africa, 1899–1929', *The Journal of Imperial and Commonwealth History*, 19:2, pp. 222–46. DOI: 10.1080/03086539108582837, p. 222.
49. Jean Comaroff and John L. Comaroff (2004) *Christianity, colonialism, and consciousness in South Africa*. Chicago: University of Chicago Press.
50. See Nathaniel Roberts (2012) 'Is conversion a "colonization of consciousness"?', *Anthropological Theory*, 12:3, pp. 271–94, https://doi.org/10.1177/1463499612469583
51. See Giliomee, *The Afrikaners*, p. 199.
52. Ibid.
53. See Frederick William Sass (1956) 'The Influence of the Church of Scotland on the Dutch Reformed Church of South Africa', unpublished PhD thesis, University of Edinburgh, pp. 14–15.
54. Ibid., p. 5.
55. Giliomee, *The Afrikaners*, p. 199.
56. Quoted in Giliomee, *The Afrikaners*, p. 199.
57. MacKenzie and Dalziel, *The Scots in South Africa*, p. 9.
58. Giliomee, *The Afrikaners*, p. 199.
59. MacKenzie and Dalziel, *The Scots in South Africa*, p. 17.
60. Olive Schreiner quoted in Giliomee, *The Afrikaners*, p. 202.
61. Giliomee, *The Afrikaners*, p. 202. See M. E. Rothman (ed.) (1976) *Oorlogsdagboek van 'n Transvaalse burger te velde*. Cape Town: Tafelberg, pp. 45–6.
62. Giliomee, *The Afrikaners*, p. 205
63. MacKenzie and Dalziel, *The Scots in South Africa*, p. 20. This debate came particularly to the fore in the post-South African War context as the fault lines between English- and Afrikaans-speaking whites in the Union of South Africa as an imperial entity became exposed. See, for example, the contributions of J. A. Retief, Nyasaland missionary and husband to the Scots Afrikaner, Helen Murray, in this regard. See Retief Müller (2014) 'War and "racial feeling"

in the writings of an Afrikaner missionary', *Studia Historiae Ecclesiasticae*, 40:2, pp. 71–84.
64. See, for example, Lucinda Manda-Taylor (2006) 'Violence and "othering" in colonial and post-colonial Africa. Case study: Banda's Malawi', *Journal of African Cultural Studies*, 18, pp. 197–213.
65. Esme Cleall (2012) *Missionary Discourses of Difference: Negotiating Otherness in the British Empire, 1840–1900*. London: Palgrave Macmillan, p. 166.
66. Ibid., p. 5.
67. Ibid., p. 145.
68. Ibid., p. 148.
69. Ibid., p. 152.
70. Ibid., pp. 152–3.
71. John Philip (1828) *Researches in South Africa*. London: James Duncan. With this work, Philip set forth his particular blend of radical evangelicalism, which emphasised the need for missionaries to be involved in politics. 1828 also saw important legal breakthroughs for equalisation measures he had long campaigned for: 'Ordinance 49 overturned the notion that the Bantu-speaking Africans across the eastern frontier should be kept entirely separate. They were now permitted to cross the border and seek work, regulated by the requirement that they must take out passes. This ordinance has been seen as the necessary corollary to the more famous Ordinance 50, for which John Philip had campaigned ceaselessly. This gave the Khoi and other free persons of colour equality before the law. It decriminalised "vagrancy" and abolished pass laws, compulsory labour service and child indenture while permitting Khoi to buy and own land as well as giving them the opportunity to enter into free contracts of labour.' MacKenzie, pp. 76–7.
72. See I. Schapera (1960) 'Livingstone and the Boers', *African Affairs: the Journal of the Royal African Society*, 59:235, pp. 144–56.
73. MacKenzie and Dalziel, *The Scots in South Africa*, p. 102.
74. Ibid., p. 69.
75. See Paul Goodman (2000) *Of one blood: Abolitionism and the origins of racial equality*. Berkeley: University of California Press.
76. See Cleall, p. 6.
77. See MacKenzie and Dalziel, *The Scots in South Africa*, pp. 101, 112.
78. Ibid., p. 124.
79. Ibid.
80. Ibid., p. 173.
81. Ibid., p. 174.
82. Duff even suggests that the DRC's apparent severance of ties with their mother church in the Netherlands was fully the Scots' doing. 'In 1824, the Scottish ministers gained full control of the DRC, having persuaded the colonial state to sever the church's ties with Classis Amsterdam, establishing it as separate and independent, with its own synod.' Duff (2018), p. 331.

CHAPTER TWO

Scots in South African Dutch Pulpits in the Early to Middle Nineteenth Century

The question of the 'other' and otherness more generally, and how such themes played out in the Scottish South African interactions over time, are central to the interests of this book. It will be shown that the most influential Scots in the DRC became willing yet partial Afrikaners over time. As I suggested in Chapter 1, this development might also have been part of an unacknowledged missionary strategy. Ironically, their essential missionary identity might have been more clearly perceived by those among whom they pastored than by themselves. Unsurprisingly, the Scots were not easily accepted as bona fide loyal members of the *volk* in the mainstream Dutch Afrikaner culture, and this underlying, sometimes open, suspicion against the Scots plays an important role in the narrative I am constructing.

An important source for this chapter is a 1956 doctoral thesis defended at the University of Edinburgh on 'The Influence of the Church of Scotland on the Dutch Reformed Church of South Africa' by Frederick William Sass. Sass briefly introduced a well-known narrative in South African DRC history, which concerns the idea that continental rationalist theology had become a trend among the Dutch clergy at the Cape in the aftermath of the handover from Dutch to British colonial rule in 1795. The prevalence of this supposedly unreliable theology in concurrence with the fact that a large number of pastoral vacancies remained unfilled convinced the British governor to take action. Although Sass merely states that this situation allowed the governor, Lord Charles Somerset, to take 'advantage of this situation',[1] I mentioned in Chapter 1 that this became a useful subset to a more general policy of anglicisation. Anglicise the DRC and you thereby defang the Dutch influence at the Cape, perhaps. Not that the Dutch influence had much teeth to speak of, as indicated in Chapter 1, but whatever residual resistance remained could now be effectively neutralised.

Hence, Somerset set about recruiting Scots Presbyterian ministers to serve in the DRC.

The first such appointee was George Thom in 1818, after Thom had resigned from the LMS. Born in Aberdeen in 1789,[2] theologically educated at the Gosport Academy and ordained at the Scots Kirk, London Wall, in April 1812,[3] Thom had an earnest desire to be a missionary overseas. He had originally prepared himself to serve in India, but he never made it all the way there. After arriving at Cape Town on 24 October 1812, he opted to remain on African soil rather than resuming the planned onward voyage across the Indian Ocean. This was after a Scots Regiment, the Sutherland Fencibles, had asked him to remain. This regiment had started a congregation and they wanted Thom to be their minister. Thom married a Cape Dutch woman, Christiana Louisa Meyer, in 1814, who tragically died two years later while giving birth to their first child. A few years later, Thom left the LMS after becoming dissatisfied with its administration in the Cape.[4]

After verifying the similarity of the doctrines of the Presbyterian Church in Scotland to that of the DRC, the governor, Charles Somerset, with the supporting opinion of the chief justice, appointed Thom to the DRC at Caledon in 1818.[5] Sass states that a special aspect of Thom's ministry was to the 'heathen around Caledon', which was an aspect of the work 'that bore much fruit'.[6] An honorary doctorate was conferred on him by the University of Glasgow in 1821. Sass credits Thom for among other things his role in advising the Glasgow Missionary Society to begin mission work in what is today the Eastern Cape.[7] Missionaries of this society constituted a presbytery in 'Kaffraria', as the region was called in colonial society in 1824.[8]

Thom served the DRC in Tulbagh between 1825 and 1833, but suffered from an unspecified mental illness, perhaps a form of depression, which enabled him to preach for only three years during this period. He died in Tulbagh on 10 May 1842. After the death of his first wife he had married Neeltje Maria Vos, also of Dutch Afrikaner stock. The Thoms became a prominent Afrikaner family over time. For example, one descendant, Dr H. B. Thom, became an apartheid-era principal of Stellenbosch University from 1954 to 1969.[9]

George Thom's most important legacy from the point of view of the DRC is the role he played as a recruiter of ministers. On 28 December 1818, Lord Somerset wrote to the Secretary of State for the Colonies, Earl Bathurst, as follows: 'I believe it has been before suggested that it would be desirable that the clerical vacancies in this settlement should be filled by ministers from Scotland, who however should be masters of the vernacular language of this place previous to their appointment.'[10]

The British government agreed to this and a subsequent step was that Dr Thom, who was on furlough in Britain in 1821, was commissioned by Somerset to recruit young Scottish ministers for South Africa.[11] Thom set about his task industriously, writing to and receiving positive responses from, among others, a Professor MacGill of the University of Glasgow and a Professor Bentley of King's College, Aberdeen,[12] agreeing to help in this recruitment drive.

Names of the eventual ministerial recruits included Alexander Smith, William Ritchie Thomson, Henry Sutherland, Colin Fraser and George Morgan. Thom also recruited six Scottish teachers, including James Rose Innes and William Robertson.[13] Perhaps the best known of the ministerial recruits was that of Aberdeen graduate, 'Andrew Murray, Master of Arts, a clergyman of about thirty years of age, of established character and of good abilities . . .'[14] After spending some time in the Netherlands to learn Dutch, Murray became lifelong minister in the Karoo town of Graaff Reinet. He married a Dutch Afrikaans woman, Maria Susanna Stegmann, in 1824.

Scots Ministers and the 'Great Trek'

Murray's Karoo parish was emblematic of a general pattern, since the Scots ministers tended to receive their appointments in parishes near the eastern frontier of the colony. Many of their congregants were Boers who steadily became more disaffected by the increase of abolitionary measures instituted at the behest of, most notably, LMS superintendent John Philip (see Chapter 1). This gave rise to what would become in the retelling the first mythical Afrikaner rebellion against what was portrayed as an oppressive and freedom-impinging British Empire.[15] The rebellion in the form of a migration became known in Afrikaner legend as the Great Trek, which eventually led to the establishment of Boer republics to the north of the Gariep River.

Because of their geographical situatedness, Scottish ministers were caught up in the mix. One name to mention is that of John Taylor, who along with another Scott, Thomas Reid, the minister of DRC Colesberg, were the first two to write and ask permission from their Presbytery (Ring) of Graaff Reinet to visit the emigrants in 1840.[16] Taylor arrived in the Cape on 13 January 1817 and like Thom, above, he originally served in the LMS, but he too resigned and was appointed as DRC minister at Beaufort West in 1818.[17] It is said that he married a Dutch woman who was born in Ceylon, Antonia Francina van Geyzel, with whom he had several children. A DRC *Gedenkboek* (memorial book) contains a photo of Revd and Mrs Taylor, as well as some background on a woman, who, although appearances in nineteenth-century photos might be deceiving, seems likely to be of indigenous Ceylonese extraction.[18]

According to the brief biography given, Ms van Geyzel was the sister of a widow of a British officer in Ceylon. The unnamed sister had met and married DRC Revd M. C. Vos after the latter had lost his first wife during a missionary excursion to Ceylon. When Vos and his Ceylonese wife journeyed back to South Africa in 1809, Antonia Francina accompanied them. She married Taylor, officiated by Vos, on 6 April 1817 at Caledon.[19]

It seems that Taylor and other LMS workers who exchanged their society positions for the more fixed government-funded positions as ministers in the DRC risked an amount of ire from their former colleagues. Hopkins mentions that Taylor on occasion defended himself by arguing that his parish in the newly founded district of Beaufort West would be larger than Yorkshire. To this his unnamed rhetorical opponent rebutted that had he gone a little deeper inland as missionary he could have had a parish the size of Great Britain![20]

In 1824 Taylor became the DRC minister at Cradock, where he remained

Ds. en Mev. John Taylor.

until his death on 21 May 1860. Sass mentions that Taylor had baptised the future president of the Transvaal, Paul Kruger, in 1826. Regarding his relationships with the emigrants (*Voortrekkers* as they would become known in Afrikaner history), the *Grahamstown Journal* reported in 1849:

> Rev. Mr. Taylor deserves also to be remembered as the Christian friend of the ill-used Emigrant farmers, when they left the Colony in despair in 1836–37. In order to arrest the migration some of the clergy determined to refuse all the rites of the church to those who had settled beyond the Orange River, but Mr. Taylor resisted the decision. He visited them, prayed with them, and for them. He stood between the living and the dead – among the faithful, faithful only he.[21]

This portrayal of Taylor as a friend of the migrants, however, tells a rather one-sided, even inaccurate story. The truth is that he, along with all other Scottish ministers in the DRC at large, were in opposition to this venture of migration. The *Kerkbode* of 30 March 1927 mentions the fact that exactly half of the ministers in the years 1836–8 were not born Afrikaners. As mentioned above, the majority of these 'foreign ministers' were situated exactly in the border congregations from whence the migration occurred.[22] One could, for example, refer to a letter by one of Taylor's congregants published in *De Zuid-Afrikaan* of 1 June 1838:

> On 18 March 1838 our minister [Revd Taylor] took his text from the Prophet Jonah, where he fled from God, and implicated thereby those

who are now readying themselves to become emigrants; but our minister is missing the point here, because nobody in the congregation here is so ignorant as to want to flee from the hand that God sends. They merely want to move to where the reign of Dr Philip is no longer honoured. [translation]²³

In a 28 September 1840 letter to the secretary of the governor, Taylor admitted to being strongly against the emigration, but he also expressed the willingness to visit them and administer the sacraments, since an invitation to do so from the emigrants had been received.²⁴

It turns out that over time the emigrants, at least some of them, were quite amenable to Revd Taylor, and he in turn seems to have become increasingly sympathetic to their situation. He was even approached to serve as their minister by members of the so-called *Potgieter trek*, but this call was not accepted. One example of the positive sentiment for Taylor is noted in a 1850 letter from Magaliesberg in which the author states among other things: 'We consider the Lord Taylor as the person most interested in our failings regarding the religion' [transl.].²⁵

Similar narratives regarding other Scots and their shifting allegiances over time might be told, including that of Andrew Murray Jr, a central character in South African church history, and much attention will be given to him in this book. Regarding the early Scottish ministers, there are at least a couple more that could be mentioned in somewhat greater detail. Scottish influence in the Cape DRC seems to have played at least a contributing role in terms of a schism of note that occurred, and which led to the establishment of the Gereformeerde Kerke, or the so-called *Doppers*.²⁶

The controversy surrounding the singing of evangelical hymns and the consequent establishment of the Gereformeerde Kerke was a subject in which Revd Thomas Reid, regarding whom I shall mention more shortly, was particularly central, but Taylor in Cradock also experienced some of the tension. He for the most part attempted as far as possible a reconciliatory approach to the proto-*Doppers*. I mentioned above the fact that he baptised the baby Paul Kruger on 19 March 1826.²⁷ Kruger would later be well known as president of the Transvaal and he was known to be a devout *Dopper*.

Thomas Reid was born in 1800 in Huntly, Aberdeenshire. After theological training and ordination, he went to Amsterdam in 1834 to study Dutch,²⁸ according to the above-mentioned mandate of Somerset. After his return to Scotland he left for South Africa and arrived in 1836, where he received legitimisation in the DRC and became minister of the Colesberg congregation. He stayed in Colesberg until his more or less forced resignation in 1854, whereafter he continued to reside there but no longer as minister.²⁹ He had a deeply contentious relationship with his congregants, among whom were many sympathisers of the *Dopper* view that opposed hymn singing. To explain this briefly, evangelical hymns sung in the DRC in Holland were introduced in the Cape Town congregation in 1814. From there these hymns were gradually taken up by other congregations throughout the Cape Colony. A conservative faction, in sympathy with like-minded dissenters in the Netherlands, in the north and north-eastern districts of the colony refused to sing these hymns, because, according to them, the hymns, unlike the Psalms, were not derived from Scripture. Hymns, they believed, imparted a foreign unscriptural theology.[30] While such dissenters were often tolerated to a degree, that is, allowed to remain silent during the singing of hymns, Revd Reid followed a much more polemical approach. He refused to baptise the children of such parents, refused them confirmation and refused to officiate in their marriages. They in turn desisted from attending church and partaking in Communion.[31]

Hymn singing was possibly only the catalyst to a developing problematic relationship between church members and their pastor over several years. The initial accusation to the Presbytery occurred in 1846. In a list of complaints against Revd Reid by which the dissatisfied members hoped to be rid of their troublesome minister, it is apparent that they mainly accused him of insulting words and behaviour towards them.[32] The impasse only ended after an agreement between him and the church council was reached that Reid would step down.

Badenhorst, who chronicled a history of the Colesberg congregation, mentions a few specific bones of contention between Reid and the congregation, which are of interest. One is that Reid allowed an English lady to act as organist. This, according to the dissenters, contravened the scriptural injunction that only men were allowed to act in the teaching office. The reasoning was that by playing the organ the unnamed organist somehow impeded the man who was in charge of leading the singing. It seems there were quite a few who objected to the very presence of the organ, and organ music in church. Another thing about Reid that they objected to was that he had invited Anglican priests to preach in his church. According to Badenhorst, these priests angered the congregants even further when they accused the 'Afrikaners of committing cruelties against the natives and that they were treating the coloured heathen badly' [transl.].[33]

Badenhorst reports only the *Dopper* indignity at these allegations. He does not comment on their possible veracity. A *Dopper* historian from the middle of the twentieth century did however have some interesting things to say that shed light on interracial attitudes in Colesberg in the mid-1800s:

> Because these people wanted to remain civilised reformed Christians, they were determined to walk in the ways of the Reformed Church reformation, as embodied in the Synod of Dort of 1618 to 1619. Any diversion from the Word of God in the doctrine, or in the moral life, or in the mixing and equalisation with uncivilised heathen natives were seen as an abomination. [transl.][34]

In the description of the proto-*Dopper* grievances against Reid it becomes apparent that racial attitudes featured as an underpinning factor for causing tension. One point of dissatisfaction was that 'he persisted in using the consistory for the giving of education to non-white women' [transl.]. He furthermore acted as 'agent for the welfare of the illegitimate children which the English [colonists] had with non-white women, and he would even allocate church money for the purpose' [transl.]. He also caused a public controversy when he removed 'a young non-white woman' from an ox-driving position in front of the *Voortrekker* wagon of Pretorius and Vermeulen.[35]

This last incident is unfortunately not further described but one might surmise that Reid's reasons for this action might have been either/or a combination of factors such as that the 'young woman' was perhaps not a woman at all but a child, or perhaps the terms of her service to these *Voortrekkers* were somewhat less than voluntary. The author, Spoelstra, concludes that 'all these unpleasant stimuli contributed to the Colesbergers identifying their minister as being in the same kraal as the philanthropic magistrate Rawstorne and the missionaries of the London Missionary Society' [transl.].[36]

Let me proceed to mention some other early Scottish ministers at the Cape who stayed until the end of their lives, many of whom eventually had towns and hamlets named after them. The dates mentioned here indicate their start date in South Africa and their year of death. John Evans served at Cradock between 1818 and 1823. Alexander Smith, a noted friend of missions, served at Uitenhage (1822–66). Henry Sutherland (1823–79) served at Worcester. Colin Fraser was minister between 1824 and 1870 at Beaufort West. He also had a similarly named son who became a minister in the Free State town of Philippolis for a time. George Morgan (1825–80) served at Somerset East and St Andrew's in Cape Town. His son, C. S. Morgan, subsequently served in the DRC in Cape Town. James Edgar (1828–48) served in Durban and Somerset West. William R. Thomson was minister at Stockenstroom, Alexander Welsh (1833–56) served at Glen Lynden and Robert Shand, who played a prominent role in the revivals of the 1860s and '70s, was minister of Tulbagh. A second group of Scottish ministers arrived in the 1860s, but I am focusing here on these early Scottish ministers, who in a number of cases together with their descendants played prominent roles in South African religious and social history. As mentioned previously, far and away the most significant name to add to this list is that of Andrew Murray (1822–66) at Graaff Reinet, and much of what follows will closely trace the roles played by Murray descendants, among whom the most famous was the second son, Andrew Murray Jr, of whom I shall say more shortly. First, let me zoom in on the life and role of another important early Scottish minister at the Cape, William Robertson. Robertson, 1831–79, served in South Africa for forty-eight years.[37] Recruited in Scotland by George Thom, he arrived in the Cape Colony in 1822 to work for the colonial government as teacher in Graaff Reinet. He occupied this position for five years, according to the historian Dreyer with great distinction. Then he returned to Scotland for higher education at Aberdeen and Edinburgh, as well as a few months at Utrecht in the Netherlands, in order to study divinity. In May 1831 he was accepted as candidate for ministry in Aberdeen, and the following month he received ordination, after which he undertook the journey back to South Africa. There he served as minister first at Clanwilliam (1831–3), then at Swellendam (1833–72) and finally at Cape Town (1872–8), where he died the following year.[38] Ten years after completing his initial theological studies, Aberdeen University conferred an honorary doctorate on Robertson.[39]

Although Robertson served in Clanwilliam for less than two years, the author of that congregation's *gedenkboek* wrote that he had made a positive impact there, including immersing himself in and adopting the culture and language of his congregants. Despite learning the Dutch language only as an adult, he was supposedly enthusiastic and dedicated about its usage, in contradistinction to some of the higher society Cape Dutch who often eschewed their language of birth. The author of Clanwilliam's congregational memorial, D. A. Kotzé, asserts that Robertson's indignation was inflamed on more than one occasion when someone, for example a lady of Dutch descent, would haughtily proclaim: 'I don't speak Dutch.'[40]

Whatever Robertson's true feelings about his church members might have been, to imagine on the basis of the above scenario that this Scot had 'gone native', that is, fully assimilated to the Cape Dutch culture, would be a stretch of the imagination. In fact, in an otherwise glowingly positive biographical chapter, Afrikaner church historian and missiologist G. B. A. Gerdener, who is best known for his crafting of early apartheid policies for church and government, describes Robertson as 'Engelsgesind' (English-oriented).

For an interesting comparative glimpse into the purely numerical strength of the Scots influence on the mid-nineteenth-century Cape Dutch society, one could take heed of Gerdener's comment that in 1833, the year that Robertson began his ministry in Swellendam, Scots comprised twelve of a total of twenty-two minsters in the DRC of South Africa. Gerdener also writes that Robertson did not take much time to, for example, start appealing the government to recruit Scots teachers with theological training for work in South Africa, albeit without success. He also endeavoured strongly for the launching of English-language services in the DRC. Some of his plans he aborted subsequently, after, presumably, much resistance from the Dutch population. These plans included an idea to enforce the availability of English-language services under certain conditions, as well as a plan to have the Scots Confession translated into Dutch. In this rare critical paragraph, Gerdener argued that Robertson's advocacy of English services contributed to a situation wherein a younger generation grew up with little or no knowledge of the Dutch language.[41]

Robertson spent the bulk of his ministry, thirty-seven years, in Swellendam, during which time he, among other things, served as moderator of the

DRC.[42] During the early part of this period his name should be mentioned in connection with the initial resistance from the Cape church leadership against the above-mentioned Revds Taylor and Reid's application for leave to serve the sacraments to the emigrants due to the suspected 'impure motivations' of the emigrants.[43]

Among the documents included in Dreyer's collection of sources on the theme of the Cape church and the Great Trek, a letter by Dr Robertson most notably offers illumination on this tension. Writing on 13 March 1836 to the journalist John Fairbairn in Cape Town, Robertson relates conversations he had had with members in a distant part of his parish who were all set on the 'idea of going to Port Natal'. He enquired regarding their reasons for wishing to undertake this venture, and upon realising that much of their motivation was based on false information and poor moral principles, Robertson sought to dissuade them.

> Many of them, particularly the women, came and thanked me for so explaining matters and I hope the most of them will give up the foolish idea. It may be amusing however to hear some of their reasons for leaving the land of their birth, . . .[44]

Robertson then proceeded to list several of these 'amusing' reasons. Let me highlight the most interesting ones here. The so-called Roman danger, which often served as a suitable bogeyman for common or garden Calvinists around the world, raised its spectre here:

> [I]t has got abroad among the poor that the Church of the Colony is to become Roman Catholic, and it has even been said, and many seemed to believe it, that more than one half of the inhabitants of Cape Town had already joined the Roman Catholic Church . . .

Popular people's (*volks*) theology about Bible and mission were evidently also present, as the following quoted motivations make clear:

> Many have also been induced to believe that it is distinctly foretold by the Prophet Joel and also in the 24th chapter of Matthew that they are to flee to another country and that their emigration is therefore necessary for the fulfilment of these parts of Scripture . . . Many have also been in some way given to understand that their emigration is necessary for the extension of the gospel among the Heathen Tribes among whom they purpose settling themselves.[45]

As seen from the above, there was an implicit self-identification with the biblical Israel, and moreover notions of a holy conquest of a mythological land of milk and honey, as the following statement by Robertson makes clear:

> The most extravagant notions have been given them by means of journals and Letters of the fertility of the Soil and the Beauty of the

> Climate – 'They may have three crops in a year' – 'It is always summer there,' 'Every sort of manufacture may be purchased for *one fourth* of the price for which it can be obtained in this Colony.' 'The new Colony is to be named *Palestina*, and some say *New Holland.*'[46]

The listing of these motivations, which Robertson found amusing, offers useful information regarding the rank-and-file emigrating farmers' views of religiosity and its connection to themes of land, nation and the indigenous inhabitants, which recalls the discussion in Chapter 1 regarding the extent to which a 'chosen people' discourse might have been operative here. It also gives a quite different view of Robertson in terms of his positioning vis-à-vis the emerging Afrikaner identity formation brought about by this process of migration. The so-called Great Trek left him apparently at best amused, at worst disheartened and appalled. In fact, he leaves his readership with no doubt as to what the main push factor for the migrants might have been:

> The chief reason, however, of those who are principal movers in the matter, is – 'the final abolition of Slavery' – the pecuniary loss which they have sustained by the 'Compensation' – and the fear of not being able to procure servants.[47]

Robertson stated that he could easily debunk most of the stated motivations by explaining their error:

> With regard to the last reason I reminded that Slavery was founded in Injustice – and contrary to the Law to do unto others as we would wish them to do unto us – I reminded them that its abolition was a compromise of difficulties and told them of the immense sum given by England for that purpose.[48]

In other words, argues Robertson, abolition had not been a case of expropriation without compensation. To the contrary, the people of England themselves carried the financial burden. They, who never had any benefit from slave-ownership, 'were now *willingly* taxed . . .'[49]

Robertson finally asserted that his appeals for staying within the confines of the British Empire were acceptable to many of those he spoke to, and he could but only hope that these would be sufficient to persuade many against the path of folly chosen by the emigrant leaders.

Notwithstanding Robertson's initial scepticism of and resistance to the migrations, in the following decade, late in 1848, he would accompany P. E. Faure on a tour to the north of the Gariep River, where he would serve for four months as evangelist among the emigrants. As described in the Swellendam congregational *gedenkboek*, this, however, was conceived more like a missionary tour than the visit of an interim minister among far-flung church members. No, the emigrants had to be evangelised, and Robertson, who harboured strong missionary interests, as will also be seen in Chapter 3, was well-suited to the task, apparently.[50]

Andrew Murray of Graaff Reinet, Patriarch of the Murray Clan in South Africa

Let us now return to the initial recruitment of Robertson by George Thom. On the ship travelling back to South Africa together with Thom were six young teachers, Innes, Dawson, Blair, Rattray, Brown and Robertson. Then there was Andrew Murray, the first Scot to be recruited to serve as minister in the DRC, after spending ten months in the Netherlands to learn Dutch. During that initial period of Robertson's career in South Africa, he stayed at the parsonage in Graaff Reinet. Murray, who was appointed there in 1822, would become lifelong minister of the Graaff Reinet congregation.[51]

Murray came from an Old Light Presbyterian family of pastoralists in Aberdeenshire that had lost their farm due to economic hardship following the Napoleonic Wars. Afterwards, his parents occupied the apparently lesser occupation of mill ownership in Clatt. There was, however, some money in the extended family which helped the millers' children to earn education – theological degrees in the case of both Andrew and his older brother, who eventually became Revd Dr John Murray of the Free New North Church in Aberdeen.[52] Andrew wanted to be a missionary, and after rejecting one call to serve a church in Newfoundland, he accepted Thom's invitation to South Africa a year later, apparently partly due to his belief that this would allow him to live out his missionary vocation.[53]

In her family memoir, *Unto Children's Children*, Maria (Murray) Neethling wrote that her father immediately immersed himself in the life of his adopted church and society. He played an active role at the DRC's first synod of 1824 in Cape Town. Among the committees he served on there was one concerning the founding of a theological seminary, a project that would come to fruition more than three decades later with his eldest son John appointed as first professor (see Chapter 3).[54]

The next year, 1825, saw Murray return to Cape Town, this time to marry Maria Susanna Magdalena Stegmann, sixteen years old at the time of her marriage.[55] She became the family matriarch, with eleven children surviving into adulthood, and she died at the age of eighty at Graaff Reinet in 1889. This Scottish-Dutch marriage and its offspring, proverbially germinated in the Karoo soil of Graaff Reinet, encapsulate more than any other comparable family the emergence of the Scots Afrikaners as a factor in South African history, and especially in the settler context of the DRC. As mentioned in Chapter 1, this might be termed a hybridity, or perhaps it is better described as a cultural bilingualism. Or, to those who would over time find it expedient to be suspicious of hybrid identities and their implicit ambiguity, it would be more akin to a Scottish kernel embedded in a Dutch husk. Whatever the case, the dual identity started at the linguistic level and was steeped in religious practice. Take the following statement by Maria Neethling regarding Andrew Murray, for example: 'His pulpit and family prayers were in Dutch. His own private devotions and prayers with his children, or on special occasions, were in English.'[56] He was perhaps publicly Dutch, but privately Scottish/English, as a cynic might argue.

Andrew Murray as DRC minister, serving a mainly Dutch settler population, apparently also kept up an active interest in the spiritual and social situation of the indigenous people of South Africa. According to a 1972 *Sunday Times* article about the Murray Clan, published to commemorate their 150-year history in South Africa, Murray was something of a proto-abolitionist as well. Paraphrasing *Unto Children's Children*, the article relates:

> Long before slavery was abolished, he had espoused the cause of the slave. When upon his marriage a female slave, according to the custom of the time, was given to his bride to accompany her to her new home, Mr. Murray gave the girl her liberty before she set out with them. And when travelling in the Karoo, often for periods of up to a fortnight at a time, and had stopped for the night at farmhouses, he always asked to conduct services. He then insisted that all the servants and shepherds be brought in to take part.[57]

This connects to Murray's missionary interests, which meant that despite supposedly fully immersing himself in the Dutch culture of the Karoo, he never came to share the prevailing anti-missionary sentiments common among the Dutch farmers. To the contrary, he himself was a missionary at heart, and he maintained friendships with a wide array of other missionaries and extended hospitality to many of them at the Graaff Reinet parsonage. Neethling writes:

> Of the visits of the missionaries how much there is to tell! English, Scotch, French and German missionaries found it not only convenient, but most refreshing, to rest themselves and their wearied oxen midway on the long journey between Port Elizabeth and the interior. . . . Men and animals found room in the spacious house and yard, the out-rooms affording lodging to a whole host of Bechuana or Basuto drivers and leaders of oxen . . . How fresh in the minds of some of the children are still today the visits of Mr. Moffat and of Dr. Livingstone, since become so famous . . . And some years later the children were called to listen while Papa read aloud letters he had received from the explorer, telling of his early journeys into the far interior, where he found tribes who manufactured gold rings and bracelets. Lively recollections are cherished of the earlier French missionaries – Pellissier, Roland, Casalis, Lemue, Lauga, Arbousset, Daumas . . .[58]

Elsewhere, Neethling relates a letter her father had written to her two brothers, John and Andrew, at the time residing with their uncle in Aberdeen as young teenage boys for the purpose of furthering their education. The subject of discussion was their hoped-for careers upon reaching adulthood, and here their father implores them to avoid law, to consider either medicine or theology as viable options at the Cape, or, it seems most laudable of all, missionary work in India![59]

It is with the Murray children that the term Scots Afrikaners really becomes an applicable designation. With a Cape Dutch mother and Scots father, there was no question about the authenticity of their hybridity. It is in reference to them and their descendants that the 1972 *Sunday Times* article could state, almost apologetically:

> The Murray family of today is a living rebuttal of the theory that there can never be national unity in South Africa between English-speaking and Afrikaans-speaking people – only cooperation and that on terms![60]

The Scottish side of this hybrid identity was strengthened particularly in the case of the above-mentioned two elder sons, John and Andrew. They were sent to Scotland at ages ten and twelve respectively, for a period of seven years, which ended up being followed by four years of seminary education in the Netherlands.[61]

> But when, ordained in the church, they returned to the Cape they brought back with them, as did their two younger brothers who followed them to Scotland, the civilising influence of Scottish scholarship, tradition and learning which has spread far and wide in South Africa.[62]

The two younger brothers in question were Charles and William. The former would succeed his father as lifelong minister at Graaff Reinet, and William would be founder of an institute for hearing-impaired learners in the town of Worcester. Of John, the first professor at the Stellenbosch Seminary, and particularly Andrew, the famous evangelical writer and advocate of missions, much more will be said.

Before moving on to the narrative of the early careers of John and Andrew Jr, let me add a couple more points of interest regarding their father, and his relations with the Cape Dutch people. There is almost no question that the assertions regarding his willingness to throw in his lot with these people are accurate. Consider this testimony related in *Unto Children's Children*:

> He cast his lot so whole-heartedly with his people that his children cannot remember ever hearing him express the wish to visit his native land . . . How often we have heard him say, 'the lines have fallen to me in pleasant places, I have a goodly heritage'.[63]

However, that was a perspective developed during the course of his career in Graaff Reinet. Initially, such eventual closeness with the Cape Dutch/ Dutch Afrikaners might have been unanticipated. I believe that the key to understanding Andrew Murray, and quite likely the same is true of peers like the above-mentioned Robertson, has to do with his initial motivation for going to South Africa, and his lifelong passion, missionary work. Might it be that he in fact fulfilled his vocation, that he, not to mention the other early Scots ministers, became a de facto missionary among the Dutch Afrikaners, even if the open acknowledgement of such an idea would have been scandalous among a people who considered themselves white and therefore Christian? Yet this is no far-fetched idea, considering for example the following glimpse offered of the early Scots ministers and their unredacted views of the Cape Dutch, as seen in an excerpt of Andrew Murray's diary during the sea voyage to Cape Town in the company of George Thom, William Robertson and the other teacher recruits:

> Thursday the wind continued favourable, so that we were able to make considerable distance of easting. In the evening had some amusement respecting the manners and customs of the Cape farmers. All seemed to enjoy the description Dr. Thom gave of the simplicity of their manners. This description reminded us of those ages when tyrant customs had not shackled man.[64]

In other words, Andrew Murray and other missionary enthusiasts from Scotland were going to a field ripe for the tilling. It was perhaps not an atypical missionary enterprise, except for the somewhat anomalous hue and provenance of their native missionary subjects, the Cape Dutch.

John Murray and Andrew Jr in Aberdeen and Utrecht

If the above perspective on the missionary motivations of the early Scots ministers holds water, then it is also not surprising that a similar missionary ethos would be instilled in the second generation. Andrew Jr and his brother John would over time become instrumental in an evangelical revival movement at the Cape, which served as a necessary substrate for further missionary engagements of the DRC (see Chapters 3 and 4). After receiving their MA degrees from Marischal College in Aberdeen, where they had been living and studying for several years under the care of their uncle (see below), Andrew and John went to Utrecht in the Netherlands for their theological education. Having exchanged Scotland for Holland they did not, however, divest themselves of Scottish influences. Their father, who had also spent time in the Netherlands prior to taking the voyage to South Africa, had worried that they would become corrupted by worldly habits such as cigar smoking and gin drinking. Instead they became heavily involved in a pietistic revivalist movement exemplified in their membership of the society *Sechor Dabar* (Remember the Word), of which more below. As for their father back in Graaff Reinet:

> Mr. Murray was delighted when in due course he heard that his sons had both become associated with the Revival movement, started by two Scottish laymen, Robert and James Haldane, which had spread to Holland.[65]

This interest in, and exposure to, revivalism was hardly a new development for the two Murray sons. Back in Aberdeen, under the tutelage of their uncle, John, and active members of the North Church congregation he led there, the younger Murrays were already deeply steeped in similar currents sweeping through Scotland in the 1840s. The name of the revivalist preacher William C. Burns could be mentioned here. Burns, a nephew of Revd Dr John Murray's wife, resided at the North Church parsonage during his time there, and apparently 'nowhere was his work more fruitful than in connection with the North Church'.[66] Burns, to resume a familiar theme, had initially wanted to be a missionary, but had come to an understanding of the great evangelistic need to be found among his own Scottish people, and this set him on the route to revivalist preaching, a ministry in which he was also keenly supported by John Murray in Aberdeen.[67]

In contemporary perspective it may seem completely logical that prospective theological students in South Africa's DRC might have wanted to study in the Netherlands, at a place like Utrecht. However, making such a move from Scotland, despite the geographical proximity, was apparently not a well-trodden path at all in the early to mid-nineteenth century. Van der Watt, in his biography of John Murray, suggests that Holland was largely an unknown entity within the circles that the young Murrays moved in in Aberdeen. Their uncle declined their invitation to journey with them to this foreign land, because this would supposedly not be worth the effort since during his life up until then he had only encountered two persons from the Netherlands. When they approached the well-known Professor John Duncan from New College, Edinburgh to request letters of recommendation, he admitted to the young John and Andrew that he had zero contacts with colleagues at any of the Dutch universities.[68]

Apparently, Utrecht was chosen over other Dutch universities such as Leiden and Groningen, less because of academic reasons and more to do with reasons of affordability in cost of living and the scenic walkways to be found in the area. There was, however, also a perception that Utrecht students were slightly more pious and less under the influence of Dutch liberalism than some of the other available options. However, the young Murrays were apparently not exactly enthralled with the quality of the lectures they received there. For example, as Andrew wrote to their parents: 'The lectures here are such that it is almost impossible to get any good from them.'[69] John in a similar vein wrote to his father in September 1846 regarding the necessity for the DRC of South Africa of having a theological institution to train ministers, catechism teachers and regular teachers. In this letter John implored his father to try to rid their church as quickly as possible of Holland, because the people of South Africa had a completely skewed view of this country. John decried the theological teaching, particularly in Leiden and Groningen, the fact that preachers spoke with disdain of *Dordtse regzinnigheid* (Dordt's orthodoxy) and saw no problem in adapting the words in the forms of unity. If people in South Africa knew about this, as well as the immorality of the Dutch theological students, they would quickly sever ties with the Netherlands, in John's opinion.[70]

The theological teachings and religious life in nineteenth-century rationalistic Netherlands thus failed initially to inspire the two Murrays, who were used to the warm evangelicalism they had imbibed in Aberdeen. In fact, it seems that connections formed through student societies not only played a formative role on specifically their spiritual formation, but also to a large degree served to shape their theological and social orientation (see below). An important countering influence to the spirit of rationalism was represented in the Netherlands in the so-called *Reveil*, a movement that emphasised the inner life of faith, and outwardly a practical and true Christian life.[71] Doctrinal orthodoxy was de-emphasised in favour of Christian living. In this sense it was thus comparable to, and perhaps influenced by, early nineteenth-century developments in Germany where Friedrich Schleiermacher, for example, responded to religion's 'cultured despisers' not by attempting to attack the opponents' rationalistic enquiry, but instead by circumventing the very logic of this type of debate, by locating the locus of religion in *Gefühl*.[72] Similarly, a life of devotional contemplation inspiring practical Christianity seems to have been the backbone of the *Reveil*.

One of the primary locations where the *Reveil* became anchored in the religious community, initially as a literary movement, was in the meetings of the *Christelijke Vrienden* (Christian Friends) in the years 1845 to 1854 in Amsterdam and elsewhere. Focused on Bible study and intense prayer sessions, these meetings delivered practical consequences through the founding of educational and social institutions, Christian residences, all premised on welfare and evangelisation. Related movements also emerged in Utrecht, including student organisations, such as *Secor Dabar*,[73] which became a spiritual home for the Murrays, and ultimately a society with immense secondary influence in the South African context.

Secor Dabar's main goal was 'to practice the sciences that were advanced for the office of gospel preacher' [transl.].[74] The Murrays became members of this society upon befriending a Dutch student, N. H. de Graaff. They were officially accepted in a meeting held on 8 October 1844. Van der Watt mentions that the Murrays' future brother-in-law, J. H. Neethling, would become a member the following year. Two more South Africans, H. E. Faure and N. J. Hofmeyr, would become members in 1848.[75] Over time, these people would become among the most influential figures in the DRC of South Africa. For example, the pair of Hofmeyr and John Murray were destined to become the first two professors of the Stellenbosch Theological Seminary. For these reasons it might not be entirely correct to imagine that the Stellenbosch Seminary was founded in the spirit of Utrecht. More to the point, it was founded in the spirit of *Secor Dabar*. I shall return to this theme in Chapter 3.

Not only did *Secor Dabar* involve itself in various aspects of practical

Christianity, such as welfare and education, it also, to a large extent due to the presence of the Murray brothers, founded a mission organisation, *Eltheto*, of which John and Andrew were founding members. *Eltheto* also published its own journal, *Berigten aangaande de uitbreiding van Gods Koninkrijk op Aarde* (Notices regarding the expansion of God's Kingdom on Earth), of which John Murray was the first editor.[76]

The formative role of *Secor Dabar* on the life of Andrew Murray is emphasised by the fact that as the DRC's most influential minister in Wellington, on 15 September 1884 he wrote to N. H. de Graaff to express his appreciation for everything that the society had meant to him, his by then deceased brother John, as well as their younger brother, William. In the letter, Andrew testified that he understood *Secor Dabar* to be one of the 'preparatory schools that had equipped them for the service of the Lord' [transl.].[77]

Andrew Jr and John Murray as Missionary Ministers in South Africa

The above captured some of the highlights of the two elder Murray sons' overseas sojourn. Let me now proceed to mention some interesting aspects regarding their ongoing identity formation vis-à-vis the budding Afrikaner *volk* back in South Africa. I have already suggested that their father and other first-generation Scots ministers might have understood themselves as missionaries to the rural and often recalcitrant Cape Dutch. Did such a missionary identity also inspire the younger Murrays in terms of their relations with the *volk*?

John Murray is best known in South African church history for the role he played as the first professor of the Stellenbosch Seminary, which indeed inaugurated an episode of pivotal importance, as this was the first educational venture in a series of developments that would eventually morph into Stellenbosch University, as it is known today. A lesser-known episode in John's biography concerns the preceding period, during which time he was minister in the Karoo town of Burgersdorp. In terms of emerging Afrikaner identity politics and the Scots Afrikaners' positioning vis-à-vis all of that, this period in John's life is likely of even greater importance. This is because Burgersdorp became intrinsically involved in the first major religious schism in the Dutch Afrikaner community. After the secession of a group in the Transvaal in 1859 to form the Gereformeerde Kerke van Suid Afrika, colloquially known as the *Doppers*, a local Gereformeerde congregation was formed in Burgersdorp. Subsequently, this denomination's first seminary would also open its doors in Burgersdorp before eventually moving to Potchefstroom in the Transvaal. Burgersdorp also emerged as a centre of activism for the reinstatement of Dutch as an official language towards the end of the nineteenth century.[78]

Murray arrived in Burgersdorp in mid-1849. According to Van der Watt's chapter heading on the subject, this was a period of 'blessed congregational ministry'.[79] Murray was known as a powerful preacher and energetic leader who actively worked towards the institutionalisation of devotional and educational programmes and missionary activities, some of which had met with resistance from the church council and congregants. In apparent anticipation of an era of revival that would envelop many DRC congregations during the following decade, Murray struggled to institute regular communal prayer events, known as *bidure*, something that would later become central to the weekly programmes of most DRC congregations, but which some of Murray's church members opposed. Such members exhibited what Murray euphemistically described as a 'unique way of thinking' (*eigenaardige denkwyze*).[80] He also agitated against the near-exclusive use of formalistic prayers as printed and used in family devotions in a context where a culture of spontaneous prayer was relatively unfamiliar.

Murray also encountered racial thinking as an indelible aspect of these noticeably unique thought patterns of rural Afrikaners. He was not pleased with what he described as their 'prejudice against colour'. He sought to change perceptions and so, in 1857, one of his actions in this regard was to have a missionary appointed specifically for work among the local 'heathen',[81] probably in reference to African farmworkers. Other concrete activities of Murray in this regard included the founding of a 'Mission School' in collaboration with government funding, the institution of English-language church services, and Van der Watt mentions what must have seemed particularly scandalous for some congregants: on Sunday evenings he held services for 'coloureds' and these proved popular also with many whites choosing to attend these events.[82]

If this set of issues between minister and congregants is already starting to sound familiar, let me also mention the fact that the 'unique way of thinking' that confronted Murray in Burgersdorp was apparently mostly to be found among those harbouring oppositional thinking with respect to the hymns. Compared to the confrontational approach of the above-mentioned Reid in Colesberg, Murray, at least initially, followed a more accommodating route, declaring that on many occasions he would make use exclusively of the Psalms when he found himself in neighbourhoods where the majority would rather not sing hymns.[83]

However, cracks in the relationship between Murray and the anti-hymn faction soon started to emerge and then quickly widened. According to Spoelstra, congregants objected to Murray's preaching, which was judged to be tinged by Methodism.[84] Murray, for his part, in 1877 as reported in the *Cape Monthly Magazine*, mentioned as problematic, apart from the issue of hymn singing, the differences over race relationships between him and these *Doppers*, as well as the fact that they insisted 'to preserve the most rigid type of Calvinist orthodoxy'.[85] In fact, Spoelstra listed a series of theological and church orderly issues, as well as reasons best described as premised on the emerging politics of identity, as contributing factors in the Burgersdorp schism. Van der Watt summarised these factors, among which the most interesting in addition to Murray's alleged Methodism, and his importation of innovations like hymn singing and communal prayer services, were their complaints about a perception that the Cape church had become anglicised (*verengelsing*), and most interesting of all: the fact that 'non-whites were allowed to use the whites' church building [which] was seen as church integration' [transl.].[86]

Chapter 3 elaborates more on this time period generally, where attention will be given to the 1857 synod and its alleged role in the construction of apartheid. I also return to the theme of the founding of the Stellenbosch Seminary, where more will be said about John Murray, because, as I have already mentioned, subsequent to concluding his career in congregational ministry he took up a new role as professor in Stellenbosch. I now turn to the early career of John's brother, Andrew.

Andrew Jr is by far the more famous of these two elder brothers in the South African Murray clan. One reason for this is simply that he had a much longer career, spanning into the first decades of the twentieth century. Consequently, more will be said about him in the coming chapters, but similar to the case of John, less about Andrew is generally known and talked about concerning the early stages of his career, subsequent to the brothers' return from Europe. When John was appointed as minister at Burgersdorp, Andrew was given a parish even deeper into the rural hinterland, outside the boundaries of the Cape Colony in the Orange River Sovereignty settlement of Bloemfontein. These appointments were made by the Cape governor, Sir Harry Smith. After an interview with the two brothers, Smith assigned John to the parish of Burgersdorp, which at least found itself within the borders of the Cape Colony. This decision was based on the hierarchy of age, and with Andrew being the younger he received the less desirable settlement of Bloemfontein.[87] This was a frontier settler community, in close proximity to and often in states of conflict with the Basotho people. It was also the northernmost parish of the imperially sponsored DRC. As such, it placed the young Andrew Murray in a unique, shall we call it missionary-like position with respect to the emigrant farmers who had exiled themselves from the British Empire in favour of an independent, Afrikaner-ruled existence beyond the Vaal River. To quote du Plessis, 'And thus Andrew became the first pastor of a territory nearly fifty thousand square miles in extent, and the first regular minister to live and labour among the *voortrekkers*.'[88] I believe it is possible to argue that just as his father and other first-generation Scots ministers in the DRC had in important if unstated respects conceived of themselves as missionaries to the rural Cape Dutch, so Andrew Jr now became a 'missionary' to these northerly emigrants.[89]

In keeping with their sentiments for leaving the Cape Colony in the first place, it should be clear that Dutch Afrikaners in both the Orange River Sovereignty and Transvaal were not generally speaking on good terms with missionaries. They were particularly averse to representatives of the LMS. I have mentioned John Philip's association with Ordinance 50, which purported to secure equalisation between the Khoisan and white population groups.⁹⁰ Philip's work, 'Researches in South Africa', was considered slanderous due to the portrayals of the unjust interracial relations existing between these settler farmers and the indigenous population.⁹¹ However, it was not only Philip and the LMS that attracted the ire of Dutch Afrikaner landholders. In the Orange River Sovereignty, the Paris Evangelical Missionary Society (PEMS) worked among the Basotho, a group of people that suffered frequent attacks and conflict over land and accusations of livestock theft from the local Boers.⁹² PEMS missionaries naturally aligned themselves with the plight of their spiritual flock. From the Afrikaner Boer point of view, on the other hand, such attitudes placed the PEMS in exactly the same boat as the LMS, which they identified as imperial agents seeking to curtail the Afrikaner drive to independence. This was an important nuancing factor in understanding the context within which Andrew Murray landed as minister of the DRC in Bloemfontein. Furthermore, as a so-called Scottish minister, he was immediately perceived to be in cahoots with these other foreign missionary societies. Spoelstra enunciates this type of sentiment in the following manner, which I translate from Afrikaans:

> Many of the first Scottish ministers in the Cape Church were originally missionaries of Societies. The Cape Church consequently fell in line with the Societies' mission . . . At church councils an appeal was made that special effort should be taken for the heathen at church services and catechisms. Some *Voortrekkers*, that left the country shortly hereafter, feared that the Cape Church was moving in the same direction as the London Missionary Society.⁹³

Spoelstra further describes the feelings against missionaries of Boers in the Orange River Sovereignty:

> Their getting acquainted with the London Missionary Society at Philippolis, the French mission stations at Bethulie and in Basotholand, and the sympathy of the Scots ministers with the Societies generated great dissatisfaction . . . [transl.]⁹⁴

Spoelstra furthermore refers to a correspondence between William Robertson and the British colonial authority, at the conclusion of the former's evangelisation tour together with P. E. Faure to the Transgariep and Transvaal. Herein Robertson argued for an extension of British sovereignty to the Transvaal, and according to Spoelstra it was as a consequence of this proposal that Andrew Murray was appointed by the colonial authority as minister at Bloemfontein in February 1849.⁹⁵ The suggestion seems to be that in this way an imperial agent was planted in the midst of the independent-minded Boers. Moreover, as indicated above, Murray fulfilled the role of the Cape Church's representative in the whole northerly region, including the Transvaal. Spoelstra intimates that the British authorities were quite happy with this arrangement, because according to an unnamed government source, his services there 'would tend more towards the security of our Frontier, than 2,000 soldiers'.[96]

A significant segment of the Dutch Afrikaner population in the Orange River Sovereignty favoured independence from Britain, and during the course of the early 1850s it became apparent that the young Andrew Murray instead supported the British-leaning opposition to the proposed independence.[97]

There are some interesting aspects regarding Murray's visits to and contact with the Transvaalers. He ultimately made four extended journeys into the Transvaal, the third one accompanied by his brother John. On the final tour, his fellow *Secor Dabar* member, J. H. Neethling, went along with him. Neethling would also become part of the family by marrying Andrew and John's sister Maria in 1852.[98]

One of the towns Murray and Neethling visited, and where they apparently preached and evangelised with much success, was Potchefstroom,[99] which by then was already a familiar congregation to Andrew. Around the turn of the year 1850/1 Murray had even received a call to be minister of the congregation at Potchefstroom, which after much internal wrangling he formally declined on 9 March 1851.[100] Murray's own musings during the decision-making process, as expressed in a letter to his father, are however instructive for the light in which he viewed the invitation to the pastorate at Potchefstroom:

> What young minister would be willing to go across the Vaal River? I have been brought in the leading of Providence to take an especial interest in this people, which may not be excited in the heart of anyone else. God has now set before the Church an open door across the Vaal River, and if we enter not in, it may soon be shut.[101]

Clearly then, as this statement indicates, Murray considered the Transvaal a mission field within which the Church remained absent as of yet. One might easily imagine how his own missionary heart must have been kindled by this prospect. His description of his 1850 tour of the region reveals a situation where he visited various *Voortrekker* settlements, sometimes baptising people, and on other occasions refusing to administer baptism to children when those parents requesting it seemed morally compromised, as Murray describes one such situation: 'I felt too that they were wholly unprepared for the administration of such an holy ordinance, drinking and cursing having been but too much the order of the day.'[102]

Although Murray reports that he generally had a good impression of the people in the area of Magaliesburg, where he baptised more than a hundred children,[103] when he set off in a westerly direction towards 'the Morikwa' he ran into some trouble, which is instructive for understanding how at least one section of the Boer population viewed Murray and others of his ilk. A short way from the 'church-place', Murray and his party were suddenly detained by a group of Boers. They refused to release him until he had given 'an account' of himself. This situation of disputation went on for several days, with Murray put on informal trial 'while some forty Boers stood round . . .' Apparently they were deeply suspicious of Murray's affiliation and loyalties. The accusers brought forth 'all sorts of nonsensical demonstrations about the duty of coming out of Antichrist . . ., in order to prove that I could not be a true minister till I came out from under the English Government to this side of the Vaal River. Of course there was no arguing with such people . . .' Despite being eventually allowed to preach there on the Sunday, the next day, Monday saw another public dispute:

> The three heroes, Paul Roos, Stoffel de Wet and Jacob Erasmus, came forward, and immediately began to prove that England is a horn of the beast, etc. I need not repeat all the nonsense, I may almost say blasphemy, which they uttered . . . [T]hey literally seek their salvation in their opposition to the Antichrist. May the Lord have mercy on them.[104]

If these journeys across the Vaal River might be understood as 'missionary' journeys, an important qualifier to emphasise here is that the missionary subjects were emphatically the Boers rather than the indigenous African population. This was perhaps not due to any racial bias on the side of Murray, but the consequence of his own linguistic capabilities and constraints. On these tours he preached in Dutch, and although local Africans were not excluded from such gatherings, they were not likely to understand much of what was said. Nonetheless, Africans sometimes participated in or at least observed the proceedings. An interesting anecdote relayed by travelling companion J. H. Neethling gives a sense of a local unnamed African attendee's perception of the nature of the relationship between Murray and his Boer evangelistic subjects:

> I never thought that the white men stood in such dread of their chiefs. Look at the young chief yonder [that is, Murray]. He points his finger at the people: they sit quiet. He threatens them: they sit quiet still. He storms and rages at them: they sit as quiet as death![105]

Andrew Murray and Boer Politics of Independence

What might be described either as Andrew Murray's developing Scots-Afrikaner hybridity, or his unstated missionary self-identification with respect to these northerly Boers, came to the fore in the fact that he was subsequently recruited by the British to act as mediator in conversations with the Transvaal leader, Andries Pretorius, starting on 25 August 1851. According to du Plessis, citing a letter of Andrew Murray to his brother John, Andrew played an important role in dissuading Pretorius from a pattern of pro-independence agitation and interference in the affairs of the Orange River Sovereignty. Instead, he encouraged Pretorius to seek a treaty with the British regarding the independence of the Transvaal. These negotiations concluded successfully with the signing of the Sand River Convention in January 1852, an event where Murray was present and acted in the role of interpreter.[106]

In spite of Murray's strong interest in the spiritual state and earthly affairs of the Dutch Afrikaners of the Transvaal, it should be noted that the perceived respect and the remarkable submission to his spiritual authority as suggested in the above anecdote told by Murray's colleague, Neethling, was either short-lived or not what it had seemed from the beginning. After his fourth visit to the Transvaal, the ecclesiastical situation there underwent a transformation, with some of the most prominent congregations, most notably Potchefstroom where Murray had acted as *consulent* (interim pastor), choosing to go independent from the oversight of the Cape Church. In effect another schism had occurred, this time almost wholly due to anti-imperial and pro-Dutch feeling in the Transvaal. On the initiative of influential pro-*Voortrekker* sympathisers in the Netherlands, Revd Dirk van der Hoff was dispatched to minister directly to these northerly Boers. Having arrived in the Cape in November 1852, he duly underwent the Cape Church's requirements for ordination, and by May 1853 he arrived at Potchefstroom to take up his call.[107] This was when the trouble started, at least from the points of view of Murray and the Cape DRC. In a show of independence, the Potchefstroom church council decided that, contrary to accepted practice in the Cape Church, there was no need for the *consulent* to officiate at the ordination of the new minister. Instead, arguing that van der Hoff was already an ordained minister, no such ceremony was needed, and Andrew Murray received the unambiguous message that a further visit from him to Potchefstroom would be deemed unwelcome. Ultimately, van der Hoff became the minister at Potchefstroom without any direct connection to the Cape Church. To quote du Plessis:

> In this manner arose the separatist body known as 'de Nederduitsch Hervormde Kerk' of the Transvaal, so named in contradistinction to the historical Church from which it had broken away, viz. 'de Nederduitsch Gereformeerde Kerk' . . .[108]

Detailing the various forces at play in this development is beyond the scope of this chapter, but one way to interpret the episode is that it illustrates the abiding tension, which sometimes loosened a bit only to be tightened again, between Murray and the Boer/Dutch Afrikaner people. Such a perspective might also help to explain why the same Andrew Murray who had helped smooth the way for Transvaal political independence would subsequently oppose the independence drive within the Orange River Sovereignty. If considered without context, such variegating loyalties might seem strange, but in fact there was no anomaly. Above and beyond the controversy involving Potchefstroom and van der Hoff, it should be obvious that Murray was no republican, and as far as he helped to facilitate Transvaal independence his motivation would have been the preservation of political peace to enable and ensure freedom of movement for missionaries belonging to the various societies, or, in his case, to the Cape Church. I believe in this conclusion of his motivation I am supported by du Plessis' summary of the three points of interest Murray most vociferously voiced during the synod of 1852:

> [T]he claims which the Transvaal congregations had to incorporate into the Synod; the duty and privilege of entering into closer fraternal relations with the French Reformed Church, engaged in missionary work in Basutoland; and the urgent need of establishing a theological seminary in South Africa, in order to supply the Church with God-fearing and orthodox ministers.[109]

One might deduce that all of these interests converged for Murray in the strengthening and ecumenical expansion of the Cape Church in order to fulfil its missionary mandate.

Regarding proposals to negotiate independence for the Orange River Sovereignty, which was much favoured by a majority of the Dutch Afrikaner population, a strong resistance developed in the southern districts, that is, those closest to the Cape Colony. Imperial negotiators ascribed this contrary view in places like Fauresmith, Bloemfontein and Smithfield in particular to the 'untiring zeal of the Scotch Presbyterian Clergyman',[110] aka Andrew Murray.

Despite such efforts, it was clear that by early 1852 the colonial authority had already understood the Orange River Sovereignty as too much trouble for its worth. Both outfoxed and outclassed in skirmishes and negotiations with the Basuto chieftain, Moshoeshoe, the colonial powers had had enough given the limitations of their contemporary capabilities in the region.[111] Thus, despite the protestations of merchants, missionaries and the 'Scotch Clergyman', the decision was made to relinquish the Sovereignty to the Boers. Not satisfied with this turn of events, an expedition was launched under full approval of the *Ring* [Classis] of Transgariep to travel to England and protest to government regarding the colonial relinquishment of this territory. The expedition consisted of Andrew Murray and Dr A. J. Frazer, who was an army surgeon stationed in the region.[112] They set off for England on 21 January 1854.[113]

Spoelstra, a *Dopper* historian, eager to emphasise the extent of the Cape Church's embeddedness in and assimilation of imperial concerns, thus to more effectively justify his own denomination's schismatic history as both theologically orthodox and pro-Afrikaner, elaborates on the wide support this pro-Crown expedition had among prominent ministers such as Revd P. Roux of Smithfield. Spoelstra also mentions that the *Ring* of Swellendam had declared that an independent Orange Free State would be contrary to the 'moral and religious interests' of Her Majesty's subjects and fatal to 'numerous native tribes'.[114] Swellendam was of course where the influential and contentious William Robertson was minister at the time. While it is probably true that a certain pro-imperial bias might have influenced people like Murray and Robertson in their decision making, it seems likely that a more deeper-lying sentiment for them would have been their identification with the concerns expressed by their PEMS friends in Basutoland. Du Plessis writes: 'The missionaries and their circle, in their antagonism to the abandonment policy, indulged in somewhat wild talk of the injustice of creating another Boer State to oppress the natives . . .'[115]

Murray and Frazer's mission proved futile. On 23 February, even before they arrived in London, the agreement was signed between the British commissioner, Sir George Russell Clerk, and the local representatives, dominated by the pro-independence party, which transformed the Orange River Sovereignty into the Orange Free State.[116]

Murray's journey was not a completely wasted effort, however. It allowed him to seek medical attention for a problem apparently affecting his 'nervous system',[117] and it also offered the opportunity to consult academics and church leaders in the Netherlands regarding the prospective theological seminary in South Africa. Murray, among other things, had the blessing of his church to consult with potential candidates for professorships at the soon to be established institution. Ultimately, the Dutch candidates that were approached for such roles declined, but Andrew made mention of the fact, in a letter to his brother, that John's name was already being proffered as a suitable candidate for such a position.[118]

When Murray returned to Bloemfontein after his nearly two-year-long overseas sojourn, his biographer du Plessis contended that the local church received him warmly enough.[119] Whether there were any ill feeling for his participation in a venture to undermine their quest for independence is a different matter regarding which du Plessis did not speculate, but this episode would certainly be useful in the following decades, and well into the next century, to cast aspersions on his loyalties, as ideologically expedient. The following chapters will elaborate on this theme.

In his final years in Bloemfontein, Murray started to immerse himself in educational ventures, an interest that would continue to inspire his ministry in the decades to come. His interest in the founding of a theological seminary has already been mentioned, but at Bloemfontein he became involved with, and even served as first principal of, Grey College,[120] to this day one of the most prestigious schools in South Africa.

However, undoubtedly the most important, life-shaping occurrence during these years was his marriage in 1856 to Emma Rutherfoord. Emma's father, Howson Edward Rutherfoord, was a Scottish immigrant and an influential Cape merchant[121] who was also a leading member and treasurer of the 1828-founded 'Cape of Good Hope Society for aiding deserving Slaves and Slave-children to purchase their freedom'.[122] What du Plessis mentions next is worth quoting directly for its importance in understanding the

Murray family within the developing discourse of Afrikaner identity politics over the next century:

> The suburban home of the Rutherfoord family, first at Green Point and afterwards at Claremont, was noted for its generous hospitality to missionaries of any society and denomination ... Through the services of Dr. Philip, the well-known secretary of the London Missionary Society in Cape Town, Andrew Murray was introduced to this Christian home, and here, on the occasion of his return from England in 1855, he first met Miss Rutherfoord.[123]

Neither the pro-missionary nor the abolitionist sentiments of Andrew Murray's in-laws are surprising, given his own proclivities and those of his parental household. However, the direct, even pivotal association with another Scottish missionary, John Philip, that infamous scourge of the Cape Dutch farmers as portrayed in Afrikaner nationalist descriptions such as by Spoelstra above, is a much more serious matter. By meeting his future bride through the helping hand of the Dutch Afrikaner's nemesis in chief, Dr Philip, Murray would not have done himself any favours if he had wanted to convince his church membership of his self-identification with them and their causes. Of course, since I am building a case here that the Murrays' primary association with the Afrikaner people was a missionary association, this all makes sense, but 'going native' was clearly not an immediate interest in the approach of the young Andrew.

Notes

1. Frederick William Sass (1956) 'The Influence of the Church of Scotland on the Dutch Reformed Church of South Africa', unpublished PhD thesis, University of Edinburgh, p. 14.
2. Ibid., p. 17.
3. Anonymous (1990) 'George Thom (1789–1842): Scottish Pioneer in South Africa', *The Banner of Truth*: https://www.christianstudylibrary.org/article/george-thom-1789-1842-scottish-pioneer-south-africa
4. Ibid.
5. J. A. S. Oberholster (1943) *Gedenkboek van die Ned. Geref. Gemeente Tulbagh: (Roodezand, Waveren) 1743–1943: 'n oorsig van die geskiedenis van die gemeente*, p. 76.
6. Sass, 'Influence of the Church of Scotland', p. 18.
7. Ibid.
8. Gordon Balfour (1899) *Presbyterianism in the Colonies with special reference to The Principles and Influence of the Free Church of Scotland*. Edinburgh: Macniven & Wallace, p. 284.
9. Sass, 'Influence of the Church of Scotland', pp. 18–19.
10. G. M. C. Theal (1898) *Records of the Cape Colony vol. xii*. London: Government of the Cape Colony, pp. 116–17.
11. Sass, 'Influence of the Church of Scotland', p. 15.

12. Ibid.
13. Anonymous, 'George Thom'.
14. George Thom, quoted in Theal, *Records of the Cape Colony vol. xii*, pp. 116–17.
15. See A. Grundlingh and H. Sapire (1989) 'From feverish festival to repetitive ritual? The changing fortunes of Great Trek mythology in an industrializing South Africa, 1938-1988', *South African Historical Journal/Suid-Afrikaanse Historiese Joernaal*, 21, pp. 19–37.
16. Andries Dreyer (1929) *Die Kaapse Kerk en die Groot Trek*. Kaapstad: Van de Sandt de Villiers en Co., p. 29.
17. Sass, 'Influence of the Church of Scotland', p. 20.
18. H. C. Hopkins (1968) *Die Ned. Geref. Kerk Cradock 1818–1968*. Observatory: Pro Ecclesia, p. 22.
19. Ibid.
20. Ibid., p. 23.
21. Dreyer, *Die Kaapse Kerk en die Groot Trek*, p. 166 footnote; *Grahamstown Journal*, 16 June 1849.
22. *De Kerkbode* (30 March 1927), p. 432.
23. Quoted in *De Kerkbode* (30 March 1927, p. 432).
24. *De Kerkbode* (30 March 1927), p. 432.
25. Quoted in Hopkins, *Die Ned. Geref. Kerk Cradock*, p. 32.
26. The origins of this word to designate these Dutch schismatics is unclear, but Hopkins suggests it might have its roots in a derogatory term in the sixteenth-century Netherlands, that is, 'Dorpers' to indicate lesser-educated villagers in contradistinction to the more 'civilised' city-dwellers. Hopkins, *Die Ned. Geref. Kerk Cradock*, p. 29.
27. Hopkins, *Die Ned. Geref. Kerk Cradock*, p. 31.
28. Sass, 'Influence of the Church of Scotland', p. 46.
29. L. H. Badenhorst (2001) *Die Nederduits Gereformeerde Gemeente van Colesberg oor 175 jaar (1826–2001)*. Unpublished manuscript, p. 51.
30. Ibid., p. 48.
31. Ibid., pp. 48–9.
32. Ibid., pp. 49–50.
33. Ibid., p. 49.
34. B. Spoelstra (1961) 'Die stigting van die Gereformeerde Kerk Colesberg', in *Die Gereformeerde Kerk Colesberg gestig 8 Desember 1860 op die plaas Hamelfontein van I. D. du Plessis: Gedenkalbum tydens die Eeufeesviering 27, 28, 29 Oktober 1961*, p. 9.
35. Ibid., p. 24.
36. Ibid., p. 24.
37. *Koerantberigte Skotse Predikante* (1906–1909) [unauthored collection of newspaper clippings pertaining to Scots ministers] (DRC Archive, Stellenbosch).
38. D. A. Kotzé (1981) *Van Roodezand tot Gariep: Die 150-jarige bestaan van die N. G. Gemeente Clanwilliam 1826–1976*. Goodwood: Nasionale Boekdrukkery, pp. 56–7.
39. G. B. A. Gerdener (1951) *Bouers van Weleer: Lewensketse van enkele groot figure uit die geskiedenis van die N.G. Kerk in Suid-Afrika*. Kaapstad: N. G. Kerk Uitgewers, p. 48.
40. Kotzé, *Van Roodezand tot Gariep*, p. 21.
41. Gerdener, *Bouers van Weleer*, p. 49.

42. A. Dreyer (1899) *Geschiedenis van de Gemeente Swellendam.* Kaapstad: Taylor en Snashall, pp. 36–9.
43. Dreyer, *Die Kaapse Kerk en die Groot Trek*, p. 27.
44. Ibid., p. 6.
45. Ibid., p. 7.
46. Ibid.
47. Ibid.
48. Ibid.
49. Ibid., p. 8.
50. Dreyer, *Geschiedenis van de Gemeente Swellendam*, p. 48.
51. M. Neethling (1909) *Unto Children's Children: lives and letters of the parents of the home at Graaff Reinet, with short sketches of the life of each of the children, and a register.* London: Printed by T. H. Hopkins, p. 9
52. Neethling, *Unto Children's Children*, p. 7.
53. George Aschman (25 June 1972) 'The Gathering of the Murray Clan', *Sunday Times Colour Magazine*, p. 40.
54. Neethling, *Unto Children's Children*, p. 9.
55. Ibid, pp. 9–10; see also https://www.geni.com/people/Maria-Susanna-Magdalena-Murray-b1c1-SM/6000000013335102883
56. Neethling, *Unto Children's Children*, p. 34.
57. Aschman, 'Murray Clan', p. 40. Cf. Neethling, *Unto Children's Children*, p. 34.
58. Neethling, *Unto Children's Children*, pp. 14–15.
59. Letter to 'My dear Boys', Graaff Reinet, 20 January 1842, in Neethling, *Unto Children's Children*, p. 21.
60. Aschman, 'Murray Clan', p. 35.
61. See P. B. van der Watt (1979) *John Murray 1826–1882: Die Eerste Stellenbosse Professor.* Pretoria: N. H. Kerkboekhandel Transvaal, p. 19.
62. Aschman, 'Murray Clan', p. 40.
63. Neethling, *Unto Children's Children*, p. 12.
64. Andrew Murray, quoted in Neethling, *Unto Children's Children*, p. 137.
65. Aschman, 'Murray Clan', p. 40.
66. J. B. Thompson (1908) *The Ministers of the North United Free Church, Aberdeen 1843–1908. Some biographical notes.* Aberdeen, p. 13, quoted in van der Watt, *John Murray*, p. 29.
67. Van der Watt, *John Murray*, p. 29.
68. Ibid., p. 43.
69. Quoted in J. du Plessis (1919) *The life of Andrew Murray of South Africa.* London: Marshall Brothers, p. 67.
70. Van der Watt, *John Murray*, p. 45 from J. du Plessis (1920) *Het Leven van Andrew Murray.* Kaapstad: Zuid Afrikaanse Bijbelvereniging, p. 73.
71. See G. J. TenZythoff (1987) *Sources of secession: The Netherlands Hervormde Kerk on the eve of the Dutch immigration to the Midwest.* Grand Rapids, MI: W. B. Eerdmans Publishing Company, pp. 59–74.
72. See Julia A. Lamm (1994) 'The Early Philosophical Roots of Schleiermacher's Notion of Gefühl, 1788–1794', *The Harvard Theological Review*, 87:1, pp. 67–105.
73. Van der Watt, *John Murray*, p. 46.
74. Unnamed personal correspondence quoted in van der Watt, *John Murray*, p. 46.
75. Van der Watt, *John Murray*, p. 48.

76. Ibid., p. 50.
77. Ibid., p. 52.
78. See https://www.places.co.za/html/burgersdorp.html
79. Van der Watt, *John Murray*, p. 75.
80. Ibid., p. 81.
81. Ibid., p. 76.
82. Ibid., p. 76.
83. Ibid., p. 81.
84. B. Spoelstra (1963) *Die 'Doppers' in Suid-Afrika 1760–1899*. Kaapstad: Nasionale Boekhandel, p. 165.
85. Quoted in Van der Watt, *John Murray*, p. 82.
86. Van der Watt, *John Murray*, p. 82.
87. Du Plessis, *Life of Andrew Murray*, p. 77.
88. Ibid.
89. This will not be the first time a 'missionary' would become involved with the *Voortrekkers*. American Presbyterian missionary Daniel Lindley also served for a time as their minister/missionary, although the reader will note that his biographer insisted on making a distinction between his roles as missionary to the black Zulu, and pastor for his work among the white Dutch Afrikaners. Edwin William Smith (1952) *The life and times of Daniel Lindley (1801–80): missionary to the Zulus, pastor of the Voortrekkers, Ubebe Omhlope*. New York: Library Publishers.
90. See Richard Elphick (2012) *The equality of believers: Protestant missionaries and the racial politics of South Africa*. Charlottesville: University of Virginia Press, pp. 28–9.
91. See Spoelstra, *Die 'Doppers'*, p. 58.
92. See M. Singh (2000) 'Basutoland: A Historical Journey into the Environment', *Environment and History*, 6:1, pp. 31–70. Retrieved 21 December 2020 from http://www.jstor.org/stable/20723119
93. Ibid., p. 58.
94. Ibid., p. 61.
95. Ibid., pp. 105–6.
96. Quoted in Spoelstra, *Die 'Doppers'*, p. 107.
97. Spoelstra, *Die 'Doppers'*, p. 108.
98. See H. C. Hopkins (7 June 1972) 'Drie Geslagte Murrays', *Die Kerkbode*, p. 730.
99. G. B. A. Gerdener (1934) *Geskiedenis van die Ned. Geref. Kerke in Natal, Vrystaat en Transvaal*. Kaapstad: S. A. Bybelvereniging, pp. 49–52.
100. Spoelstra, *Die 'Doppers'*, p. 126.
101. Andrew Murray Jr quoted in du Plessis, *Life of Andrew Murray*, p. 125.
102. Andrew Murray Jr quoted in du Plessis, *Life of Andrew Murray*, p. 121.
103. Ibid.
104. Ibid., pp. 122–3.
105. Unnamed listener to Murray's sermon, quoted by J. H. Neethling in du Plessis, *Life of Andrew Murray*, pp. 134–5.
106. Du Plessis, *Life of Andrew Murray*, pp. 129–31; see also Spoelstra, *Die 'Doppers'*, p. 148.
107. See du Plessis, *Life of Andrew Murray*, p. 139.
108. Ibid., p. 141.
109. Ibid., p. 146.
110. Quoted in Spoelstra, *Die 'Doppers'*, p. 148.

111. See du Plessis, *Life of Andrew Murray*, pp. 147–8.
112. Ibid., p. 164, note 1.
113. Ibid., p. 152.
114. See Spoelstra, *Die 'Doppers'*, p. 149.
115. Du Plessis, *Life of Andrew Murray*, p. 153.
116. Ibid., pp. 155–6.
117. See Andrew Murray's letter to 'members of home circle' in du Plessis, *Life of Andrew Murray*, p. 162.
118. See Andrew Murray's letter to John in du Plessis, *Life of Andrew Murray*, p. 163.
119. Du Plessis, *Life of Andrew Murray*, p. 165.
120. Ibid., pp. 167–8.
121. See John M. MacKenzie and Nigel Dalziel (2007) *The Scots in South Africa: ethnicity, identity, gender and race, 1772–1914*. Manchester: Manchester University Press, p. 70.
122. Du Plessis, *Life of Andrew Murray*, p. 168. Robert Ross writes that the abolition movement at the Cape was 'surprisingly moderate in their anti-slavery. The only significant abolitionist society was the Cape of Good Hope Philanthropic Society, which hoped to end slavery gradually by purchasing young slave women for emancipation.' R. J. Ross (1995) 'Abolitionism, the Batavian Republic, the British and the Cape Colony', in Gert Oostindie (ed.) *Fifty years later: Antislavery, capitalism and modernity in the Dutch orbit*. Pittsburgh, PA: University of Pittsburgh Press, p. 184.
123. Du Plessis, *Life of Andrew Murray*, p. 168.

CHAPTER THREE

Scottish Ministers, Evangelical Revival and Church-based 'Apartheid'?

When Andrew Murray left Bloemfontein to take up the pastorate at the Overberg town of Worcester in 1860, he thereby contributed to a strengthening of the intellectual ferment of imperial-leaning Afrikaners in the Cape Colony. This precipitated a period of theological advance, such as seen in the founding of the theological seminary in 1859, but also a period of theological competition between the so-called orthodox/conservatives, on the one hand, and the liberals, on the other. This next decade also saw the emergence of the Cape DRC's participation in a transatlantic evangelical revival movement. Preceding all these developments was the 1857 synod, which is often touted as the ecclesiastical foundation of apartheid as a factor in South African history. In all these developments, Scots-descendent ministers, and especially the Murrays, played central roles.

What complicates matters for anyone interested in taking a fresh look at this past is that much about these developments is entrenched in the popular imagination of students of South African, especially DRC, history. Unfortunately, much of what is imagined about this era is rather undernuanced ideological construction, which tends to rely on binary thinking. In this chapter, and as the narrative unfolds, I shall attempt to provide a nuanced perspective to the role of the Scots in terms of these central moments in theological and political development. Although this somewhat disrupts the normal chronology, we may begin with the founding of the Stellenbosch Seminary, especially since, as I have indicated in the previous chapter, this was a project long in the planning by some central characters in this book. Although this is often seen as a movement attempting to assert orthodoxy against the liberalism feared as prevalent among Dutch-trained ministers at the Cape, the fact is that the founders had some divergent and even contradictory interests and motivations. The truth is that since the Scottish takeover of the church,[1] described in the previous chapter, evangelicalism had comprised the majority sentiment.

The Stellenbosch Seminary

A number of influential ministers wanted a local seminary, but apparently for different reasons. In addition to Andrew Murray, the four most important characters involved in this project were N. J. Hofmeyr, G. Van der Lingen, J. H. Neethling and John Murray. The Murrays belong to the central group of figures in this book. Hofmeyr has been briefly mentioned together with the Murrays, and Neethling as part of *Secor Dabar* in Utrecht.

That leaves the much older Van der Lingen, minister at Paarl, and a vociferous opponent of modernism, as a bit of an outlier in the mix. A strictly Dordt-centred Calvinist and adherent of the notion of double predestination, Van der Lingen, although not the first person to proffer the idea of a local seminary, was an early and ardent advocate of the plan. Born in South Africa in 1804, the son of a Dutch missionary to the Khoekhoe, he relocated to the Netherlands together with his parents in 1818 when the South African Mission Society, to which his father belonged, disbanded. There he stayed for thirteen years, which included theological studies at Utrecht, and a start was made towards his doctoral studies. However, apparently without completing his doctorate, he decided to return to South Africa, where he took up the pastorate at Paarl, just north-east of Stellenbosch, in 1831.[2] This was more than a decade prior to the arrival in Utrecht of the Murrays and the founding of *Secor Dabar* in 1844.[3] This means that while the founders of the Stellenbosch Seminary had all studied at Utrecht, among this group only Van der Lingen had missed out on membership of *Secor Dabar*.[4]

Furthermore, whereas Hofmeyr, the eventual uncle of influential Cape politician and Afrikanerbond leader 'Onze' Jan Hofmeyr,[5] had local, Cape national sentiments, Van der Lingen was a Nederlandophile. The following lines from Jean du Plessis' Masters thesis on Van der Lingen show the tension between the two views. Van der Lingen is quoted as distinguishing himself from Hofmeyr as follows:

> ... I imagine that I live in my fatherland. Yet I am a Netherlander and exclusively so ... [Hofmeyr] wants to promote a national sentiment, develop national talent and establish a nationalist tendency all by means of the Seminary. I envisage nothing of the kind. Nationality has little to do with the issue. Those individuals working for the greatest and most noble purpose of this country have mainly been foreigners: people such as Dessie, van Lier and Van der Kemp ... .[6]

When it came to the appointment of the first professors, no Netherlanders availed themselves for the task (see Chapter 2), which meant that Hofmeyr's local sentiment became the de facto victorious position. John Murray was first called, and he accepted the appointment. Van der Lingen himself was called next, but he declined after his church council unsuccessfully insisted that he should only accept the call if the seminary was founded in Paarl rather than in Stellenbosch.[7] The very same Hofmeyr, at the time minister at Calvinia, was then called instead. Hofmeyr had health problems, which made him doubt whether he would be able to survive the cold, wet Stellenbosch winters. Wavering over whether or not to accept the call, it was allegedly none other than Andrew Murray Sr who convinced him to do so by asking the following question: 'Are you willing to place your life on the line for this great task?'.[8]

Regarding the theme of the founding of the seminary in Stellenbosch, it should be noted that William Robertson of Swellendam was also a strong advocate of this project. In fact, his son and namesake, who would later become the minister of the DRC, Tulbagh,[9] was among the first intake of only four students at the seminary. Another son of a Scots DRC minister was also among the original four, C. S. Morgan. Yet another interesting Scottish connection to the Stellenbosch Seminary is James Mackinnon, who would be Professor of Ecclesiastical History at Edinburgh from 1908 to 1931. Mackinnon was a student at the Stellenbosch Seminary in the period 1881–4.[10] It is thanks to Mackinnon that we have a written portrayal of Daniel Gizani, the first known black African (Mfengo) student at the seminary during this same period.

Mackinnon attempted to describe some of the experiences of this student, including the prejudices of his Dutch Afrikaner classmates, and in the process Mackinnon also happened to betray his own embeddedness in colonial racial discourse, ironically, in spite of the enlightened view of self he wished to convey. When, upon their initial encounter, Mackinnon thought it appropriate to give Gizani a handshake, the Dutch Afrikaner students, evidently insulted by Gizani's presence among them, only looked on critically.[11] However, racism comes in many shades, and so, for context, let me also include the following lines as part of Mackinnon's own descriptive evaluation of Gizani:

> He had of course the Kaffir features, but not so pronounced as to make them disagreeably prominent. The nose and lips, for instance, were less heavy and thick than in the common Kaffir, and in addition to two rows of shining teeth, he had quite a profusion of black, curly hair. There was likewise a mildness and intelligence and kindliness about the whole face, which made you forget the Kaffir and think of the man.[12]

The Scots and Church-based Apartheid?

Some years earlier, the eventual seminary founding figures, that is, the Murrays, Hofmeyr, Van der Lingen, as well as J. H. Neethling, minister of Stellenbosch, were all present and played their parts in the 1857 synod, which had in recent decades become notorious in South African Reformed theological discourse for its alleged institutionalisation of a kind of proto-apartheid in the congregational settings of the Cape Church. The controversy all boils down to a motion introduced by Andrew Murray Sr as part of an attempt to resolve an impasse after a question was posed by another Scot, Robert Shand of Tulbagh. Shand wanted the synod to give clarity over whether it was permissible, or not, for black converts to congregate in a separate building from the whites. Shand, who at the time was standing in as *consulent* of the vacant charge of Ceres, had refused to allow the white congregants there to erect a separate building for the 'coloured' members. Shand now brought the question to the synod, and it resulted in a very heated discussion, as a result of which some feared a schism in the church.[13] The controversy was only resolved with the introduction of Murray's motion, which was accepted by a large majority, reading as follows:

> The Synod considers it desirable and according to the Scriptures that our members from heathendom should be taken in and incorporated into our existing congregations, everywhere, where it can be done; but where this measure, owing to the weakness of some, will stand in the way of the furtherance of the cause of Christ amongst the heathen, the congregation formed or still to be formed of heathen shall enjoy their Christian privileges in a separate building or institution.[14]

Little could anyone know at the time that his well-known and often commented-upon motion would on the one hand be seized upon by subsequent apartheid apologists in defence of a mission policy predicated on the notion of separateness.[15] On the other hand, critics of the theological roots of apartheid could easily revert back to this as the primordial catalyst, setting in motion the development of a heretical notion of church.

In fact, a reading of the 1857 synod as the apartheid synod[16] is hermeneutically somewhat problematic. It could only be read in this way if the reader steadfastly ignores the intentions of the leading actors. If that is the case, one should also remain unsympathetic to or unaware of the context of opposition Murray et al. had to negotiate.[17] While I am not at all suggesting that the church leadership acted correctly, the fact is one can only give these synodical proceedings fair treatment by taking seriously the central themes that the church leadership occupied themselves with at that meeting, most important of which was mission.[18]

Undoubtedly, racial feeling and white fear of equalisation with freed slaves and Africans generally, were perennial preoccupations for many of the Dutch-Afrikaner people,[19] particularly in rural areas.[20] Therefore, mission was always going to be a problem, because when missionary activities proved successful they delivered converts that had to be taken up into existing congregations. Sass gives valuable background involving some of the Scots ministers and their positioning regarding this issue. The first thing to note is that their introduction to the DRC, and particularly their missionary fervour, had from early on, in tandem with the work of various missionary societies, disrupted established patterns of segregation. Allegedly, church buildings were becoming crowded in the 1820s, and questions were raised about the appropriate places of worship for converted Malay slaves. This led among other things to the establishment of a church for 'slaves and slave children' in Stellenbosch in 1824.[21] Elsewhere questions were raised about the decorum of allowing whites and 'coloureds' to be served holy communion simultaneously and at the same venue. This necessitated the synod of 1829 to unequivocally emphasise the joint celebration of the Lord's Supper as 'an unalterable axiom founded on the Infallible Word of God . . . and that all Christian congregations and each Christian in particular has to think and act in accordance with it'.[22]

Despite the ongoing presence of race prejudice among many of the white congregants, Sass notes that joint congregational worship was a common feature during the first half of the nineteenth century. 'James Backhouse, a Quaker gentleman who visited the Colony for religious purposes in 1839, states that he addressed mixed Coloured and European congregations at such places as Graaff Reinet (Andrew Murray), Beaufort West (Colin Fraser), Worcester (Henry Sutherland), Tulbagh (Robert Shand), and Stellenbosch.'[23] Considering the Afrikaner nationalist *volkskerk* that the DRC would devolve in less than a century later, it is hard to imagine what is stranger about this image – racially mixed congregations, or a Quaker successfully acquiring permission to address DRC congregations!

Regarding race relations and mission at the 1857 synod, it seems that the mission commission of the synod reported a more than healthy financial balance at that meeting, but some of the younger members, including Andrew Murray Jr, N. J. Hofmeyr and J. H. Neethling, expressed dissatisfaction with the lack of progress made by this commission, especially the fact that no missionary project had yet been launched across the Vaal River.[24] This proposal was quite shocking to some of the older synod members. The upshot was that these three *Secor Dabar* members, along with P. K. Albertyn of Caledon, became the core of the new permanent missions committee that was then constituted. Andrew Murray Jr remained a member of this committee until his retirement in 1906.[25]

It was, however, the closer-to-home congregational missionary and evangelistic actions by some ministers not abiding by the growing culture of colour prejudice that led to the 'weakness of some' motion. I mentioned the question brought forward by Robert Shand (above). One precursor to this situation involving Shand's congregation concerned the somewhat irregular appointment of W. R. Thomson in 1830 as the minister of the new settlement of Stockenstrom. In the Cape there existed an informal colonial policy that relied on missionaries to keep the peace between Africans and colonists on the eastern frontier, and Thomson was one such missionary who doubled as a government agent. Since 1821 he had served under the joint supervision of the colonial government and the Glasgow Missionary Society at 'Chumie in Caffraria', but since his dual identity had become untenable for various reasons, he had asked to be moved away from there. The governor then appointed him as minister of the entirely 'coloured' congregation at Stockenstrom, which at the time was not yet officially part of the DRC, but Thomson's appointment placed him on the same level as DRC clergy. Thus, although the founding of this congregation was not a direct result of DRC missionary outreach, the congregation together with its minister was included in that church body at the 1834 synod.[26]

In 1855, after a number of 'Boer' families had moved into the district, they asked the Stockenstrom church council whether they could be permitted their own communion services to take place after the regular dispensation of such services on the first Sunday of every month. Stockenstrom refused the request, but after an appeal to the *Ring* of Albanie, under which Stockenstrom resorted, it was decided that a separate communion table might be organised to accommodate these race-conscious Boers.[27] This decision would be vigorously debated at the 1857 synod. Also notable here is the fact that this resolution at the *Ring* regarding the additional communion table was proposed by one of the original Scots ministers, Alexander Smith.[28] Regarding Smith, who was minister at Uitenhage from 1823 to 1863, it should also be noted that he had a history of negotiating race prejudice in his congregation. In the 1830s, prior to the Boer emigration from the Cape Colony, there were objections from white congregants to the ways in which he conducted the marriages of 'Hottentotte', and even the fact that such ceremonies were conducted in the church building.[29] A congregational historian notes the fact that in 1859 Smith made weekly visits to the local prison to preach to the 'Kaffers' via an interpreter.[30] However, another bit of interesting information regarding Revd Smith is the fact that he was no stranger to innovation, or perhaps deviation, in terms of the communion services. At the Easter services of 1824 he conducted communion to the Dutch-speaking portion of the congregation, and the following week communion was served to the English-speaking portion. Quite likely this was the first English-language communion service to be held in the DRC in South Africa.[31] Smith was also notable for conducting the first known Sunday schools in the DRC, again along segregated lines, with a school for Christian (white) children and another one for the children of heathen (Mfengu and other 'coloureds').[32] In 1824, Abraham Faure, DRC minister in Cape Town, also mentioned that Smith conducted separate services once a week for 'slaven en Hottentotten' (slaves and KhoeKhoe).[33]

The complicated position trodden by the pro-mission contingent, in which the Scots ministers stood central, could be accentuated by various perspectives. Sass mentions the fact that missionaries of the Free Church of Scotland in what was then named *Kaffraria*, where Lovedale was located, had something to do with the arousal of mission interest in the DRC during this time and especially in that conspicuous year of 1857. Early in the year, the tragic events of the Xhosa cattle killings leading to mass starvation and migration had occurred, and this affected the Lovedale mission directly, prompting it to seek cooperation with the DRC.[34] It might be interesting to relay this quoted paragraph from the letter, the author unfortunately unnamed, received from Lovedale regarding the cattle killing and the needed missionary response:

Who knows but that the manifest judgments of God, under which they are now suffering, because of their obstinate rejection of the gospel, may be designed to break and subdue them under the Sceptre of our Almighty and Merciful King: and that the seed which our fellow labourers among the Kaffirs have for many years been sowing in much sorrow, it may be left to you to reap? It does not become us to indicate how your Venerable Synod may best seek to accomplish this important and interesting work. I have only to say in the name and by direction of my brethren of this Presbytery that, if in any way we can take part with you in it by supplying native agents or otherwise, the opportunity for such co-operation will be regarded by us as a privilege to be rejoiced in as well as a duty to be earnestly and conscientiously performed.[35]

The synod expressed itself favourable to this communication and recommended its mission commission to look further into the realisation of practical cooperation with the Scots missionaries. Sass comments that this process of growing ecumenicity between the Scottish missionaries and the DRC was unfortunately derailed in subsequent decades due to the DRC's growing preoccupation with racial segregation.[36]

An interesting incident occurring in 1856, and reported on by A. Dreyer in a commemorative publication concerning the Swellendam DRC during the nineteenth century, involved an unnamed Mozambiquan congregant who caused offence allegedly by not maintaining enough social distancing during church services. This was, at least, according to one anonymous complaint directed at the minister, Dr William Robertson. The letter advised the minister 'to not allow the proud Mozambiquan to crowd out the whites so much in front of the pulpit'.[37] The church council decided to look into the matter at the time, but what is interesting is that Dreyer also mentioned that Robertson had started programmatic evangelistic activities among the 'heathen' from as early as 1837. The first African converts he baptised in 1839,[38] and obviously the reported incident involving the Mozambiquan worshipper confirms that by the time just prior to the 1857 synod, the Swellendam DRC had, similar to the above-mentioned mainly Scots-led mixed congregations, black members as part of its regular service. Clearly, though, not all white members were happy with this situation.

An apartheid-era Gereformeerde Kerk historian, B. Spoelstra, has an interesting perspective on the 1857 synod of the DRC. Ironically in hindsight, Spoelstra seemed determined to claim the credit for ecclesiastical apartheid for the proto-*Doppers*. His rather sarcastic interpretation, which I translate from Afrikaans, goes as follows:

With the emphasis on mission and because they were striving for a Christianity above religious difference, the Cape Church went into alliance with different philanthropic mission organisations. Hence the Cape church have still declared it as 'Scriftuurlijk' that white and non-white should congregate in one church building and receive communion together. After they heard of the strange view that was current among the *Doppers*, the Synod was willing, because of the 'weakness' to forsake their 'Scriptural' principle and to allow distinctive congregations to non-whites in emergency situations.[39]

Revd J. P. M. Huet, due to his ecumenically prophetic text, *Eene Kudde en Een Herder*, is often cited as the opponent in chief to the compromise decision finally adopted by the 1857 synod. That his book, published in 1860, a few years after the synod, unambiguously railed against the decision and the colour prejudice underpinning the whole situation is certainly true. Quite apt is his critical observation that with the above-mentioned motion the synod acknowledged it to be scripturally mandated that all believers congregate in the same church, but then it gave its members permission to effectively act unscripturally, that is, congregate separately if their prejudice demanded it.[40] However, as Borchardt infers, it was apparently only in the aftermath of the synodical proceedings that Huet reached the strong opinion expressed in his famous text. At the time of the synod he had more optimistically hoped that separate buildings could serve as an interim measure for the instruction of newly converted blacks until they reached a suitable enough educational level to be congregated together with the whites.[41] No doubt Andrew Murray Sr had hoped something similar when he introduced the ill-fated motion in the first place. Another source, C. J. Kriel, makes this kind of point when he states that Murray had meant it strategically. The idea was to stave off the growing resistance to mission, while he optimistically, and perhaps naively, hoped that the scriptural principle would win out in the long term.[42] Moreover, Kriel adds that Andrew Murray Jr, G. W. A. van der Lingen and N. J. Hofmeyr all expressed concern about the colour prejudice that was prevalent in some congregations.[43] Therefore, did Huet's missive against the sin of non-equalisation and segregation at church place him at odds with the Murrays who seemed content to compromise? Apparently not, because the very next year Huet and Andrew Murray Jr would undertake a joint missionary tour in the Free State and Basutoland. 'Huet's company I enjoyed very much. We spent a fortnight together,' Andrew subsequently wrote to his brother, John.[44]

Revivalism and a Strengthening of the Scottish Hand in the DRC

The revival at the Cape, ardently propagated by local ministers, including G. W. A. van der Lingen, albeit belatedly, since he initially considered it akin to 'spiritual quackery' [transl.],[45] and Andrew Murray, was very much an offshoot of similar events in North America and Britain, but also parts of the European continent, starting from 1857 to 1858.[46]

De Kerkbode, in 1859, became a strong advocate of revival through at least six editorial pieces on the subject of prayer as well as specific calls for revival by prominent ministers such as those already mentioned above. Scottish-origin names were prominent among those mentioned in connection with these calls to prayer, such as Murray, Morgan and Cameron. Other names included Faure and Van der Lingen.[47]

This indicated international linkages, and the evident desire to be part of an international movement of revival is also expressed through subsequent events. This includes Andrew Murray's efforts to embed the DRC into a wider Protestant missionary movement, to be elaborated on in subsequent chapters, as well as American involvement in the founding of the Huguenot Seminary (see below). Another aspect to mention is the involvement of a few South African publications, but also individual clergy within international contexts. One could refer in this regard to an eighty-five-page pamphlet, *De Kracht der Gebeds* (The Power of Prayer), which describes the American revival, and which J. H. Neethling, for example, distributed and utilised effectively to inspire enthusiasm for revival among his congregation in Stellenbosch.[48]

Duff points to a notable difference among sectors of support for revivalism. While the Murrays and other younger members of the DRC leadership quickly adapted to aspects of modernisation as part of the revival movement, especially print culture through the publication and successful local and international distribution of books and pamphlets, the older Van der Lingen did not. He detested all modernist inventions, whether ideological or technological, and was, for example, a well-known opponent of the railway running through Paarl.[49] Generally speaking, though, the *Secor Dabarians* were in the ascendancy in the 1860s and beyond, and as Duff, basically, puts it: 'Evangelicalism opened the DRC to the world.'[50]

The theme of Revival came particularly to the fore at the first interdenominational Christian conference that was held at Worcester on 18–19 April 1860.[51] Convened upon the initiative of three of the *Secor Dabar*-rooted influencers, Profs Hofmeyr and Murray and Revd Neethling, it received 374 delegates from all over the country.[52] Du Plessis mentions that notably only five of the older DRC ministers were present, and among the eleven younger ones present a good seven belonged to the Murray clan, either as sons or sons-in-law of Andrew Sr.[53] It is noteworthy, though, that just prior to the conference, Andrew Jr, still in Bloemfontein but on his way to his new parish of Worcester, was not particularly enthusiastic about the prospects of the conference. In a letter to John, among other things concerned with plans to fill the many soon to be opened vacancies in the church resulting from retirements with immigrant ministers from Europe and America, Andrew also expressed his reservations over the DRC's participation in the planned international conference as follows:

> We have no chance of competing with Churches in which the blood and power of a European life and organization circulates. We need to conquer the difficulties of our isolation and of the slow action of our

Church courts. The prospect of this being done made me rejoice. But I must confess I do not see much that will result from a Conference of English-speaking missionaries and ourselves. Our people are still so separated from the English on the one side and the natives on the other, that you will find harmonious action to any great extent an impossibility.[54]

The tone of the above seems rather atypical for this otherwise fiery missionary statesman and ecumenist. Perhaps the Bloemfontein experience had finally managed to dampen the young Andrew's spirit somewhat. Does the fact that he refers to his church members as 'our people' indicate a growing sense of identification? Perhaps so, but his commentary about them also conveys the sense that he does not share their sensibilities.

The chair of the Worcester conference was Revd Robert Shand of Tulbagh. The Scottish connection at the conference was strong from the start. Dr Robertson of Swellendam was one of the prominent speakers. He also had an interesting subsequent responsibility that strengthened the Scottish connection in the DRC (more on that below). Another was of course Andrew Murray Sr, but there was also a Dr Adamson, a former minister of the Scotch Presbyterian Church in Cape Town, who had just returned from America, and who spoke eloquently of the Second Great Awakening in North America. Robertson interpreted his speech into Dutch.[55]

Mission was high on the agenda of this conference. It was acknowledged that this was a controversial subject and the conference lamented the fact that the term missionary evoked much revulsion from within the DRC. The era of revival was an era of growing individual agency, of course, and therefore the conference emphasised mission as a personal duty for each church member. One strategy that was employed to strengthen the DRC's participation in mission was to send Dr Robertson overseas to recruit ministers, missionaries and teachers. The newly founded seminary was not yet able to supply the demand. The plan was for Robertson to visit the Netherlands for this purpose.[56] Although Europe and America were generally mentioned as places where good candidates might be found, it is important to note that Andrew Murray Jr, who proposed this mission, and who also nominated Robertson for the role of recruiting agent, proposed that he should go to Holland specifically. The motivation seemed to be the fact that the local DRC members were generally distrusting of foreigners, and no doubt Dutchmen would be more readily perceived as acceptable.[57]

M. W. Retief writes that there was quite an amount of opposition to Robertson's overseas mission, as expressed through op-ed columns in the secular press. The first bone of contention was that he as a Scot might have had a bias against the Dutch. The fear was thus that he could specifically recruit individuals who would strengthen the anglicising of the church in the Cape Colony. Possibly related to this was the objection from the so-called liberals that his mission could open the way for a stream of 'orthodox' ministers to enter the Cape. According to M. W. Retief, this was a legitimate fear since the conference was convened by *regsinnige* [orthodox] ministers, who intended to find *regsinnige* recruits from overseas.[58]

The use of the term 'orthodox' in binary opposition to 'liberal', as has been the norm in the way this history was usually constructed, is problematic for various reasons. Duff has recently shown how Andrew Murray and other revivalists embraced 'liberal ideas' in some respects,[59] and I shall indicate in subsequent chapters that the Scots became viewed as both liberal and heterodox in influential sectors of twentieth-century Afrikanerdom. The Dutch/South African theologian Vincent Brümmer has argued, furthermore, that the nineteenth-century Utrecht-trained evangelicals, including John and Andrew Murray and Nicolaas Hofmeyr, should be understood as piously evangelical rather than doctrinally orthodox in the narrow Dordt Reformed sense.[60] Somewhat contrary to M. W. Retief's mid-twentieth-century assessment, it seems clear that in the mid-nineteenth century there was an anti-evangelical, anti-British and specifically anti-missionary sentiment among certain sections of the DRC, and that this provided the grounds for opposing Robertson's mission.

Whatever the case, when Robertson arrived in the Netherlands he was indeed discouraged by the preponderance of liberal theology. He was only able to recruit two Dutch ministers, a Revd Van de Wall and H. Van Broekhuizen. Robertson's evaluation of the general state of Dutch Christianity is expressed in a letter he sent to the Cape on 12 October 1860:

> All Christians admit that the condition of the Reformed Church in Holland is exceedingly parlous. Liberalism – for so the prevalent form of unbelief is called – has spread itself over the whole land and seeks to rob the Church of Christ of its cherished truths. The trinity, the divinity of Christ, the personality of the Spirit, the vicarious suffering of Christ, and naturally all that stands in closest connexion with these truths, are not merely denied but assailed . . . [O]f the 1,400 or 1,500 ministers in Holland, only about one hundred can be looked upon as thoroughly orthodox; while others who judge more favourably think that they could find about two hundred. Is it to be marvelled at that under such circumstances I could secure but few orthodox ministers in Holland?[61]

In Scotland, on the other hand, Robertson was able to recruit eight candidates from the Free Church of Scotland. One of them, Alexander McKidd, volunteered himself for the DRC's foreign mission. He became one of the Cape DRC's first couple of missionaries to the north of the Vaal River. The other Scottish recruits for ministry in the DRC were W. Cormack, D. McMillan, J. McCarter, T. McCarter, T. M. Gray, A. McGregor and R. Ross.[62] Du Plessis judged Robertson's mission a great success:

> The wisdom of the resolution adopted by the Worcester Conference, and the wisdom of the choice of Dr. Robertson as deputy, were now

clearly apparent. The men who came out in response to the appeal of the Cape Church proved in almost every case worthy of the trust reposed in them, and continued, some for a longer and some for a shorter period, but most of them for many years, to serve with the greatest fidelity and devotion the land and people of their adoption.[63]

A South African Revival Takes Root

At the Worcester conference, William Robertson had read a paper on revivals, after which he implored the listeners to consider whether such a phenomenon was not also necessary in South Africa. Adamson's news about the revivalist movement in America also generated much deepened discussion, and du Plessis mentions that in the aftermath of this conference signs of revival started to occur in a quiet fashion, principally in the districts of Montagu and Worcester, and interestingly enough not in towns, initially, but in the countryside where people had organised themselves into prayer groups.[64]

It is not the intention of this chapter to give a full overview or chronology of the revival as such, but rather to comment on the role of the Scots in the DRC in the whole process as well as its aftermath. Therefore, the role played by Robert Shand in Montagu is noteworthy:

> On Sunday evening [22 July] a prayer meeting was conducted by Revs. Shand and de Smidt when the spiritual fervour was so great that people complained that the meeting ended an hour too soon. A year ago prayer meetings were unknown. Now they are held daily, and sometimes as frequently as three times a day – even amongst children.[65]

In Worcester, where Andrew Murray was the newly inducted minister, the revival started among farmworkers in informal prayer settings rather than within organised church meetings. 'Young and old, parents and children, White and Coloured all gathered together to cast themselves before God in cries of penitence from the depths of their souls.'[66] It seems that Andrew Murray was less than thrilled about the fact that such occurrences took place in forms and settings often beyond his control, perhaps even as a challenge to his authority as minister. There is for example the testimony of one prayer leader, J. C. De Vries, who commented on how Murray objected to a prayer session where everyone was praying out loudly, typical of Pentecostal and proto-Pentecostal settings. De Vries mentioned the remarkable fact that an unlikely source in this DRC setting proved to be the catalyst to the revivalist outpouring:

> After three or four others had (as was customary) given out a verse of a hymn and offered prayer, a coloured girl of about fifteen years of age, in service with a farmer from Hex River, rose at the back of the hall, and asked if she too might propose a hymn. At first I hesitated,

not knowing what the meeting would think, but better thoughts prevailed and I replied, Yes. She gave out her hymn-verse and prayed in moving tones. While she was praying we heard as it were a sound in the distance, which came nearer and nearer, until the hall seemed to be shaken, and with one or two exceptions, the whole meeting began to pray, the majority in audible voice, but some in whispers.[67]

Murray, who arrived when this prayer session was already in full swing, attempted to get De Vries' attention, but the latter was according to his own description fully caught up in the fervour. Murray then

> called out, as loudly as he could, *People, silence!* But the praying continued ... Mr. Murray then called again aloud, *People, I am your minister sent from God, silence!* But there was no stopping the noise. No one heard him, but all continued praying and calling on God for mercy and pardon. Mr. Murray then returned to me, and told me to start the hymn-verse commencing *'Help de ziel de raadloos schreit'* [Aid the soul that helpless cries]. I did so, but the emotions were not quieted, and the meeting went on praying. Mr. Murray then prepared to depart, saying, 'God is a God of order, and here everything is confusion.' With that, he left the hall.[68]

Apart from uncontrolled prayer, there were also other bodily manifestations of spiritual euphoria/strife. The same J. C. De Vries mentions instances of worshippers fainting, and most notably this happened during a prayer session to Hessie Bosman, future spouse of Alexander McKidd.[69] Recruited by William Robertson, McKidd together with Henry Gonin had arrived in Cape Town in 1861 and they promptly became the first 'foreign' missionaries of the DRC.[70] 'Foreign' in this case meant that they served beyond the territorial borders of the Cape church, in the Transvaal, and does not reflect on the fact that these missionaries were foreign to the DRC itself.

Andrew Murray's initial aversion to the actual manifestations, if not the idea, of revival apparently experienced a reversal once he became able to preach in ways that fostered further instances of revival, both from within the church at Worcester, but also far beyond. In reference to *De Kerkbode*'s description of these events, Duff writes:

> ... in some villages, the numbers attending church were so great that separate meetings for 'mannen [...] hunne vrouwen [...] hunne zonen, hunne dochteren, en [...] hunne kinderen' (men, their wives, their sons, their daughters, and their children), and masters as well as servants flocked to services. Andrew Murray jun. observed that 'poorer and younger people' were often the first to convert during revivals.[71]

Occurring as it did during a period of economic hardship and drought,[72] there was no short supply of poor young people.

Andrew Jr's involvement in the revival was perhaps also predestined, to use a Calvinist idea in reference to a more typically Wesleyan phenomenon, by the fact that the Murray family as spearheaded by their father in Graaff Reinet was deeply invested in the theme of revival. Once Andrew Jr became enthused by the revival there was no stopping him, and according to different reports he became quite the preaching phenomenon. As Henry Vicars Taylor, pastor of the Presbyterian Church in Wellington, stated:

> Audiences bend before the sweeping rain of his words like willows before the gale. The heart within the hearer is bowed, and the intellect is awed. Andrew Murray's oratory is of the kind to which men willingly go into captivity.[73]

Gains for Mission

More revivals, again connected to overseas movements, followed in the next decade, and an important consequence of these developments was a renewed interest in mission. Indeed, the DRC missionary enterprise was really birthed out of these spiritual awakenings. As evidence for this one might consider publications from the period. Olea Nel mentions a 15 September 1860 editorial of *Het Volksblad* where it was 'claimed that an interest in missions had started to blossom amongst DRC members, and that they were displaying a new zealousness for this cause. In April 1861, *De Wekker* wrote a more intentional article that encouraged believers to preach the gospel to their servants, and to allow their sons and daughters to become missionaries.'[74]

In 1862, from April to June, Murray left to accompany the above-mentioned Gonin and McKidd to their mission fields in the northern Transvaal.[75] In order to establish these two at a suitable mission field, Murray turned for help to the future Transvaal president, Paul Kruger. The two were already well acquainted since the time when Murray conducted a preaching tour in the Transvaal (see Chapter 2). Murray considered Kruger 'a great man of influence among the natives'.[76] A letter written to his children was quite revealing in terms of what it conveys of Murray's appreciation of Kruger, but also his views of the Transvaal Boers more generally. I quote a brief excerpt:

> [Kruger] is a good, pious man. Perhaps Mamma has told you that some of the white people here do not wish the black people to be taught about Jesus. This is because they do not love Him themselves. But Mr. Kruger says that when God gave him a new heart, it was as if he wanted to tell everyone about Jesus' love, and as if he wanted the birds and the trees and everything to help him praise his Saviour; and so he could not bear that there should be any poor black people not knowing and loving the Saviour whom he loved.[77]

However, this particular missionary initiative was initially unsuccessful. The two chiefs with whom Murray along with Kruger negotiated (Magato followed by Ramkok) both declined to accept missionaries in their areas of jurisdiction.[78] This was the end of Murray's participation in finding a field for Gonin and McKidd. They remained in the Transvaal, while he returned to the Cape Colony. In May 1863, Alexander and Hessie (Bosman) McKidd received an invitation from the Buys clan in the Soutpansberg area to start work among them. This ended tragically when Hessie (1864) followed by Alexander (1865) both died of malaria, and the work they had started had to be continued by others.[79]

Andrew Murray and Anti-liberalism?

It is a pity that some contemporary authors writing about this period in South African history, particularly regarding the liberal/'orthodox' divide, have tended to do so with remarkably little nuance. An exception is the above-mentioned book by Brümmer on the theological history of the Cape DRC. Olea Nel, on the other hand, introduces the theme by all but identifying the nineteenth-century Cape liberals in the DRC with Satanism when she writes regarding Andrew Murray, who became moderator of the DRC in 1862: 'Although the ordeal would leave him emotionally bruised and physically spent, it would leave us with an enduring example of how to overcome Satan in battle.'[80] Of course, there is no denying that this concerns a highly polemical episode in DRC history. Andrew Murray himself had uncompromising views about the liberal faction, as will be elaborated on below. Undoubtedly, stark theological differences existed between the two camps. However, in retrospect the whole controversy might also perhaps be interpreted as a power struggle between a Scottish originating, mission interested, evangelical leaning faction on the one hand, and a Dutch rationalist, intellectualist grouping on the other. The revivals in the Cape might even be interpreted as an ultimately very successful ploy by the former group to neutralise the influence of the latter, but that would only be part of the story, of course.

The 1862 synod saw the emergence of a remarkable controversy when elder Loedolff of Malmesbury registered an objection to 'the sitting in the Synod of deputies from congregations lying beyond the boundaries of the Cape Colony'.[81] This occurred after Andrew Murray Jr, as moderator, had called out the name of the minister of Pietermaritzburg to the synod as part of the routine opening roll call. Interestingly, the minister from Pietermaritzburg who had his credentials unexpectedly questioned was none other than the above-mentioned Revd Huet, vehement opponent of ecclesiastical segregation and author of *Eene Kudde en Een Herder*. It is also interesting as a side-note that Loedolff was the brother-in-law of Revd J. C. Le Febres Morrees of Malmesbury,[82] who would steer his congregation in subsequent years to an institutionalisation of segregation. Under Morrees' direction the church council would choose to interpret the 1857 'weakness of some' decision to mean that it mandated segregated communion services for 'white' and 'coloured' members.[83]

Loedolff's objection, which was defeated in the synod by a large majority, was in effect the first salvo to be fired in a series of church and legal battles between the so-called 'liberals' and 'orthodox'. The liberal camp, which Loedolff represented in this objection, argued that the Cape church was, according to a colonial ordinance of 1843, legally confined within the boundaries of the Cape Colony.[84] The reason, according to F. L. Cachet, for the liberals to insist on this territorial confinement of the church was due to the fact that almost all the ministers to the north of the Orange River were orthodox, whereas the liberals believed that they might attain a majority if the Cape ministers were exclusively counted.[85]

Despite being voted down in the synod, Loedolff and his supporters immediately took the case to the Cape Supreme Court, where the plaintiff's case against the church was upheld. Consternation reigned in the orthodox camp, but the synod then had no choice but to exclude all delegates from beyond the Orange River, including Huet from Pietermaritzburg and the delegation from Bloemfontein, Andrew Murray's former congregation. This successful legal challenge mounted by the liberal camp also excluded the Stellenbosch Seminary professors Hofmeyr and John Murray from sitting in the synod.[86]

Who were these liberal ministers supposedly behind the machination executed by Loedolff and the Supreme Court? Cachet mentions the names of J. J. Kotzé of Darling, T. Burgers of Hanover and S. P. Naudé of Queenstown. These 'liberals' or 'modernists' were representative of 'the unbelief which is proclaimed as truth in Holland and in Dutch academies . . .'[87]

The following years saw a ramping up of tensions between the 'liberals' and 'orthodox' in the Cape Colony. This involved more court cases against the DRC, with Andrew Murray standing as accused against the liberal opponents in his capacity as moderator. Burgers was in turn accused of heresy by an elder from a different congregation. Kotzé got himself into trouble for denying the validity of question 60 of the Heidelberg Catechism, according to which humanity is 'continually inclined towards all evil'.[88] Both cases ended up in the Supreme Court after both Kotzé[89] and Burgers[90] were suspended. In both cases the ministers had to be reinstated after it was found that the DRC had followed incorrect procedures in its dealings with them.[91] The 'orthodox' faction was dismayed by these developments, and did whatever they could to have these reinstated ministers hamstrung in terms of actually carrying out their ministerial activities. It seems that the case of Burgers, whose Hanover congregation was part of the Graaff Reinet *Ring*, where Andrew Murray Sr still held the fort, was particularly irksome. Thus, when Burgers now involved the church in further litigation, in 'April, 1866, the Synodical Committee decided to carry the case Burgers versus the Synodical Committee in appeal to the Privy Council' in England. It was decided that Andrew Murray Jr, as moderator, would be the man to handle the case on behalf of the DRC, so he and his wife Emma and their five children boarded a ship bound for England.⁹² This mission, however, ended in failure: 'On 6 February 1867, the Privy Council upheld the High Court ruling in favour of Burgers.'⁹³

This was, then, Murray's second failed mission to England in appeal of a losing local cause, the first being the attempt to prevent the imperial relinquishment of the Orange River Sovereignty during the previous decade (see Chapter 2). However, like the previous time, Murray achieved other goals, as his personal international fame as writer and preacher had started to bud. During a ten-month period he spoke at a conference in Bath, his paper was published in *Evangelical Christendom*, and he preached in several London churches with such success that he was presented with a call to the pastorate of the Marylebone Presbyterian Church, which he declined.⁹⁴

When Murray arrived back in Cape Town, he might have wished he had accepted that call to a London church instead, because controversy reigned yet again. Du Plessis writes that 'in 1867 the Liberal Movement at the Cape was at the height of its power and influence'.⁹⁵ Burgers had managed to accrue much support for his cause from within the DRC and from without. The famous Bishop Colenso of Natal, who had been involved in a similar struggle in the pursuit of rationalism, but within the Anglican Church, was one of the prominent names contributing to Burgers' legal expenditure.⁹⁶

Murray's pastorate during this period was the Groote Kerk in Cape Town. During his absence, his senior colleague had retired, which prompted 527 members out of a total of three thousand to sign a petition to their church council to have J. J. Kotzé appointed to fill the vacancy, early in 1867. However, the council rejected this sizeable minority opinion and opted instead to call Murray's maternal cousin, G. W. Stegmann Jr.⁹⁷

A further development in the protracted controversy occurred when a Leiden-trained ministerial candidate, David P. Faure, returned from the Netherlands. He was of unitarian persuasion and he realised of his own accord that he could not sign the *colloquium doctum*,⁹⁸ the statement of orthodoxy that the Cape church demanded of its ministers. Faure eventually founded the Free Protestant Church in Cape Town, a body that attracted many liberal members in the DRC, and thus weakened the liberal contingency in the latter body.⁹⁹ In 1868 he published thirteen of his talks on modern theology in booklet form, which promoted among other things the findings of historical criticism.¹⁰⁰

Andrew Murray responded to *De Moderne Theologie*¹⁰¹ in a series of counter-lectures in defence of traditional church doctrine held at the Groote Kerk, and subsequently published as *Het Moderne Ongeloof* (Modern Unbelief).¹⁰²

Ultimately, liberalism was all but vanquished in the Cape.¹⁰³ Regarding the recalcitrant ministers, Kotzé and Burgers, the synod had to decide whether to abide by the civil rulings and reinstate them, or to cease its connection to the state by becoming a fully voluntarist society responsible for paying its own salaries. Such a radical move proved to be a bridge too far for a church that in spite of its budding evangelicalism was very much a state church, and dependent on all the benefits accruing from such a position. Hence the ministers were reinstated. Kotzé continued as minister of Darling until old age and ill health forced him into retirement. Burgers would continue for another couple of years in his congregation at Hanover, whereupon he would resign and move northwards to become the president of the *Zuid-Afrikaansche Republiek* (South African Republic) in 1872.[104]

Burgers' career is an interesting case in point of a DRC pastor turned pro-Boer, proto-Afrikaner nationalist politician. It inadvertently reminds one of a subsequent generation character who found his way from the DRC pulpit onto the political stage, D. F. Malan. In fact, comparing these two makes sense given that both men might be described as theologically liberal or modernist, although this was less pronounced in the case of the latter. Malan was certainly in favour of employing higher criticism in the interpretation of the Bible.[105] Like Burgers, Malan was trained in the Netherlands at a time before neo-Calvinism had become such a dominant discourse both there and in South Africa. Malan's taint of modernism was not serious enough to cause trouble with his synod. However, that might have been different had he not opted of his own accord to first follow a journalistic path as editor of the newly founded *De Burger*, followed by a political role as leader of the National Party that won the election of 1948 under an apartheid agenda.

What is furthermore interesting about Burgers and Malan is that over time Andrew Murray would clash with both. I shall consider the debate between Murray and Malan in detail in Chapter 7.

Before going on to the next section, which concerns Murray's consolidation of the evangelical ascendancy, it might be important to briefly refer again to Brümmer and his assertion that there was somehow a connection between the nineteenth-century liberals and the early twentieth-century fundamentalists who accused Murray's protégé, Johannes du Plessis, of heterodoxy. This argument leans perhaps quite heavily on the fact that during the tumultuous time of the nineteenth-century liberal controversy, one of the accused, Kotzé, after having his name cleared, proceeded to accuse Murray himself of having a heterodox view of predestination as expressed by the Canons of Dordt. This occurred after Murray apparently issued a challenge during the 1870 synod to anyone who wanted to prove that he did not subscribe to a pure doctrine of predestination.[106] The very fact that such a challenge would be issued indicates that there existed broader suspicion regarding Murray's orthodoxy, of course. Murray defended himself for all he was worth, but Brümmer suggests that his defence was not fully convincing, because he centred ultimate truth in the Love of God, whereas Dordt placed the Sovereignty of God in the centre.[107]

On one level, Murray, Hofmeyr and the *Secor Dabar* influence sphere won that particular battle, due to the fact that most of the influential liberals subsequently proceeded with their activities outside of the official DRC channels. All except Kotzé, of course. The fact that Kotzé remained in the ministry until retirement, and that he particularly managed to get under Murray's skin with his doctrinal argument, does make one wonder if he did not inadvertently open the door for the later defenders of orthodoxy, who were most definitely not liberal, S. J. and J. D. du Toit et al., to label the evangelical stream in the DRC as Methodists, that is, non-subscribers to predestination[108] (see Chapter 7).

Murray, in the meantime, left the somewhat troubled Groote Kerk congregation for a call to the Boland town of Wellington in 1871. Here his interest in education was taken to a different level through a pioneering initiative. After becoming acquainted with a biography of the life of Mary Lyon, founder of the Mount Holyoke institute, Murray became convinced that this model of Christian women serving as educators should also be used in South Africa. On 2 December 1872 he wrote to the principal of Mount Holyoke, in which he explained his wish for one of their graduates to come and teach in South Africa. The net result of this exchange was that the training institute for women teachers subsequently opened its doors in Wellington on 19 January 1874, with two American teachers and fifty-four local students from around the Cape. With the establishment of the Huguenot Seminary, as it was known, Andrew Murray became a pioneer visionary of women's education in South Africa (see Chapter 4).[109] This underlines the point made by Robert and Duff that evangelicalism in the nineteenth century could be quite progressive.[110] Perhaps that would in turn make it less surprising to also find aspects of the nineteenth-century liberal tradition joining forces with a much more conservative movement, that is, neo-Calvinism in the early twentieth century. One important commonality was the Dutch rather than Scots origins of these divergent streams, of course.

The above will suffice for suggesting that Andrew Murray subscribed to rather 'liberal' views[111] regarding the roles of women and their rights in society. Yet another indication of Murray's views of humanity, specifically slavery, might be found in an excerpt of a testimony by one of his (unnamed) daughters, and quoted in du Plessis, where she recalls growing up in the Worcester pastorate in the 1860s. She mentions the many missionaries frequently passing through their household as well as one of her earliest recollections, a map of the Religions of the World hanging on the wall, and her father pointing out the United States, saying: 'They are fighting that the slaves may be free'.[112] Murray's anti-slavery stance, although perhaps not intellectually well developed or theologically argued, is really part and parcel of the general British evangelical milieu out of which he emerged and into which he married (see Chapter 2).

If social involvement in causes such as missionary work, anti-slavery and women's education contributed to a consolidation of the evangelical position at the Cape, the more decisive victory over theological liberalism was achieved through the prominent role played in the ensuing years by the theological seminary at Stellenbosch. As du Plessis summarises the conclusion of this particular episode:

> [T]he force of Liberalism within the Church was broken by the admission to the ministry, in increasing numbers, of young men who had undergone their training in the Theological Seminary at Stellenbosch, at the feet of those two eminent and devout professors, John Murray and Nicolaas Hofmeyr. Between 1862 and 1870 the ranks of the orthodox party in the Church were strengthened with between thirty and forty ministers, the majority of whom received appointments to Colonial congregations, though some went to serve the more needy Churches beyond the Orange and Vaal rivers. The Liberal party, which seemed so powerful and influential in the Synod of 1862, had shrunk to a shadow of its former self in 1870, and could muster on critical questions only eleven votes in a Synod of over one hundred members.[113]

It is furthermore instructive that an 1898 pamphlet on the struggle against liberalism would directly connect the defeat of the liberal position in the DRC with a growing emphasis on mission work. Dreijer, the author of this work, states conspicuously in the concluding paragraph, which I translate from the Dutch:

> 'Liberalism' in the DRC in South Africa belongs to the past. The struggles of 1862–1870 have done her well and have made her understand her strengths as well as her weaknesses. Under the providing hand of the Lord much good has emerged from the evil ... Our Church is becoming increasingly more a mission-loving church. During the last years a mission enthusiasm emerged that increases year on year, giving hope that the South African Christendom would become the light bearer for the whole of Africa.[114]

Ecumenical Overtures

I mentioned above how Scottish and DRC missionary projects coalesced in the 1850s. Next I shall briefly discuss a situation where the liberal challenge to orthodoxy led to an attempt at ecumenicity between the DRC and the Anglican Church. However, as part of a narrative in which I argue that the DRC was itself evangelised and conquered from within by Scots, let me mention a couple of instances of attempted church unity between the DRC and Scots Presbyterians. The first occurred already in 1824 when George Thom, who had been the government-assigned recruiter of the original group of Scots ministers and educators, placed before the synod a motion arguing in favour of unity between the DRC and the Church of Scotland. This was referred to the government, but ultimately due to legislation introduced and remaining in force since the Batavian Republic, such fraternisation, comparable with what had existed between the DRC and the Reformed Church in the Netherlands, although desirable, was not possible.[115]

Subsequently, there were some further moments of interest regarding such a development. At the 1862 synod, Andrew Murray pleaded for unity with the Scots church. The synod voted against this, 'although the link with the DRC of the Netherlands had been severed, and all correspondence with that Church had ceased'.[116] While 1862 marked the first occasion that Murray served as moderator, 1894 marked the sixth and final time he would serve in that capacity. By then the synod apparently accepted his position, as the following decision indicates:

> The Synod desires to have it minuted that it is in favour of a closer union between the branches of Presbyterians in South Africa. It regrets the circumstances which appear to stand in the way of immediate organic union, but trusts that ere long some means will be devised whereby that very desirable object shall be obtained. Meanwhile it would urge all Presbyteries and Consistories to do all they can to further not only spiritual unity, but external and organic union, among the different branches of the Churches, who hold the Reformed faith and Presbyterian principles.[117]

Subsequent years saw an escalation of tensions between the memberships of these churches as political tensions culminating in the South African War effectively ended the DRC's search for ecumenical partnerships among the English-speaking churches. While closer nineteenth-century ties between Reformed and Presbyterian churches could have been a natural development, such ties with the Anglican Church would have been farther-fetched. Yet precisely such an attempt was made.

I briefly referred to Bishop Colenso's support of Burgers above, and to be sure, comparable to the evangelical-liberal controversy in the DRC, the Anglican Church in South Africa experienced its own conflict, principally between Bishop Robert Gray and Colenso. The former accused the latter of heresy due to Colenso's affirmation of higher criticism, and this led to a protracted battle in church and court which resulted in Colenso being excommunicated. Gray represented the conservative wing of his church, and he looked upon the predominance of liberalism within the DRC with much alarm. Jonathan Draper quotes Gray in a letter dated 10 August 1863[118] to Revd Bullock as follows:

> I reckon that about two fifths of the Dutch Clergy, are liberals, i.e. more or less rationalistic. They are to have another Synod in October to expel liberalism that is spreading. Thank God not one [of our] clergymen as far as I know holding a spiritual office in this Province sympathizes with their views, nor do I think that more than a very

few of our laity do; but the public do in some measure, especially the Dutch portion of it, do.[119]

There are many important differences between the Anglican and DRC cases making the various opposing sides to these controversies unlikely cross-denominational partners, principally the fact that Colenso as a missionary enthusiast might on one level have had more affinities with some of the evangelicals in the DRC than with the Dutch-trained liberals. Yet, in the aftermath of these controversies, it so happened that both churches had their synod sessions in 1870, and there occurred a remarkable initiative from the Anglican side to achieve a church union with their Reformed brethren. Du Plessis suggests that the victorious sides in the two churches had drawn closer after their respective heretics were purged or otherwise sidelined. At any rate, the suggestion for unity was favourably received by the DRC, and a special committee was convened consisting of the moderator, the actuary and the scribe of their synod, who were P. E. Faure, Andrew Murray and William Robertson.[120] Bishop Gray, perhaps not surprisingly in the light of his earlier dealings with Colenso, proved an uncompromising negotiator from the point of view of the DRC colleagues. Gray insisted that the episcopate, as an essential aspect of the gospel, should be foundational to any prospective church union. The DRC representatives disagreed, and ultimately the church unity project had to be abandoned.[121]

The failure to achieve church unity between churches with such distinct positions in terms of polity should not be surprising, but what is surprising is the fact that such a project was even attempted. The English–Afrikaans rupture formalised by the South African War, and carried further with the rise of Afrikaner nationalism in the early twentieth century, would make this nineteenth-century venture seem rather quaint, perhaps even a source of shame for some among the subsequent generations of Afrikaners in the DRC. The strong Scottish element in the preliminary victorious evangelical grouping within the DRC undoubtedly played a role in initially bridging the divide between the two colonial churches, the one English and the other supposedly Dutch. That very same Scottish element would become suspect of harbouring divided loyalties when anti-imperialism became a leading trend in the mainstream DRC in its subsequent ideological development as a *volkskerk* for white Afrikaner people.

Conclusion

One thing that stands out in considering the above is the almost ironic reversal of perspectives regarding liberal and evangelical positions to social (and ecumenical) affairs over time. In the late twentieth century and beyond, evangelicalism came to signify social conservatism, not only in South Africa, but globally. However, in the late-nineteenth-century liberal–evangelical struggle it seems that the evangelicals were more typically the social reformers. Local education, including women's education, was a cornerstone of their mantra in DRC circles, as represented by the Murrays in particular, as the next chapter will elaborate in further detail. In contrast, the liberals primarily concerned themselves with doctrinal affairs involving the church's confessions. Although this certainly was the result of exposure to excellent education in the Netherlands, including historical criticism, the liberals were apparently less able to effectively translate their learning to the wider context in South Africa. Particularly, the liberal opposition to the expansion of the DRC beyond the Orange River, and the implied anti-missionary bias one could read into that, might seem like a negative and ironically non-progressive strategy.

Notes

1. Cf. Duff: 'In 1824, the Scottish ministers gained full control over the DRC, having persuaded the colonial state to sever the church's ties with the Classis Amsterdam, establishing it as separate and independent, with its own synod.' S. E. Duff (2018) 'The Dutch Reformed Church and the Protestant Atlantic: Revivalism and Evangelicalism in the Nineteenth-Century Cape Colony', *South African Historical Journal*, 70:2, pp. 324–47, DOI: 10.1080/02582473.2018.1468810, p. 331.
2. See M. C. Kitshoff (2010) 'Meesterbouer aan die Teologiese Kweekskool – Ds GWA van der Lingen, 1804–1869', *Nederduitse Gereformeerde Teologiese Tydskrif*, 15:1, pp. 121–2.
3. See A. Vos (1981/2002) 'Inventaris van het archief van het theologisch-litterarisch gezelschap "Secor Dabar" te Utrecht 1844–1969', *Het Utrechts Argief*, hetutrechtsargief.nl/onderzoek
4. In fact, in contrast to the Murrays who were arguably more enthralled by *Secor Dabar* than the general university experience at Utrecht, Van der Lingen wanted specifically to model the seminary on Utrecht. Kitshoff mentions that Van der Lingen was not only responsible for the inscription of the Utrecht motto *Sol Iustitiae Illustra Nos* at the seminary building in Stellenbosch, but also at his church in Paarl, as well as at the Paarl Gymnasium, the prestigious school he founded in the town where he ministered for nearly forty years. Kitshoff, 'Meesterbouer', p. 128.
5. See Duff, 'The Dutch Reformed Church and the Protestant Atlantic', p. 343.
6. Jean du Plessis (1988) 'Colonial progress and countryside conservatism: An essay on the legacy of Van der Lingen of Paarl, 1831–1875', MA thesis, University of Stellenbosch, p. 118.
7. Kitshoff, 'Meesterbouer', p. 126.
8. J. D. Kestell (1912) *Het leven van Professor N. J. Hofmeyr*. Kaapstad: Hollandsch-Afrikaansche Uitgewers, p. 75.
9. See *Jubileum-Soewenier van die Ned. Geref. Kerkgebou, Tulbagh (1878–1928)*, p. 19.
10. Frederick William Sass (1956) 'The Influence of the Church of Scotland on the Dutch Reformed Church of South Africa', unpublished PhD thesis, University of Edinburgh, p. 157.
11. James Mackinnon (1887) *South African Traits*. Edinburgh: J. Gemmell, pp. 60–1.

12. Ibid., p. 61.
13. Sass, 'Influence of the Church of Scotland', p. 138.
14. Acta Synodi 1857, p. 60. transl. from Dutch., as quoted in Sass, 'Influence of the Church of Scotland', p. 139.
15. Some, like Van der Walt, even, incorrectly, argued that this decision necessitated the formation of separate churches along racial lines. I. J. van der Walt (1960) 'Eiesoortige Kerkvorming as Missiologiese Probleem met Besondere Verwysing na Suid-Afrika', thesis for the Doctorate of Theology, Potchefstroom University for Christian Higher Education, p. 473.
16. The South African missiologist and anti-apartheid stalwart, Willem Saayman, was a notable exponent of this type of reading: 'the "weakness of some" is actually exploited for (what is considered to be) "the progress of the Kingdom of God among the heathen"'. Saayman, furthermore, in hindsight, implanted the following motivation to the drafters of the resolution: 'Politically we are going to commit an injustice (albeit temporary), so let us at least in religious terms exonerate the injustice as far as possible by casting ourselves into mission unreservedly.' W. A. Saayman (2007) *Being missionary, being human: an overview of Dutch Reformed Mission.* Pietermaritzburg: Cluster Publications, p. 92 Cf. Chris Loff (1983) 'The history of a Heresy', in John W. De Gruchy and Charles Villa-Vicencio, *Apartheid is a heresy.* Grand Rapids, MI: W. B. Eerdmans Pub. Co.; Dirk Smit (2009) *Essays on Being Reformed: Collected Essays 3.* Stellenbosch: SUN Press, p. 461.
17. Giliomee shows how in the synod debate between those who favoured ecclesiastical unity versus those who wanted *afscheiding* (segregation), N. J. Hofmeyr played a crucial role as proponent of a 'third way', a position he had been advocating since earlier in that decade. Following the example of St Stephen's Church, a congregation of mainly former slaves in Cape Town, and a Presbyterian church, Hofmeyr argued that each DRC congregation should be serviced by a minister and a missionary. The latter's work should be based in the *Gesticht*, a building separate from the main church building and specifically intended for religious instruction of a missionary nature to blacks and 'coloureds'. In other words, this was a nod towards the accommodation of existing racial prejudice, while simultaneously strengthening mission, but without segregating the church congregation as such. See Hermann Giliomee (2003) '"The Weakness of Some": The Dutch Reformed Church and White Supremacy', *Scriptura*, 83, pp. 212–44, pp. 218–19.
18. Of course, one might credibly argue that nineteenth-century mission was indelibly a discourse of otherness, so there is really no tension between a mission-centred synod and an apartheid synod. In fact, apartheid and mission could very easily be conceptually connected, because what was apartheid if not a system of institutionalised otherness? Cf. Esme Cleall (2012) *Missionary Discourses of Difference: Negotiating Otherness in the British Empire, 1840–1900.* Houndmills: Palgrave Macmillan. Yet missionary discourse, while accentuating otherness in many respects, also attempted to erase difference in other areas. For this reason, in South Africa, nineteenth-century missionaries were typically the enemies of the most ardent racialised discourses.
19. Elphick's recent work on the theme of equalisation vs. non-equalisation has been one of the most important contributions to South African church history, and his treatment of 1857 falls in line with that general discourse, but he

appears to acknowledge that more has been read into the 'weakness of some' decision in the subsequent century than what was meant with it at the time: 'In retrospect, the 1857 synodical resolution may seem a portentous precedent of the DRC's later advocacy of apartheid. Yet it merely gave official sanction to arrangements already common in practice, and did not appear highly important to observers in immediately subsequent generations.' Richard Elphick (2012) *Equality of Believers: Protestant Missionaries and the Racial Politics of South Africa.* Charlottesville: University of Virginia Press, p. 44.

20. An example of this divide between a more 'liberal' centre and a more prejudiced periphery could be seen in the fact that in 1860 whites and blacks were still baptised in the same building in Cape Town, Wynberg, Stellenbosch, Paarl, Swartland and Montagu, but in the eastern Karoo towns of Cradock, Somerset East, Burgersdorp and Colesberg this was not the case. Carl Borchardt, 'Die "Swakheid van Sommige" en die Sending', in J. Kinghorn (ed.) (1986) *Die NG Kerk en Apartheid.* Johannesburg: Macmillan, p. 76.
21. Sass, 'Influence of the Church of Scotland', p. 115.
22. 3 Acta Synodi 1829, III, pp. 71–2, transl. from Dutch and quoted in Sass 'Influence of the Church of Scotland', p. 117.
23. Sass, 'Influence of the Church of Scotland', pp. 117–18.
24. Johannes du Plessis (1919) *The life of Andrew Murray of South Africa.* London: Marshall Brothers, pp. 174–5.
25. Sass, 'Influence of the Church of Scotland', p. 119.
26. Ibid., p. 136.
27. Ibid., pp. 137–8.
28. Ibid., p. 138, note 1.
29. A. P. Smit (1967) *Ligbaken aan die Swartkops. Ned. Geref. Kerk Uitenhage 1817–1967.* Uitenhage: Nederduitse Gereformeerde Kerk, p. 43.
30. Ibid., p. 42.
31. Ibid., pp. 43–4.
32. This was gleaned from a land report in 1838. Smit, *Ligbaken*, p. 44.
33. Abraham Faure, *Het Ned. Z. A. Tydschrift*, part 1, no. 2, p. 156, quoted in A. Dreyer (1930) *Gedenkboek van Jansenville, Driekwart-Eeufees, 1855–1930.* Stellenbosch: Pro-Ecclesia, p. 11.
34. Sass, 'Influence of the Church of Scotland', p. 140.
35. Acta Synodi 1857, CCA S1/10 p. 990, quoted in Sass, 'Influence of the Church of Scotland', pp. 141–2.
36. Sass, 'Influence of the Church of Scotland', pp. 143–4.
37. A. Dreyer (1899) *Geschiedenis van de Gemeente Swellendam.* Kaapstad: Taylor en Snashall, p. 51.
38. Ibid., p. 33.
39. B. Spoelstra (1961) 'Die stigting van die Gereformeerde Kerk Colesberg', in *Die Gereformeerde Kerk Colesberg gestig 8 Desember 1860 op die plaas Hamelfontein van I. D. du Plessis: Gedenkalbum tydens die Eeufeesviering 27, 28, 29 Oktober 1961*, p. 13.
40. P. Huet (1860) *Eéne kudde en één herder: verhandeling over de toebrenging van heidenen tot de christelijke kerkgameenschap.* Kaapstad: Marais, p. 50.
41. Borchardt, 'Die "Swakheid van Sommige"', p. 77.
42. C. J. Kriel (1963), *Die Geskiedenis van die Nederduitse Gereformeerde Sendingkerk in Suid-Afrika, 1881–1956*, Paarl: Paarlse Drukpers, p. 59.

43. Ibid.
44. 'To Professor John Murray', 30 November 1858, in du Plessis, *Life of Andrew Murray*, p. 157.
45. M. W. Retief (1951) *Herlewings in Ons Geskiedenis*. Kaapstad and Pretoria: NGK Uitgewers van Suid-Afrika, p. 14.
46. Ibid., p. 10. Also see Duff, 'The Dutch Reformed Church and the Protestant Atlantic'.
47. See Olea Nel (2010) *South Africa's forgotten revival: The story of the Cape's Great Awakening in 1860*. Canberra: Olive Twig Books, pp. 70–3.
48. Retief, *Herlewings in Ons Geskiedenis*, p. 13.
49. See S. E. Duff (2015) *Changing childhoods in the Cape Colony: Dutch Reformed Church evangelicalism and colonial childhood, 1860–1895*. Basingstoke: Palgrave Macmillan, p. 38.
50. Duff, 'The Dutch Reformed Church and the Protestant Atlantic', p. 325.
51. See H. Giliomee (2011) *The Afrikaners: biography of a people*. London: Hurst & Co., p. 205.
52. Retief, *Herlewings in Ons Geskiedenis*, p. 14.
53. Du Plessis, *Life of Andrew Murray*, pp. 186–7.
54. Andrew Murray to Professor John Murray, 19 January 1860, quoted in du Plessis, *Life of Andrew Murray*, p. 185.
55. Retief, *Herlewings in Ons Geskiedenis*, pp. 14–16.
56. Ibid., p. 16.
57. Du Plessis, *Life of Andrew Murray*, pp. 187–8.
58. Retief, *Herlewings in Ons Geskiedenis*, p. 17.
59. Duff, 'The Dutch Reformed Church and the Protestant Atlantic', p. 334.
60. See V. Brümmer (2013) *Vroom of Regsinnig?: Teologie in die NG Kerk*. Wellington, South Africa: Bybel-Media.
61. 'Dr. Robertson to the Members of the Committee appointed by the Worcester Conference', quoted in du Plessis, *Life of Andrew Murray*, pp. 190–1.
62. Du Plessis, *Life of Andrew Murray*, pp. 191–2; Retief, *Herlewings in Ons Geskiedenis*, p. 17.
63. Du Plessis, *Life of Andrew Murray*, p. 192.
64. Ibid., p. 193. Duff sketches a background context of rural poverty, drought and hardship, and she also mentions the fact that the Scottish ministers were placed in rural areas, which partly helps to explain why they were specifically associated with this movement. See Duff, 'The Dutch Reformed Church and the Protestant Atlantic', p. 331
65. Du Plessis, *Life of Andrew Murray*, p. 194.
66. Ibid.
67. Revd J. C. de Vries, quoted in du Plessis, *Life of Andrew Murray*, pp. 194–5.
68. Ibid., p. 195.
69. Ibid., p. 196.
70. See Sass, 'Influence of the Church of Scotland', p. 120.
71. Duff, 'The Dutch Reformed Church and the Protestant Atlantic', p. 336.
72. See Duff, 'The Dutch Reformed Church and the Protestant Atlantic', p. 335 ff.
73. Henry Vicars Taylor, quoted in W. M. Douglas (1957) *Andrew Murray and his message*. Fort Washington: Christian Literature Crusade, p. 230.
74. Nel, *South Africa's forgotten revival*, pp. 152–3.

75. Du Plessis, *Life of Andrew Murray*, p. 201.
76. Ibid., p. 202.
77. Andrew Murray Jr, quoted in du Plessis, *Life of Andrew Murray*, p. 203.
78. Du Plessis, *Life of Andrew Murray*, pp. 202–3.
79. Nel, *South Africa's forgotten revival*, pp. 155–6.
80. Ibid., p. 177.
81. F. Lion Cachet (1875) *Vijftien jaar in Zuid-Afrika: Brieven aan een vriend.* Leeuwarden: H. Bokma. quoted in du Plessis, *Life of Andrew Murray*, p. 212.
82. J. G. Botha (1981) *Gedenkuitgawe van die Nederduitse Gereformeerde Sendinggemeente van Malmesbury in die Eeufeesjaar 1981.* Malmesbury: NG Sendingkerkraad, p. 13.
83. See Giliomee, '"The Weakness of Some"', p. 220.
84. Du Plessis, *Life of Andrew Murray*, p. 213.
85. See Cachet in du Plessis, *Life of Andrew Murray*, p. 212.
86. Du Plessis, *Life of Andrew Murray*, pp. 214–15.
87. Cachet in du Plessis, *Life of Andrew Murray*, p. 213.
88. Du Plessis, *Life of Andrew Murray*, p. 215. Although Vincent Brümmer, *Vroom of Regsinnig?*, does not use the term deism in his exegesis of the Cape Liberals' theological orientation, his description of a deterministic world view wherein God could not be persuaded by prayer, for example, is reminiscent of deism. An interesting example of this is Kotzé's opposition to and refusal to have his Darling congregation participate in a day of prayer for rain, as called out by the synod in 1866, the reason being that God could not be swayed by prayer since, according to this world view, God and humans are locked into predetermined patterns. Brümmer, *Vroom of Regsinnig?*, pp. 62–3.
89. Du Plessis, *Life of Andrew Murray*, p. 217.
90. Ibid., p. 224.
91. Ibid., pp. 222, 226.
92. Ibid., p. 228.
93. Nel, *South Africa's forgotten revival*, p. 184.
94. Du Plessis, *A Life of Andrew Murray*, pp. 243–4.
95. Ibid., p. 244.
96. Ibid.
97. Nel, *South Africa's forgotten revival*, pp. 184–5.
98. This was an examination for ministerial candidates instituted by the Cape synod in 1862 as a direct response to combat the perceived liberalism of Dutch-trained clergy. See Brümmer, *Vroom of Regsinnig?*, p. 55.
99. See du Plessis, *Life of Andrew Murray*, p. 231.
100. See Brümmer, *Vroom of Regsinnig?*, p. 81, 83ff.
101. D. P. Faure (1868) *De Moderne Theologie. Dertien Toespraken gehouden in de Mutual Hall, Kaapstad.* Cape Town.
102. Eventually it was also translated into Afrikaans. See Andrew Murray (1942) *Die Moderne Ongeloof. Dertien Leerredes.* Afrikaanse vertaling in deel II van die *Versamelde Werke* van Andrew Murray. Stellenbosch.
103. See A. du Toit (1987) 'The Cape Afrikaners' Failed Liberal Moment', pp. 49–56. Jeffrey Butler, Richard Elphick and David Welsh, *Democratic liberalism in South Africa: its history and prospect.* Middletown, CT: Wesleyan University Press.
104. Du Plessis, *Life of Andrew Murray*, p. 235.

105. V. Brümmer (2013) 'DF Malan en die Hoër Kritiek', *Nederduitse Gereformeerde Teologiese Tydskrif*, 54, pp. 3–4.
106. *De Ondersoeker* (1871), p. 9.
107. See Brümmer, *Vroom of Regsinnig?*, pp. 118–19.
108. See Brümmer, *Vroom of Regsinnig?*, p. 163ff.
109. Nel, *South Africa's forgotten revival*, pp. 195–6.
110. See Dana L. Robert (1993) 'Mount Holyoke Women and the Dutch Reformed Missionary Movement, 1874–1904', *Missionalia*, 21:2, pp. 103–23, and S. E. Duff (2005) '"Oh! for a blessing on Africa and America": the Mount Holyoke system and the Huguenot Seminary, 1874–1885', *New Contree*, 50, pp. 95–109.
111. See Duff, 'The Dutch Reformed Church and the Protestant Atlantic', p. 334.
112. Quoted in du Plessis, *Life of Andrew Murray*, p. 201.
113. Du Plessis, *Life of Andrew Murray*, p. 231.
114. A. Dreijer (1898) *De Strijd onzer Vaderen tegen het Liberalisme*. Kaapstad: Jacques Dusseau & Co., p. 48.
115. See Sass, 'Influence of the Church of Scotland', p. 237.
116. Ibid., p. 238.
117. Acta Synodi, 1894, CCA Sl/19, pp. 129–30, quoted in Sass, 'Influence of the Church of Scotland', p. 238.
118. This seems to refer to the 1862 synod of the DRC, so this date might have been erroneously transcribed as 1863.
119. J. Draper (2003) 'The Trial of Bishop John William Colenso', in J. A. Draper (ed.) *The Eye of the Storm: Bishop John William Colenso and the Crisis of Biblical Inspiration*. Pietermaritzburg: Cluster, p. 313.
120. Du Plessis, *Life of Andrew Murray*, p. 255.
121. Ibid., pp. 255–9.

CHAPTER FOUR

The Scottish (and American) Foundations of a Trans-frontier Afrikaner Missionary Enterprise[1]

In the late nineteenth century, the DRC started to send missionaries first to the Northern Transvaal, followed by Nyasaland, Mashonaland and Bechuanaland, and eventually as far north as what was then the western Sudan (present-day Nigeria). A primary driving force behind this missionary initiative was the influential Andrew Murray Jr. Having proven themselves victorious in securing the social and theological ascendancy in the DRC, Andrew Murray and his compatriots were subsequently able to institute a strong missionary interest within a church that was more typically characterised by its long tradition of seeing itself as the religious custodian of Dutch cultural norms at an expanding frontier into darkest Africa. I deal elsewhere with the complexities inherent in Andrew Murray Jr's hybrid identity, but here I highlight the fact that he became the first president of the *Predikante Sending Vereniging* (Ministers' Missionary Union: MMU) that negotiated with the Scottish Presbyterian mission about taking up missionary activities in Nyasaland in an area where the Free Church of Scotland had already made a start. The main thrust of this chapter, and much of the rest of the book, will be on developments in Nyasaland/Malawi, because here there developed a noteworthy partnership between Scots missionaries from both the Free Church and the Church of Scotland, on the one hand, and Scots Afrikaner missionaries from South Africa, on the other.

An American–Scots Afrikaner Missionary Impetus

The above-mentioned growth in mission interest did not simply occur spontaneously, nor were Andrew Murray and the Scottish Afrikaners solely responsible for engendering such a sentiment. A very important side-stream into the general narrative concerns a women-led American impetus. Dana Robert writes that over forty women arrived in South Africa from the USA between 1873 and 1887, approximately half of whom were representatives of Mount Holyoke Seminary in Massachusetts.[2] Robert makes a compelling argument that the DRC missionary enterprise would never have taken off were it not for the fact that it was to a large extent driven by women's fundraising ability, organisational skills and willingness to go themselves as missionaries to remote places, among other factors.[3]

Significant for my purposes here is the fact that Andrew Murray, described by Robert as the 'greatest dominee of the DRC in the late nineteenth century',[4] was the catalyst for this development. Having read a biography of Mary Lyon, founder of Mount Holyoke Seminary in 1872, Murray, deeply impressed by the equal footing Lyon had given in her educational system to the 'Head, the Heart, and the Hand',[5] initiated a correspondence with Mount Holyoke when he became aware of a teaching vacancy in his parish at Wellington. This correspondence set in motion a series of events that resulted in the arrival in South Africa of Abbie Ferguson and Anna Bliss and, after successful propagation and fundraising by Murray, the founding of the Huguenot Seminary in Wellington. Once the idea caught on, similar schools were also founded in other towns in South Africa – Stellenbosch, Worcester, Graaff Reinet, Swellendam and Pretoria. All these were girls' schools based on the Mount Holyoke model.[6]

The school's main purpose is stated in a piece written by Ferguson, who subsequent to her arrival in South Africa became principal of the seminary: 'the Huguenot Seminary was designed to provide the daughters of the Boers who were of French and Dutch descent an education which was on the level of that which was provided to the young ladies in our boarding schools in America and England'.[7] The formation of the Huguenot Seminary was also proposed as a remedy to the lack of trained educators within South Africa, an issue which had been felt for some time prior to the Seminary's founding. Andrew Murray, while addressing the question of why he had brought in teachers from America rather than Scotland, given his familial connections, answered that his reasoning lay in the character of Mary Lyon and the institution she had created. 'She believed women should receive the best intellectual training possible to enable them to fill their place alright. With this she believed the cultivation of a truly moral and religious character to be of supreme importance.'[8] He went on to state that, although it was not her express 'purpose to train missionaries, there has been no institution that has produced so many. Entire devotion to God, and our fellow men, was her watchword.'[9]

These schools and the ethos they instilled dramatically changed the culture of a significant segment of young women, and with it the missionary and social outreach profile of the DRC at large. This was perhaps especially so for rurally based young Afrikaner women, who had had rather limited and limiting visions of adulthood, with marriage being a prerequisite step for almost every viable option. The Mount Holyoke model opened up the prospect of an independent career in the foreign mission field, where DRC women operated in many respects on a relatively equal footing with the men, and often in leadership positions that would have been unheard of in the patriarchal rurally based Afrikaner society in South Africa. Anna Bliss, for example, made the following telling comment: 'one of the first complaints brought against us was that we taught the girls that they were almost as good as their brothers and could do as good work in their classes.

Time has proved that even in South Africa girls can do as well as the boys if they are faithful students.'[10]

Due to the unfamiliarity of female missionaries in South Africa, these efforts were received with some scepticism. Within one of the Seminary's yearbooks this matter is touched on by C. E. Waite, a member of the Seminary's staff who was involved in the mission training class. She addresses some concerns which they had received regarding the young women's ability to function as missionaries by means of employing an appeal to the readers' logic as well as expressing confidence in their training and spirit. 'If we want a house built, we are careful to hire the man most thoroughly trained in the business; or if we want a dress made, we act on the same principle. Shall we be less careful in the dealing with precious souls[?]'. Miss Waite then continues: '... these dear girls have not only given themselves but all the money they have, and means of earning money are more easily found by young men than by girls'.[11]

Dana Roberts suggests that even though the schools themselves were segregated according to the general pattern of South African society, they did help to counteract racism in some insidious ways. Particularly the 'hand' part in the Mount Holyoke model of head, heart and hand would have been a novel idea for daughters of farmers emerging from contexts where most aspects of domestic work would have been carried out by black servants.[12] 'The Mt. Holyoke system helped to move Afrikaner women and girls from a passive, tribal view of salvation to an activistic one, where conversion walked hand in hand with outreach to peoples of diverse ethnic backgrounds.'[13]

Robert furthermore notes that Andrew Murray and Abbie Ferguson shared an interest in the Holiness movement, with both being invested in the idea that Christians, including the pupils in the girls' schools, should reach deep levels of 'spiritual consecration'. It seems that the Congregationalist Mount Holyoke representatives and Murray shared a religiosity of 'evangelical pietism' that was theologically informed by 'moderate Calvinism'.[14] Robert intimates, and I agree, that the Mount Holyoke impetus strengthened Murray's hand significantly in terms of arousing mission interest among Afrikaners. To quote her directly: 'Andrew Murray's solicitation of teachers from Mt. Holyoke was thus not only an attempt to raise the educational level of Afrikaner girls, but was a plot to plant evangelical piety and support for home and foreign missions among the women of the Dutch Reformed Church.'[15] As we shall see in Chapter 7, Afrikaner nationalist opponents of Murray would have been in agreement with the idea of Murray instigating a 'plot' by founding the girls' schools, but for such opponents that only served to illustrate Murray's treachery against everything Afrikaans and Reformed.

A number of Murray women became involved in the Mount Holyoke/ Huguenot Seminary project, including Andrew's wife, sister, daughter and at least one niece. Andrew's third daughter, Catherine Margaret Murray, worked as a teacher for some time following her graduation before taking on the position of principal at the Bethlehem branch of the Huguenot Seminary in 1892.[16] One of Andrew's sisters was Helen 'Ella' Murray, who after spending a couple of years at the Huguenot Seminary declared herself ready at the end of 1875 to open a school on the Mount Holyoke model at the Murray family home town of Graaff Reinet. This was to be the Midland Seminary, where Ella became teacher and principal, initially holding the fort on her own until another teacher, 'Sarah Thayer arrived from the United States in 1876'.[17] Maria Neethling notes in *Unto Children's Children* that Helen Murray and Ferguson became lifelong friends.[18]

In the late 1870s, Huguenot Seminary pupils organised themselves into a Huguenot Mission Society, which supported and sent out a number of early women missionaries to various parts of southern Africa, including Andrew and Emma (Rutherford) Murray's daughter Mary, who together with Deborah Retief served as single women missionaries in British Bechuanaland.[19] This society also worked to raise awareness regarding mission work which was taking place on a larger scale across the globe, while remaining focused on the work being done by women. The notebook of the Society, which held the minutes of their meetings, provides an early example of this in an account of an address given by Miss Klance, an American missionary who was stationed in Natal at the time. She spoke of her experiences in the mission field, difficulties faced and lessons learned. In the months which followed, many other guest speakers gave accounts of their experiences in the mission fields to the young women of the Society.[20] These speeches offered insight into the reality of the work which was currently done and, as is commented on by Ferguson in one of her own speeches to the group, were given with the hope of igniting the missionary spirit within the audience.[21]

By 1889 missionary enthusiasm among Dutch Reformed women had been garnered to such an extent that Emma Murray became the first president of the countrywide *Vrouesendingbond* (Women's Missionary Union), which was founded at the Huguenot Seminary as an offspring of the Huguenot Mission Society.[22] This union acted as a uniting force for the large number of smaller missionary circles and societies which had sprung up across the country, due in no small part to the work which was being done by Andrew Murray and Ferguson.[23]

Dana Robert comments on the surprisingly progressive role of the *Vrouesendingbond*, which not only paid the salaries of its missionaries, but also had the power of appointing its own missionaries. Robert states that this was not a typical situation even in the United States, and she credits the fact that the *Vrouesendingbond* could occupy such a position in the late-nineteenth-century South African DRC to the 'close relationship between Andrew Murray and Abbie Ferguson, as well as Huguenot's distinguished record in supporting women as missionaries . . .'[24] One important distinction, however, is found in the Women's Missionary Union's connection to the DRC. Many similar societies elsewhere at this time operated independently. The *Vrouesendingbond*, on the other hand, effectively operated as one of the missionary arms of the DRC, and therefore was given access to both their support and connections, as well as suffering their criticism.[25]

Writing in 1924 about this era of strong missionary interest in the DRC, it is interesting to note that Johannes du Plessis, the foremost twentieth-century mission historian in the DRC, seemed oblivious to the importance of the Mount Holyoke factor in engendering this ethos. He singled out the important role of Andrew Murray criss-crossing the country on visits and evangelistic journeys as one undoubtedly strong factor, but more generally he called this missionary ethos a surprising development, the causes of which were 'hard to determine' (*moeilik te bepalen*).[26] However, thanks to more recent additional and correcting perspectives such as by Robert and Duff,[27] we can now furthermore point out that the mission interest engendered through the Mount Holyoke-modelled girls' schools culminating in the founding of the *Vrouesendingbond* also dovetailed neatly with the opening of a foreign mission field for members of the DRC.

The Ministers' Missionary Union and Scots Presbyterians

Ultimately based at Kondowe in the north of Nyasaland, the Livingstonia mission of the Free Church of Scotland had earlier started mission stations in the central region and at the south end of Lake Malawi, including at Cape Maclear and Livlezi.[28] For different reasons, including the unhealthy malaria-prone climate, the Scots were happy to vacate these areas and leave them to be occupied by DRC missionaries, who started to arrive in Nyasaland in 1888 in answer to an invitation by the Free Church. It should be noted at this point that there was possibly some confusion from early on already regarding the question of whether or not the Scots and the DRC in the Cape were on the same page about the exact nature of this relationship. More specifically, to whom did the early DRC missionaries owe their allegiance? The ambiguity surrounding answering this question has much to do with the role of the *Predikanten Zendingvereniging* (Ministers' Missionary Union: MMU), which commissioned the first male missionaries to Nyasaland and paid their salaries. When they arrived and started to work there, a question, never definitively answered, was whether they belonged to an independent missionary body or were they perhaps more correctly understood as properly belonging under the wide umbrella of the Livingstonia mission? Founded in 1886 at a conference held at the eastern Cape town of Cradock,[29] the MMU was a voluntary body of mission-interested ministers in the DRC who contributed funds out of their own pockets, and hence the initial missionaries to both Nyasaland and a few years later to Mashonaland in 1891 were technically not sent by the DRC synod but by the MMU. The Murray and Huguenot Seminary connections also extended directly into the Mashonaland venture. Andrew (A. A.) Louw, the first Mashonaland missionary,[30] was a maternal nephew of Andrew Murray. His mother, Jemima, was a daughter of Andrew Murray

Sr and the first vice-president of the *Vrouesendingbond*.[31] Prior to leaving for Mashonaland, he spoke at the Huguenot Missionary Society and he subsequently married Francina 'Cinie' Malan, who was a Huguenot graduate.[32]

It is safe to assume that the idea of mission represented something of a factional concern within the wider DRC, a factional concern in which the Scots Afrikaners stood central as already averred in the previous chapters. However, the theme regarding confused or intermeshed identity within the DRC mission enterprise in Nyasaland, which I shall explore below, is perhaps further complicated by the fact that the Free Church of Scotland missionaries might have viewed the South Africans as part of their own enterprise. The primary instigator of mission interest from the side of the DRC was, of course, Andrew Murray. The implied ambiguity of identity in the missionary enterprise that Murray inspired was possibly reinforced by the fact that the first DRC missionary to be sent by the MMU was none other than Andrew Charles Murray, a nephew of Andrew Murray Jr.

Similar to his cousin, A. A. Louw, A. C. Murray had also spoken at the Huguenot Missionary Society prior to setting off for Nyasaland. At the Huguenot meeting he had pleaded for more workers, and it seems he was a successful recruiter. He married Huguenot-trained Lydie Lautré when he returned to the Cape on furlough. In fact, Dana Robert points out that all the founding missionaries in Nyasaland married Huguenot women, and numerous single women from that institution ended up in Nyasaland as missionaries. Robert mentions the following names: 'Martha Murray, Martha Zondagh, Bertha Helm, Lettie Stegman, Mrs. A.C. Murray, Mrs. Blake, Mrs. Margaret Vlok, Annie le Roux, and Jane Soyland had all gone to Nyasaland by 1898.'[33]

Negotiating over a Mission Field

The first DRC missionaries to Nyasaland were A. C. Murray and T. C. B. Vlok.[34] While an early Scottish historian of the Livingstonia mission, James W. Jack, referred to Vlok as Murray's 'Dutch assistant',[35] he introduced Murray in words conveying rather more gravitas, but perhaps this is also indicative of how Murray was perceived in Scotland more generally:

> Mr. Murray belonged to a well-known Aberdeenshire family. It was in 1822 that the Rev. Andrew Murray left his Scottish home and settled in Graaf-reinet, where he trained a large family to become ministers and missionaries. Among the earnest, devoted workers for Christ that Scotland has given to South Africa, few have been more respected than Professor John Murray of Stellenbosch, who was cut off in the mid-time of his days, and Rev. Andrew Murray of Wellington, whose books on devotional religion are known throughout the world.[36]

Both Murray and Vlok later published memoirs of their missionary experiences. In the case of Murray, there are two separate accounts. The first he wrote while he was on medical leave in South Africa, recovering from a leopard attack that had left severe wounds on the skin of his head. This account details among other things the start of the DRC mission in Nyasaland. Here Murray first gives some helpful background on the founding of the MMU, which according to his description occurred in the aftermath of an evangelistic tour that Andrew Murray Jr had undertaken to the Transvaal. This awakened in him an understanding of the fact that there was a vast mission field out there, which was being tilled by many different mission societies, but troubling for him was the fact that the DRC was all but absent. For Andrew Murray it seemed obvious that the DRC should take its rightful place among sending agencies, but this idea led to the question of where to begin such work. At one stage it seems Andrew Murray even considered China as a possible mission field for the DRC, but his colleagues in the MMU convinced him that their obligation was towards Africa.[37]

The ultimate decision of where to go was in any case expedited by the fact that, according to Andrew Murray as related in his nephew's memoir, there was the territory in the vicinity of the Nyasa lake, where 'the Presbyterian church of Scotland worked, and where we as fellow Presbyterians would be very welcome, and where we could be assured of the support of the Scottish brothers'. A further important factor for the Scots in issuing this invitation was the fear that if the DRC did not occupy that field then the Roman Catholic Church surely would.[38]

It seems, furthermore, that A. C. Murray was not only the first DRC missionary to go to Nyasaland, but that he was himself instrumental in the ultimate decision to select this specific location as a site for mission work. Various Scottish connections are entangled in this narrative. After it had been decided that he was to be the first missionary of the MMU, but before a final decision regarding his mission field had been made, A. C. Murray went to Scotland in 1886 for an eighteen-month period of training in rudimentary medicine.[39] A number of ordained DRC missionaries subsequently followed a similar route prior to entering the mission field.[40]

While in Scotland, Murray kept thinking about the Nyasaland option and his thoughts went back to an event some years earlier when he was the secretary of the Student Mission Society in Stellenbosch. He recalls that during his student years he had, following a decision of the organisation, written to Dr James Stewart of Lovedale to receive advice about any yet unevangelised area that Stewart could recommend as a new mission field. Stewart answered that there were plenty of open doors in Nyasaland, and that the Free Church of Scotland would heartily welcome DRC missionaries there. Stewart furthermore arranged for his brother-in-law, John Stephen of Glasgow, to pay these mission enthusiasts in Stellenbosch a visit. Stephen was fortuitously in Cape Town at the time. In the meeting, Stephen, who happened to be a member of the mission committee of the Free Church of Scotland, told the Stellenbosch group many things of interest about the Nyasa lake region. He furthermore emphasised Stewart's point about the warm welcome they could expect from the Scots should they decide to go there.[41]

When the time came for the leadership of the MMU to make a recommendation to their members about a mission field, the choice was between Transvaal and Nyasaland. The commission consisting of Andrew Murray Jr and other leading figures sat with the two maps of the respective regions in front of them, as well as a letter from A. C. Murray expressing his desire to go to Nyasaland. There seemed to be very little contest. On all accounts Nyasaland won the day, and the Scottish connection is strongly emphasised in the recommendation that was ultimately issued. Not only did the Free Church offer them a field encompassing hundreds of miles. The members of the MMU would not have felt comfortable to send a single missionary so far away on his own. Therefore, it was a reassuring fact that the Free Church of Scotland 'declared itself ready to take him into its midst as one of its own missionaries'.[42]

A. C. Murray writes that shortly after this recommendation was published in *De Kerkbode* in August 1887, he sent a letter to the Chair of the commission detailing among other things the costs involved for a missionary to Nyasaland as well as specifics regarding the relationship that would exist between 'us' and the Free Church of Scotland.[43] Although Murray does not give further specifics in his book about what this relationship would have entailed, it is evident that medical training was only one aspect that occupied him in Scotland, and that detailed discussion must have occurred about missionary collaboration, or perhaps, from another point of view, his own participation in what was essentially a Scottish enterprise.

In his later publication, *Ons Nyasa-Akker*, Murray gives more details about the arrangement. The Scottish invitation came with the precondition that the South Africans should become members of the Livingstonia mission council. This was accepted, and for the first eight years after the DRC's entry to Nyasaland there was close cooperation, mentorship and even dependence on the Scots. In an article that is overall highly sympathetic to the DRC mission in Nyasaland, Janet Parsons describes Robert Laws of Livingstonia as Murray's 'mentor'. Parsons also uncovered evidence of material contributions from Laws to Murray in the form of 'Livingstonia'-inscribed bricks excavated from the foundations of Murray's original manse at their founding mission station, Mvera.[44] For his part, Murray expressed his appreciation of everything he and his fellow DRC missionaries had learned from the Scots during that early period, but he also indicated that the month-long yearly visits to the Livingstonia base at Bandawe were experienced as somewhat disruptive to their own work.[45]

In order to better explain the background to this relationship, let me briefly return to the preparatory stages of A. C. Murray's mission. Murray wrote that the Foreign Mission Commission of the DRC had agreed that this mission project might resort under its supervision, under certain conditions. However, this was not much more than a token acknowledgement from the side of the commission, because there was no synodical decision to accompany the statement. The fact was, as mentioned above, that the funding for the operation would not come through official DRC channels, but via the independent sub-formation of the MMU.[46] Therefore, the Nyasa mission, rather than a thoroughgoing DRC enterprise, was from its inception a fairly independent project driven by a specific faction in the DRC in which the Murray family, in alliance with American and Scottish partners, had a prominent position.

A. C. Murray wrote that prior to his departure from Scotland he had met with the Mission Commission of the Free Church of Scotland. He informed them of the decision of his own organisation, the MMU, regarding which the Scots expressed their joy and 'welcomed us as co-workers in central Africa'.[47]

Back in South Africa, A. C. Murray attended a ministers' conference at Bethulie in the Orange Free State. Andrew Murray Jr played an important role there. One evening was devoted to mission, and Nyasaland was extensively discussed. The 'brothers' also decided to devote Wednesdays to a day of prayer for mission. The reason given for the chosen day of the week was that the Scots also prayed for mission on Wednesdays.[48]

In spite of the high value A. C. Murray seemed to give to all things Scottish, this was not part of a more general admiration for Europe or Europeans, apparently. On his journey to Nyasaland he crossed through Portuguese East Africa, and his comments about Portugal and of course its religious authority, the Roman Catholic Church, are anything but complimentary. There is furthermore no doubt that he considered himself an 'Afrikaner', as he makes clear when he writes that European civilisation if distributed partially has a corrupting influence on the native. What they needed was the gospel, and: 'It is also my conviction that we, Afrikaners, can fare better at bringing the gospel to heathens, than missionaries from Europe' [transl.].[49] He does not give reasons for this statement, but this perhaps alludes to a developing discourse that would later also play a role in Afrikaner justifications of their racial policies, which amounted to the notion that Afrikaners knew and understood Africans and their needs better than anyone. The more such a discourse could be affirmed, the less need there was for outside critique to be taken seriously. But this is moving ahead of the narrative. Although A. C. Murray was no apartheid ideologue, he clearly identified himself as an Afrikaner, at least when writing for an Afrikaans readership, and his writing betrays examples of the type of racial bias that would over time feed into apartheid theory. More on this follows below.

En Route to the Mission Field

The first meeting with Scots on the way to Nyasaland occurred on the river 'Kwakwa', when A. C. Murray hailed a fast-travelling boat going downstream. Murray had been travelling upstream, having landed on the coast at Quelimane[50] following a sea voyage from the Cape. The travelling party turned out to include a Dr Henry of the Free Church of Scotland, as well as a Mr Duncan, who was an artisan in the employ of the Church of Scotland's Blantyre mission. The two groups subsequently spent more than two hours on the nearest shore in conversation. Dr Henry was in charge of Livlezi, which unbeknown to all present would later become a DRC mission station. Henry agreed with Murray's plan to refrain from immediately choosing an exact location for his mission but encouraged him to first take a tour of the Scottish stations. He did, however, express the view that the area to the west of Livlezi would serve as an excellent new mission field.[51]

Murray's journey continued, and eventually he made it onto a steamboat on the Zambezi River. The boat stopped at the gravesite of Mary Livingstone, and Murray spent a few pages relating the tragic circumstances of her death from malaria, and the resultant heartbrokenness of her husband. This occurred after she had come to Africa to re-establish physical contact with her husband, the famous missionary explorer, whom she had not seen for several years. Murray relates in some detail the emotional turmoil described by David Livingstone in his diary. Dr James Stewart, subsequently of Lovedale in South Africa, was also present and played a supporting role during these tragic proceedings.[52]

Having arrived in Nyasaland in 1888, Murray first visited the Blantyre mission of the Church of Scotland. He commented on the beauty of the cathedral-like church, but despite finding the missionary, a Revd Scott, and his wife's company pleasant and hospitable during his stay, Murray had few good words to say for the methods and approach of Scott. According to Murray's assessment, Scott did not seek to overtly evangelise and convert the Africans as such, but rather to 'civilise' them in a general manner by educating them and exposing them to aesthetically uplifting things such as the wondrous church building, for example. Murray comments thus: 'I do not condemn their work, but I differ completely from their goals as well as their methods. We are not sent out, I believe, to civilise the nations but to convert them' [transl.].[53] This criticism exposes a tension between the more generally evangelistic approach of the early DRC missionaries and Scottish missions, perhaps particularly those of the Church of Scotland, and their strong emphasis on education. Brian Stanley, for example, has remarked on the 'unusually pronounced emphasis on the civilising role of education'[54] as a motivating factor of the Church of Scotland's decision to institute foreign missions in 1824.

As Murray's journey through Nyasaland continued, he had occasion to meet representatives of the Universities' Mission to Central Africa (UMCA) at Matope. A telling criticism he had regarding this mission was that: 'One of their principles was that natives and Europeans should stand on an equal footing. As a consequence of this point of view many natives look down upon the missionaries and refuse to work for them' [transl.].[55]

Another problem with the UMCA was that they refused Holy Communion to members of other missions. Murray related how Revd Bain of the Free Church of Scotland, while travelling on one occasion on the UMCA's steamboat, was told that he could not partake in the sacrament, but was allowed to witness the proceedings since he was considered at the same level as a catechumen. On a subsequent occasion, Murray and his colleague Vlok would experience a similar level of exclusion from Holy Communion at the UMCA station of Likoma.[56]

Murray travelled northwards along Lake Nyasa and disembarked at Bandawe, the then head station of the Livingstonia mission. Dr Laws awaited him on the beach and provided accommodation to Murray for a period of time, during which Murray experienced much kindness from the doctor and his wife.[57] From Bandawe, Murray travelled northwards, together with the above-mentioned Revd Bain, to explore the country in search of sites for one or two stations for the MMU.[58] It is noteworthy in terms of the negotiated relationship that he specifically mentions representing the MMU in his memoir, rather than the DRC. The reason for this, as alluded to above, is that this mission remained fully independent for more than a decade. It was only in 1903 that the synod of the DRC agreed to officially take ownership of this project, and then it came under the purview of its Foreign Mission Commission.[59]

What follows in Murray's description is quite an adventure together with Bain and Dr Cross of the Free Church of Scotland. Over several chapters as detailed in Murray's original memoir they encounter slave-trading 'Arabs' with whom the Great Lakes Company was involved in warfare, wild animals both large and small, indigenous people hitherto unknown to Murray, and also a bout of severe fever (malaria). The Scots were apparently convinced that Murray's death was nigh. A location for his grave was even decided upon, but then he miraculously survived. Murray paraphrases Dr Cross: 'I believe, Mr Murray, that your recovery was in answer to the prayers of your friends at the Cape; otherwise I do not know how you could have pulled through' [transl.].[60]

Having overcome the worst of the fever, Murray was taken back to Bandawe, where he recovered in the care of Dr Laws. Laws, who was both a physician and a theologian, at first wanted Murray to return to the Cape in order to make a full recovery, but Murray convinced him that such a long delay would sound the death knell for their budding missionary project. Hence, Laws allowed Murray to stay put, and Murray wrote appreciatively of the care given to him until the end of that year, 1888.[61]

In the end he stayed for one month at the home of the hospitable Laws couple,[62] after which Robert Laws sent Murray by machilla (a hammock strung between two poles carried by African runners at each end) to further recuperate at the higher-lying, cooler and consequently healthier, according to the belief of the time, station of Dr Elmslie of the Free Church of Scotland.[63] Elmslie would later write the interestingly titled autobiography *Among the Wild Ngoni*,[64] and Murray learned much about these apparent Zulu descendants, the Ngoni, from Elmslie. The true value of staying with Elmslie was the first-hand knowledge Murray was now able to accrue regarding the running of a mission station. In his initial account he did not mention this, but this point is emphasised in a more extensive autobiography published after his retirement. Perhaps such insights regarding what he had learned and how he had learned it required time to develop. In this later publication, *Ons Nyasa-Akker*, Murray wrote that the time spent here at 'Njuyu was undoubtedly an intervention of the Lord', because 'it would have a great influence on the future of the DRC mission in Nyasaland' [transl.].[65] Murray further quotes from another DRC missionary source, A. L. Hofmeyr's *Het Land Langs Het Meer*,[66] which elaborates further about the divinely inspired illness that caused Murray to spend several months with Mr and Mrs Elmslie. Murray could learn the methods and practices of Scottish missionaries, who themselves had to learn much of what they knew through trial and error. Hofmeyr concludes: 'Our mission is more indebted to the Livingstonia-mission than we realise; and in retrospect we see the hand of God in it . . .' [transl.].[67] A most interesting aspect about the connection between Elmslie and Murray relates to similar discourses in their respective autobiographies involving missionary entanglements in indigenous rainmaking practices. I shall return to this theme below.

On 8 July 1889 a second MMU missionary, T. C. B. Vlok, arrived at Bandawe, and on the advice of Laws the two Afrikaner missionaries undertook a south-westerly tour in search of a suitable site for a mission station.[68] On the Sunday prior to their departure, they shared Holy Communion with the Scots and their congregation. Laws preached in Chinyanya and Murray in English.[69]

On their travels, Murray and Vlok eventually ended up in the area of king Chiwere, where they were impressed with the fertility of the land, as well as the climate. Chiwere himself seemed friendly and invited them to preach so that he and his people could listen to what the missionaries had to say. Murray then proceeded to do just that. He read to them the Ten Commandments and a section from the New Testament where a blind man was healed. He then asked the 'captain' of their travelling party, a certain Chipojola, to interpret what he had said. He understood as much of what followed to be able to admit that what Chiwere's people then learned was only the gist of the fourth commandment, that one should rest one day out of seven, and that the Lord Jesus was a Great Mzungu (white man). Murray wrote, seven years later, that despite such early misunderstandings, that event had indeed been the start of their work there and that several 'blind heathen' had gained their spiritual eyesight in the intervening years.[70]

En route back to Bandawe they were relieved to receive tidings that Nyasaland might possibly become a British protectorate. This was a positive development, because as Murray put it: 'It lies between the English and the

Portuguese, and who, that is thinking clearly would prefer the Portuguese?' [transl.].[71] At Bandawe they discussed with Laws the positive experience they had had at Chiwere. It seems that Laws' word was very much the rule at that stage of proceedings as far as Murray and Vlok were concerned. He was also a spiritual mentor. Murray reports that Laws had written down two prayers to take with them, one for the morning and one for the evening. Murray related a Dutch translation of the evening prayer in his memoir.[72]

At Chiwere's place the mission work started, but not without incident or danger. Murray describes how Chiwere would on the one hand claim to want their presence in his territory, but then he would occasionally act in ways that appeared to contradict this stated intention. On one instance they were told to leave the area by a messenger who brought them a sheep from Chiwere as a parting gift. However, when the missionaries confronted Chiwere directly about this, he denied ever issuing such an order. On another occasion they were all but forced into the role of rainmakers under fear of death.[73] And on yet another occasion, according to Murray's description, they were nearly murdered at night under apparent order of Chiwere, but only survived due to the fact that a majority of the chiefs, and Chiwere himself, reportedly considered them powerful sorcerers, perhaps too powerful to attack.[74] A more mundane reason for avoiding the missionary influence, according to Murray, was that Chiwere occasionally dabbled in the slave trade, selling both from his own people as well as those he had captured in wars.[75]

Murray stated that they found out about many of these intrigues only much later, including the fact that Chiwere himself had never wanted them there, but had simply agreed to their desires out of fear of their ability to magically kill him if they were not given what they asked for. This invitation on Chiwere's part not only led to much internal and political strife once it was acted upon by the missionaries, but it also infuriated Chiwere's head wife, Mshawashi, who was not at all inclined to be friendly towards the mission.[76]

Feminine Resistance and Acquiescence to Missionary Power

This attitude by Mshawashi is not surprising given the threat posed to female religious power in the matrilineal Chewa society by the missionaries' patriarchial culture and androcentric conception of Christianity. This aspect of Malawian religious change has been analysed by Isabel Phiri,[77] in particular. In the negotiations between missionaries and Africans, it was often African women who were at the real losing end of the equation.

The following story of Chauwa and her 'conversion' is a particularly poignant example regarding the case of the DRC mission. Chapter 5 describes DRC missionary J. A. Retief's background and entrance into missionary work in 1909, but since Retief is instrumental in the story of *O Chauwa – the rain goddess*, as he referred to her in his memoir, let me briefly mention something of importance about this early twentieth-century DRC missionary to Nyasaland. Retief was married to Helen Murray, a Huguenot Seminary graduate and a niece of Andrew Murray Jr. Helen's life, after seventeen years of missionary service in Nyasaland since her arrival in 1910, was tragically cut short when she contracted and died from 'blackwater fever' early in 1928.[78] It might be disingenuous to suggest that she had managed to sensitise her Afrikaner husband to the power of the feminine, but perhaps this is exactly what had occurred. Although this might seem like an unrelated point, the fact is that in Retief's narrative of the female rainmaking chief Chauwa, which I translate at length below, it seems clear that he was aware of the strategic importance of Chauwa's conversion. He gives the following description:

> She was a well-known and honoured woman chief, and she lived about six miles south of Mkhoma on the Linthipi river. Not only was she a chief with her own village, but for many miles in the surrounding area she was known as the rain goddess. In times of drought all eyes were fixed upon Chauwa. Chiefs came from all over to visit her. She had to conduct sacrifices for rain and whatever accompanies that. In her village there was at the time a trustworthy and devoted evangelist teacher with the name of Shadrach. We had tried to befriend her [Chauwa]. She was friendly towards the mission and even attended the Sunday services on occasion. Shadrach and a group of the faithful also frequently prayed for her and attempted to win her for the church. Their prayers were unexpectedly answered. On a certain day Shadrach came to tell me that there was a change in her heart and that us whites should also think of her in our prayers. Not long thereafter Chauwa arrived at Mkhoma with her entourage. She came to sign up for the baptism class! Sometime after this she was presented along with a number of others in the church. It gave cause to a great uproar. The chiefs and heathen population were very upset. Strong attempts were employed from their side to dissuade Chauwa away from her intentions, because her joining the church would impact on their tribal life, customs, and traditions. Feelings had started to run high. A movement in opposition to her was initiated, and she felt the need to call in the help of the district chief, Mazangera, who was very friendly towards the mission. He acted as her protector and put a stop to all heathen dances and practices in her village. The step taken by Chauwa gave courage to a whole number of men and women to break with the heathendom. For more than a year Chauwa had to attend the baptism class and on a certain Sunday she was solemnly baptized with a great number of elders at the great church at Mkhoma in the presence of a great crowd of chiefs and other people. That was the first time that a goddess, a rain goddess, was baptized in Mkhoma: probably the only one in Nyasaland.[79]

Negotiations over Rainmaking

Converting a 'rain goddess' such as Chauwa was obviously a significant feat and a gain for any Christian mission. However, if missionaries, or anyone else, imagined that this would put a stop to indigenous interest in the theme of rainmaking, they would have been mistaken. Instead, there are some signs that interest and expectation likely shifted to the missionaries themselves. From the indigenous point of view, rainmaking, or at least the ability to successfully pray for rain, seemed to be something of an unacknowledged entrance requirement for anyone wishing to wield religious authority during the late nineteenth century in Central Africa. It is particularly noteworthy that both the MMU and the Livingstonia missionaries had been subjected to the requirement to pray for rain in the early days of their respective missions. In the case of Livingstonia, one of its missionaries, W. A. Elmslie, related some harrowing but ultimately triumphant experiences in terms of dealing with the indigenous demand for rain. In a chapter on 'the rain question and its results', Elmslie describes how in the year 1886 a period of severe drought first gave rise to some indigenous suspicion regarding the possible missionary cause of the calamity, followed by requests for missionary rain prayers to end it. Coming to the climax of the narrative, Elmslie describes how Ngoni warriors had started to assemble at their chief's kraal, striking a threatening pose and, according to their informants, readying themselves for a strike against the missionaries, who, as some believed, were withholding the rains. Then, during a night-long prayer service at the mission, some light rain started to fall.

> Next day we had agreed to hold another service to pray for rain, and at noon the people collected, some of the chief's councillors being present again. At two o'clock, before the meeting had dispersed, heavy rain fell . . . The incident made a profound impression upon the minds of the natives, and no doubt indirectly, if not directly, advanced our work.[80]

Writing about the early days at Mvera, when he and Vlok were still busy with the construction of their house, A. C. Murray describes a situation where he was called to attend Chiwere's council. Upon arrival the councillors immediately started to quiz him about the lack of rain and accused him of withholding it until his house was finished. While explaining his powerlessness over the weather patterns, Murray still agreed to pray for rain. One councillor particularly insisted that it must rain 'tomorrow'. Although Murray made no suggestion that he was directly threatened, he mentioned that he and Vlok felt that their lives were possibly in danger since some chiefs were antagonistic towards them. He agreed to pray for rain to fall 'tomorrow', all the while insisting that God could not be prescribed in this way. Back at the mission, Murray and Vlok proceeded to pray in all earnestness, and they continued the next day when no rain was forthcoming. That evening good rains finally fell. Murray came to the following conclusion regarding this phenomenon: 'I believe that this incident contributed much to ensure our safety in the land, and to place us in the favour of the people.'[81]

Given the way in which Murray evidently looked up to Laws and the Livingstonia mission for guidance, it is tempting to think that Murray's own rainmaking narrative presents itself as a form of mimicry, or even a kind of plagiarism. However, more likely, this simply reveals the central role of rainmaking within Central African religiosity. Missionaries, as supposedly powerful sorcerers, were expected to be adept at managing this role, and the greater they were able to successfully fulfil it, the more their power increased to the detriment of specifically female ritual practitioners, such as Chauwa. It is also a good example in action of a classical missionary strategy, which was to seek points of contact within the belief system of the people one hopes to evangelise.

Controlling the Wilderness and Negotiations with Africans

African sensibilities regarding rain was hardly the only aspect of African life and religiosity that was negotiated or manipulated in the missionary encounter. People's often realistic terror of wild animals such as human-eating lions was occasionally effectively exploited for the purpose of evangelisation. Lions were encountered and mentioned by the Scottish missionaries, to be sure. Livingstone was attacked by one, and on one occasion Laws and Elmslie had a close shave when a lion ripped open the tent they were sleeping in, 'and it was only through great presence of mind that they managed to drive off this daring king of the forest'.[82] From the Afrikaner side, with their background as huntsmen and civilian soldiers, the taming of the wilderness seemed to recur as a constant theme in their writings. Often, life-threatening and life-ending encounters with big cats contributed to a strengthening of a kind of martyrdom theme within the missionary discourse. Such creatures could also be identified with the satanic by missionaries, and as such they could feature as motivational props in conversion drives.

DRC missionary A. J. Liebenberg tells a very interesting yet gory story of how a 'lion advanced the mission'.[83] In some such narratives, the beast in question is slayed by missionaries, which of course helped to bolster their position as powerful sorcerers (controllers of the forces of nature). However, this was not the case in the narrative presented by Liebenberg. This missionary wrote about how they were awoken at the station of Kongwe in the early hours by two 'heathens' from a nearby village. They told the horrific tale of a lion that had entered their village at night, broken open the wall of a hut, and dragged a man out into the bushes. The unfortunate victim, with help from other villagers, had attempted to fight off the lion with sticks and assegai, but to no avail. When the missionaries arrived on the scene, all they found of the man was a skull bone and the remains of one arm. At the village, the missionaries emphasised to an assembly of about four hundred people how 'dangerous it is to live without the Word of God, and to die in such a way'.

This tactic, of implicitly identifying protection from human-eating lions with Christianity, evidently paid dividends, because a few days later the supreme chief of the area arrived at the mission with the request that missionaries bring them the 'Word of God, and thereby prevent (so they say) that we too be killed by a lion'.[84]

The One-blood Doctrine and the Infantilisation of the Other

It is easy to point out the faults in the missionary armour with the benefit of hindsight. They had plenty of blind spots, not least regarding their own racism and sexism. However, on at least one aspect their views were more laudable and closer to our contemporary mores than many of their cultural peers as well as the African society in which they operated. This has to do with the belief which A. C. Murray et al. shared with most of their contemporary missionaries, Protestant and Catholic alike, regarding the biblical theme of human creation out of one blood,[85] which is an important theological justification for both mission and ecumenism. Murray discusses this theme in the context of 'points of contact'. The first point of contact was in the unknown God that the Chewa worshipped, according to Murray, which he equates with the apostle Paul's evaluation of the religion of the people of Athens. The second point of contact was this very issue of one blood. This, according to Murray, stood in contrast with the 'heathens' who believed that whites were made out of elephant tusks or something else, yet distinct from their own creation. And, Murray admits, there were also whites who did not believe the doctrine of one blood, but rather thought that whites were *people*, whereas blacks were merely *creatures*.[86]

Adherence to the one-blood doctrine may therefore be mentioned as a positive aspect of the DRC's missionary enterprise. However, this is hardly all that could be said about the matter. A question remains regarding exactly how missionaries like A. C. Murray saw Africans, because, as indicated above, they were not seen as equals. Murray clarifies this explicitly in a discussion of the missionary education efforts, which is so important that I quote it at some length:

> We are also very careful not to raise the natives beyond their class. When the native is taught that he is just as good as the white, and that he stands on equal footing with him, there arise grave problems... He is yet a child and should in many respects be treated as a child... We do not believe that there is in the face of God any distinction between a white and a black skin. We reject in the strongest possible terms the expression 'Ham's descendants'... But we repeat, the natives of

central Africa are still children in comparison with us, and they cannot yet occupy the place of adults alongside us. How many generations would still be needed for this to occur, we cannot say. [transl.][87]

In the above, in addition to exemplifying Cleall's critique of mission as a 'discourse of difference',[88] we have a good example of Afrikaner Christian paternalism in respect to black Africans, a kind of paternalism that would subsequently become defined by the term guardianship (*voogdyskap*),[89] and which would serve as a primary motivating factor in early apartheid apologetics. Basically, guardianship might be categorised as a pessimist's rendition of the generic White Man's Burden,[90] because it similarly upheld the notion of whites' tutelage over people of colour but withheld the notion that the latter should or could be 'uplifted' much.

Consolidating a Mission Field and Further Negotiations

In June 1891, Murray felt the need to undertake a 150-mile journey to Bandawe in order to discuss a number of issues with the Scottish 'brothers' there. Murray mentioned that he experienced much kindness from Dr Laws at Bandawe. In a short paragraph, he also attempted to clarify his own relationship to the Livingstonia mission, stating that as a member of the Livingstonia Mission Council he had attended their meeting on a number of occasions. However, since 1894 'we were no longer part of that council, since we had our own executive council in Nyasaland consisting of four members'.[91] This is, interestingly, contradicted in his later book, wherein Murray writes that they remained members of the Livingstonia council until 1898, when the first independent council meeting was held, and present at that meeting were DRC missionaries A. C. Murray, W. H. Murray, T. C. B. Vlok and R. Blake.[92]

What is striking in terms of the way the DRC missionaries had tended to position themselves vis-à-vis Livingstonia as independent and self-sufficient, is that the Livingstonia missionaries perhaps had a different view. According to Bolink: 'Up to 1900 the Livingstonia people would continue to speak of the Dutch Reformed field as the South Livingstonia Mission (Dutch Section).'[93] Although Laws makes it clear in his autobiography that the DRC mission was indeed under Livingstonia's supervision early on, the following statement, however, also indicates that its subsequent independence was a natural development:

> The Ministers' Missionary Union later became an organisation representing the whole Church. This enabled them to send more helpers. From Mvera they extended their sphere of influence as far as the Lake shore, and eventually took over all the work of the Livingstonia Mission at Cape Maclear and southern Angoniland. This was very much more satisfactory than having it superintended from Bandawe, which was much farther away.[94]

Early on it seems that it was not merely one-way traffic between Mvera and Bandawe. Murray writes that in October 1891, Laws visited Mvera. Of course, if he had indeed seen Mvera as his southern outpost, the purpose might have been that of a supervisor overseeing the work, or a patron checking up on his investment. Of course, as already indicated in reference to Parsons above, Laws had supplied bricks and perhaps other materials to Mvera. Whatever the case, his visit was experienced as a 'nourishment, which greatly encouraged us in our work' [transl.]. According to Murray, Laws also complimented them on the sense of sin that they were able to instil in the Chewa hearts, as became apparent in a prayer spoken by one of the youths in a meeting attended by Laws, who is then reported by Murray to have said: 'I have hardly if ever encountered a deeper sense of sin in a native than that attested to by the prayer of this young man' [transl.].[95]

The last decade of the nineteenth century saw quite a bit of expansion in the budding DRC mission. The number of names of Scottish background among the newcomers as mentioned by A. C. Murray is noteworthy. Robert Blake arrived in Nyasaland in 1892, and he would become an influential missionary founder of a new station, Kongwe, in 1894. Then there was A. C. Murray's own cousin, William Hoppe Murray, also arriving in 1894, who would eventually be head of the DRC missionary enterprise in Nyasaland for several decades into the twentieth century. Then there was yet another Murray, although in this case not directly related to the other two, Miss Martha Murray, who arrived in 1893, specifically in order to minister among women and young girls.[96] Still, the number of missionaries belonging to the original Andrew Murray lineage became so plentiful that Parsons, for example, could remark: 'Mission for the Dutch Reformed, to a far greater extent than the Scots at Blantyre and Livingstonia, was becoming "a family affair".'[97]

In 1894 another important development in the negotiations with the Free Church of Scotland occurred. After the death of Dr Henry of Livlezi there was a general sentiment, according to A. C. Murray, from the side of the Scots that since the DRC had started missionary work in the central region, that had created a geographical division in the field. Consequently, the Scots offered the whole area known as the kingdom of Chikusi to the south of Mvera as a mission field to the South Africans. This included Livlezi and the outpost of Cape Maclear, along with its Chewa evangelist Albert Namalambe.[98]

A. C. Murray believed that Livlezi had acquired an unjustifiably bad name for killing missionaries, because in his opinion the Scottish missionaries had simply been careless with their health while there. This, stated Murray, was illustrated by the fact that Dr Henry had lived in a flat-roofed house, with holes in the walls instead of windows![99] The South Africans considered Livlezi an important station, and they were delighted to have it. Determined to continue the work there, T. C. B. Vlok and his wife Bessie were placed in charge of the station. In 1896 Bessie passed away from 'fever', thus becoming the first DRC missionary casualty in Nyasaland, and tragically disproving Murray's optimistic earlier assessment of health conditions there.

Early in 1895 a serious incident nearly cost A. C. Murray his life.[100] Having gone after a leopard that had been feeding off the mission's livestock at Mvera, the wounded animal was eventually cornered, but then it pounced on Murray, who sustained serious head injuries from the claws of the leopard before it disappeared back into the bushes. Since Murray himself was the only person with medical training in the area, the outlook seemed particularly grim. The wounds should not have been life-threatening had they been properly stitched, cleansed and dressed. In the case of Murray's injuries, none of those things were done by experts, however, and with predictable results. Infection set in, followed by drawn-out bouts of high fever. Many visitors, including Chiwere, assumed Murray would not recover, because one simply did not survive a leopard attack under these conditions. Different people helped from various directions, and apparently the most important medical service was ultimately rendered by Dr Prentice, the Free Church of Scotland physician from Bandawe, who upon learning of the incident while journeying along the length of Lake Malawi, ordered the steamboat on which he was travelling to turn around, so that he could come to the aid of Murray. Prentice stayed with Murray until he was out of danger – all of three weeks, apparently.[101]

Although A. C. Murray survived the attack and went on to have a long career as missionary administrator within the DRC, also serving as editor of the missionary journal *De Koningsbode*, this incident did to a great extent curtail his Nyasaland career. As a result, he relinquished his role as head of the DRC mission there to his cousin, William Hoppe Murray.

Bible Translation

W. H. Murray was if anything even more Scottish-inclined than his cousin and predecessor. His personal correspondences with family members back in South Africa were for the most part all in English, and he was a trusted missionary colleague and confidant to the Scots Presbyterians, both at Blantyre and Livingstonia. E. G. Alston, a British Army captain who passed through and spent some time at Mvera in 1895, described W. H. Murray as 'more English than South African Dutch'.[102]

The area of Bible translation is particularly the place where W. H. Murray left his mark. He worked quite closely over a long period of time with, among others, Revd Robert Napier and Dr Alexander Hetherwick of the Blantyre mission on the translation of the Bible into Chinyanya. According to A. C. Murray, Drs Laws and Hetherwick were for many years the most influential persons in Nyasaland, and about Hetherwick he wrote that 'with our mission he always worked very graciously together, and from him our mission always experienced the greatest kindness and hospitality'.[103] This is confirmed by Hetherwick's biographer, W. P. Livingstone, who mentions that Murray often spent long periods of time at the manse in Blantyre while the translation work was in progress.[104]

A. C. Murray also gives a perspective on the pre-history of cooperative translation work. Initially, DRC missionaries made use of material acquired from the Scottish missions, especially educational materials such as a reading book for children, *Garu* (the dog), and a hymnal and New Testament that was translated by Laws. However, the more adept the Afrikaner missionaries became with the vernacular, the less adequate they found these books. Hence, they started their own book projects. A. C. Murray wrote a children's reading book, *Mkweri* (the monkey), and a new hymnal was instituted by the DRC missionaries in 1899, which still included songs from the old hymnal as well as additional ones from the Blantyre mission's hymnal.[105]

In 1898 a united commission of four missions, the DRC, Livingstonia, Blantyre and the Zambezi Industrial Mission, was formed to work on translation projects. According to A. C. Murray, this was useful for laying the foundations of translation work, but not in terms of the actual translation of the Bible. A. C. Murray started that work himself by translating the gospel according to Matthew, which was printed in Edinburgh in 1901. When he had to retire from the mission field for health reasons, W. H. Murray became the Bible translator in chief from the DRC side in 1903, together with Hetherwick from Blantyre. A. C. Murray states that his cousin did the actual translation work, with the help of 'the best of our Nyasa Christian men', which was then edited and improved upon in consultation with Hetherwick.[106] The Scottish missionaries' biographical sources give a somewhat different perspective of this working relationship. Although Livingstone mentions the fact that the DRC had freed up W. H. Murray to work full-time on this project, the way this is described makes it seem like a Scottish missionary project, in which the DRC representatives basically assisted. Parsons, on the other hand, gives Murray most of the credit for the translation work. After describing how Murray would from time to time vacate his missionary post to ascend on the back of his donkey the wooded hill, Kaso, behind Mvera in order to have more focused time working on the translation at this remote site, she states unambiguously: '[T]he bulk of the work had been Murray's and to that monumental task he contributed twenty-three years of his life.'[107]

The first part of the work came to fruition in 1905, when the translated New Testament was ready. W. H. Murray then went to Scotland with the manuscript, where it was printed by the National Bible Society of Scotland. A. C. Murray furthermore writes that the entire Bible translation, the *Union Nyanja Version*, was completed in 1922 under similar circumstances.[108] It appeared the following year, and *De Koningsbode* made special mention of the young native Christian, 'Gerson', actually more accurately named Gersom Chipwaira,[109] who grew up near Mvera and had the responsibility of transcribing the entire Bible with a 'writing machine' before it went to the printers.[110] On the translation of the Old Testament, *De Koningsbode* mentions that W. H. Murray worked together with Robert H. Napier of the Blantyre Mission.[111] Katsulukuta and Pretorius give more detailed information on the persons involved, as well as who was responsible for what. They mention additional names on the DRC side, the medical doctor W. A. Murray, the Revd Louis Hofmeyr, and on the Scottish side, Revd Napier and Dr Hetherwick, as well as three Malawian linguistic advisors, Mr Jonathan Sande from Blantyre, Mr Ishmael Mwale from Mlanda and Mr Wilibes Chikuse of Mvera.[112] While Murray and Napier were busy with the revisions of the last remaining Bible books in 1917, Revd Napier was called up to military service, during which he was mortally wounded. According to W. H. Murray's testimony, Napier was a 'highly gifted linguist, and a dedicated soul seeker'.[113]

Katsulukuta and Pretorius write that a 'deep friendship' had developed between Murray and Napier prior to the latter's untimely death.[114] Murray's daughter Pauline, who subsequently became a missionary medical doctor, assisted in the transcription of her father's notes concerning the translation project, and on 20 November 1916 she added some interesting personal commentary regarding Napier:

> ... Napier is such a nice young man. He is very clever, was the cleverest in Glasgow Theol. College. Dad says he is very good in Hebrew, a great help to Dad. He took me for rides on motor bike, and next year will be coming again, perhaps more than once. We are so thankful it is not necessary for dad to take that journey of more than 100 miles. He is B.A. B.D. – very good at Hebrew, and Ancient and Biblical history, and Chinyanja. Spoke of himself as a son in the house, did little things like cutting bread at table. A great stock of Scottish stories at mealtimes.[115]

Alas, the war had the final word in this developing friendship. As a sidenote it is perhaps worth mentioning here that not all romantic relationships between Scots and Dutch in Nyasaland ended in tragedy. There had been marriages between members of the different missions. A. C. Murray, for example, mentions the case of their nurse, Ms J. Haarhoff, who married one of the Scottish missionaries, Revd McMinn, in the early twentieth century, although he does not give a specific date.[116]

To return to the translation work, Parsons notes that printing equipment had meanwhile arrived from Scotland, and different kinds of literature were produced to be consumed by the new literary class in Malawi:

> *Mtenga* ('Message'), became Mvera's vernacular Christian newspaper. While the Scots were publishing in English, the DRC chose Chinyanja, only one of many indications that Mvera missionaries emphasised vernacular and 'grass roots' approaches to reach as many Malawian people as possible with basic education and Christian teaching.[117]

Hetherwick's biographer, Livingstone, writes that it was announced at the 1924 conference in Livingstonia 'that the union version of the Bible had now been placed in circulation and that its sale had been phenomenal ... It had been the work of five Europeans – mainly Dr. Murray and himself – and twelve Native assistants.'[118]

Finally, W. H. Murray and Hetherwick did not only correspond with one another about translation work. The DRC archive in Stellenbosch has a 1914 record of Murray's handwritten answers to what seems to be a wider circulated questionnaire that Hetherwick had sent out regarding 'Native Religious Beliefs'. Here Murray provides some very detailed answers after consultation with local Mvera elders to help construct what must have been a growing body of missionary data on Malawian religions.[119] I cannot go into the specifics of these questions and answers about spirits, sacrifices, names of deities and the destinies of the souls of the dead, other than to add that the construction of Chewa religion could be read in addition to the translation project as yet another piece of data to fill out the picture of intellectual collegiality that developed between the DRC, increasingly via W. H. Murray, and the Church of Scotland's Blantyre missionaries.

Conclusion

This chapter emphasised the international origins and entanglements of the DRC's foreign missionary enterprise, from the Mount Holyoke connection to Andrew Murray and the founding of the Huguenot Seminary to the close and willing partnerships that existed between the Scottish and DRC missionaries in Nyasaland, all the way from the latter's initial interest, eventual entrance and ongoing work in the field. While this has now ventured into the first decades of the twentieth century, the next chapter will backtrack a bit, to cast light on the near-fatal wedge driven into these cordial relations by the turn-of-the-century South African War.

Notes

1. This chapter was written with the collaboration of Pascal Pienaar, PhD candidate (church history), Stellenbosch University.
2. Dana L. Robert (August 1993) 'Mount Holyoke Women and the Dutch Reformed Missionary Movement, 1874–1904', *Missionalia*, 21.2: pp. 103–23, p. 103.
3. Ibid.
4. Ibid., p. 105.
5. Andrew Murray (1898) 'The Mount of Sources', *The Huguenot Seminary Annual*, 3, p. 2.
6. See Robert, 'Mount Holyoke Women', pp. 103–6.
7. Unknown author, likely A. P. Ferguson. Huguenot Seminary Report and Catalogues (1874–81). NGK archive: Stellenbosch. K-DIV 621, p. 6.
8. G. P. Ferguson (1927) *The Builders of Huguenot*. Cape Town: Maskew Miller Limited, pp. 3–4.

9. Ibid.
10. A. Bliss (1898) 'Educational growth', in *Annual report of the Huguenot mission society*. Wellington. NGK archive: Stellenbosch. K-div 638, p. 20.
11. C. E. Waite (1900) 'A plea for the mission class', in *Mission Newsletter*. NGK archive: Stellenbosch, p. 14.
12. Robert, 'Mount Holyoke Women', p. 110.
13. Ibid., p. 111.
14. Ibid., p. 112.
15. Ibid., p. 108.
16. Unknown Author (1890) *Catalogue of the nineteenth year of the Huguenot seminary Wellington SA and branch seminary*. NGK archive: Stellenbosch.
17. Robert, 'Mount Holyoke Women', p. 116.
18. M. Neethling (1909) *Unto Children's Children: lives and letters of the parents of the home at Graaff Reinet, with short sketches of the life of each of the children, and a register*. London: Printed by T. H. Hopkins, p. 115.
19. Robert, 'Mount Holyoke Women', p. 118.
20. Unknown Author (likely Ferguson) (1878) *Records of the Huguenot mission society*. Wellington. NGK archive: Stellenbosch. K-div 638.
21. Ibid.
22. Robert, 'Mount Holyoke Women', p. 119.
23. Unknown Author (1884) *Records of the Huguenot missionary society: Book 2*. Huguenot seminary, Wellington. NGK archive: Stellenbosch. K-DIV 621.
24. Robert, 'Mount Holyoke Women', p. 119.
25. Unknown Author (likely Ferguson) *Records of the Huguenot mission society*.
26. J. du Plessis (December 1924) 'Een Eeuw van Zendingarbeid. Haar Onstaan, de Ontwikkeling en de Bloei van ons Zendingwerk', *De Koningsbode*, p. 15.
27. S. E. Duff (2006) 'Head, Heart, and Hand: The Huguenot Seminary and College and the Construction of Middle Class Afrikaner Femininity, 1873–1910', MA thesis (history), Stellenbosch University.
28. Hamish Mcintosh (1993) *Robert Laws: Servant of Africa*. Carberry: The Handsel Press Ltd, p. 122. See T. Jack Thompson (2000) *Touching the heart: Xhosa missionaries to Malawi 1876–1888*. Pretoria: University of South Africa, for yet another example of South African participation in this Scots mission.
29. Du Plessis, "Een Eeuw van Zendingarbeid", p. 15.
30. See A. A. Louw (1917) *Dageraad in Banyaland: een verhaal van 25-jarigen arbeid onder de Vakaranga of Banyai in Mashonaland*. Kaapstad: Uitgegeven op last van de Algemeene Zending Commissie door de Publicatie Commissie der Zuid Afrik. Bijbel Vereeniging.
31. Robert, 'Mount Holyoke Women', p. 121.
32. Ibid., pp. 120–1.
33. Ibid., p. 120
34. Martin Pauw, who wrote a doctoral thesis on the DRC mission and its legacy in Malawi, gives extensive coverage to the formation of the MMU mission in Nyasaland and its connection to the Livingstonia mission. See C. M. Pauw (1980) 'Mission and Church in Malawi: The History of the Nkhoma Synod of the Church of Central Africa, Presbyterian, 1889–1962', DTh thesis, Stellenbosch University, p. 60ff.
35. James W. Jack (1900) *Daybreak in Livingstonia: The Story of the Livingstonia*

Mission, British Central Africa. New York: Young People's Missionary Movement, p. 178.
36. Ibid., p. 176.
37. A. C. Murray (Andrew Charles) (1897) *Nyasaland en mijne ondervindingen aldaar*. Amsterdam: HAUM, p. 6.
38. Ibid.
39. Ibid., p. 9.
40. A. C. Murray (1931) *Ons Nyasa-Akker: Geskiedenis van die Nyasa sending van die Nederd. Geref. Kerk in Suid-Afrika*. Stellenbosch: Pro Ecclesia, p. 175.
41. Murray, *Nyasaland en mijne*, p. 11.
42. Quoted from letter of commission signed by Andrew Murray (chair) and G. F. Marais (secretary), A. C. Murray, *Nyasaland en mine*, p. 13.
43. Ibid., pp. 13–14.
44. Janet Wagner Parsons (1998) 'Scots and Afrikaners in Central Africa: Andrew Charles Murray and the Dutch Reformed Church Mission in Malawi', *The Society of Malawi Journal*, 51:1, p. 22.
45. Murray, *Ons Nyasa-Akker*, p. 117.
46. Murray, *Nyasaland en mijne*, p. 14.
47. Ibid., p. 15.
48. Ibid., p. 28.
49. Ibid., p. 48.
50. See Pauw, 'Mission and Church in Malawi', p. 60.
51. Murray, *Nyasaland en mijne*, p. 51.
52. Ibid., pp. 64–6.
53. Ibid., p. 79.
54. Brian Stanley (2019) 'The Theology of the Scottish Protestant Missionary Movement', in David Fergusson and Mark Elliott (eds) *History of Scottish Theology*. Oxford: Oxford University Press, p. 58.
55. Murray, *Nyasaland en mijne*, p. 87.
56. Ibid., p. 153.
57. Ibid., p. 98.
58. Ibid., p. 101ff.
59. Murray, *Ons Nyasa-Akker*, p. 120.
60. Murray, *Nyasaland en mijne*, p. 121.
61. Ibid., pp. 122–3.
62. Ibid., p. 124.
63. Ibid., p. 127.
64. W. A. Elmslie and J. C. White (1899) *Among the Wild Ngoni: being some chapters in the history of the Livingstonia mission in British Central Africa*. With introduction by Lord Overtoun. Edinburgh and London: Oliphant & Co.
65. Murray, *Ons Nyasa-Akker*, p. 58.
66. A. L. Hofmeyr (1910) *Het land langs het meer*. Stellenbosch: Christen Studenten Vereniging van Zuid Afrika.
67. 'Ons sending het meer aan die Livingstonia-Sending te dank as ons besef; en van agter sien ons die leiding van God daarin . . .' A. L. Hofmeyr, *Het land*, p. 58.
68. Murray, *Nyasaland en mijne*, pp. 138–9.
69. Ibid., p. 140.
70. Ibid., pp. 144–5.

71. 'Het ligt tusschen de Engelschen en de Portugeezen, en wie, die bij zijn volle verstand is, zal de Portugeezen verkiezen.' Ibid., p. 150.
72. Ibid., pp. 151–2.
73. Ibid., pp. 161–3.
74. Ibid., pp. 183–7.
75. Ibid., p. 233.
76. Ibid., p. 182.
77. Isabel Apawo Phiri (2007) *Women, presbyterianism and patriarchy: religious experience of Chewa women in central Malawi.* Zomba, Malawi: Kachere Series.
78. See 'In Memoriam. Mevr. Ds. J. A. Retief, Mkhoma Nyasaland' and 'Helen Murray Retief' (15 February 1928) *De Kerkbode*, p. 239.
79. J. A. Retief (1951) *Ontdekkings in Midde-Afrika.* Stellenbosch: C. S. V. Boekhandel, pp. 218–19.
80. Elmslie and White, *Among the Wild Ngoni*, pp. 176–7.
81. Murray, *Nyasaland en mijne*, p. 163.
82. Jack, *Daybreak in Livingstonia*, p. 285.
83. See A. J. Liebenberg in J. du Plessis (ed.) (1906) *De Kerk en Haar Roeping: het verhaal van het Zendingwerk in Nyasaland, met een beroep op de Ned Ger Kerk van Zuid Afrika.* Kaapstad: Citadel, p. 15ff.
84. Ibid., p. 16.
85. In 1852 the well-known Scottish-born educator and journalist John Fairbairn could even write regarding Cape society in general that, 'The belief that God has made of one blood all the nations that dwell together on the face of the earth is universal . . .' Quoted in Robert Ross (2009) *Status and respectability in the Cape Colony, 1750–1870: a tragedy of manners.* Cambridge: Cambridge University Press, p. 67.
86. Murray, *Nyasaland en mijne*, p. 191.
87. Ibid., p. 224.
88. See Esme Cleall (2012) *Missionary discourse: negotiating difference in the British Empire, c. 1840–95.* Basingstoke: Palgrave Macmillan.
89. See Geoffrey Cronjé (1948) *Voogdyskap en apartheid.* Pretoria: J. L. van Schaik.
90. This well-known imperialist missionary trope had its genesis in the poem by Rudyard Kipling (1899) 'The white man's burden', *McClure's Magazine*, 12:4.
91. Murray, *Nyasaland en mijne*, p. 236.
92. Murray, *Ons Nyasa-Akker*, p. 118.
93. P. Bolink (1967) *Towards Church union in Zambia: A study of missionary co-operation and church-union efforts in Central-Africa.* Franeker: T. Wever, p. 83.
94. R. Laws (1934) *Reminiscences of Livingstonia.* (With plates, including a portrait.) Edinburgh and London: Oliver & Boyd, p. 204.
95. 'Ik heb zelden of nooit een dieper gevoel van zonde bij een inboorling aangetroffen dan dat waarvan het gebed van dien jongen getuigt.' Murray, *Nyasaland en mijne*, p. 241.
96. Ibid., p. 256ff.
97. Parsons, 'Scots and Afrikaners in Central Africa', p. 26.
98. Murray, *Nyasaland en mijne*, p. 258.
99. Ibid., pp. 259–60.
100. Ibid., pp. 289–98.
101. Ibid., p. 297.
102. Quoted in Parsons, 'Scots and Afrikaners in Central Africa', p. 30.

103. Murray, *Ons Nyasa-Akker*, p. 28.
104. See W. P. Livingstone (1931) *A Prince of Missionaries: The Rev. Alexander Hetherwick C.B.E., D.D., M.A. of Blantyre, Central Africa*. London: James Clarke & Co., p. 160.
105. Murray, *Ons Nyasa-Akker*, p. 131.
106. Ibid., pp. 132–3.
107. Parsons, 'Scots and Afrikaners in Central Africa', p. 30.
108. Murray, *Ons Nyasa-Akker*, p. 133.
109. See E. E. Katsulukuta and Johan L. Pretorius (n.d.) 'The Translation of the Bible into Chichewa, 1900–1923', DRC Archive Stellenbosch [PPV 1483].
110. *De Koningsbode* (June 1923), p. 147.
111. *De Koningsbode* (February 1918), p. 26; *De Koningsbode* (March 1918), p. 57.
112. Katsulukuta and Pretorius.
113. *De Koningsbode* (July 1919) p. 132.
114. Katsulukuta and Pretorius, 'The Translation of the Bible into Chichewa'.
115. Pauline Murray's personal commentary on Bible translation (n.d.) DRC Archive Stellenbosch [PPV 1483].
116. Murray, *Ons Nyasa-Akker*, p. 176.
117. Parsons, 'Scots and Afrikaners in Central Africa', p. 30.
118. Livingstone, *A Prince of Missionaries*, p. 184.
119. W. H. Murray's (1914) answers to A. Hetherwick's (n.d.) 'Queries on Native Religious Beliefs', DRC Archive Stellenbosch [PPV 1478].

CHAPTER FIVE

The South African War (1899–1902) and the Scots Afrikaners

The South African War (1899–1902), and the preceding Jameson Raid, which served as its major catalyst, possibly contributed more than any other factor to the *Afrikanerisation* of Scottish-descendent ministers in the DRC. John MacKenzie even goes as far as to state: 'By the third generation [Scots in the DRC] were unquestionably assimilated Boers ...' One example he mentions: 'The Rev. David Ross was accused of high treason for his Boer sympathies during the Anglo-Boer War and spent twenty-four days in prison.'[1]

Andrew Murray, James Stewart and Questions of War and Peace

More prominently within the general milieu of the DRC, Andrew Murray Jr, at this point the oldest serving minister in the DRC and several times its moderator, progressively eschewed his former imperial leanings and for all purposes identified himself with the independence quest of the Boer people. Several of his writings during this period attest to this positioning, and I shall elaborate on these shortly. Important to note, however, at this point is the fact that this shift in sympathy towards their northern brethren also characterised much Cape Afrikaner discourse during this period, as seen for example in a letter drafted and circulated by the *Moderamen* (church leadership), the synodical mission board and professors of the Stellenbosch Seminary.[2]

Such a shift is noteworthy in light of the fact that the Cape DRC had strongly resisted the nineteenth-century migration of their church members to these northern territories, even to the point of excluding them from access to Holy Communion (see Chapter 2). Yet at this very point a growing rift among members of the Scottish religious leadership in South Africa also becomes evident. The contrast between Scots Afrikaners and other Scots in religious circles is perhaps nowhere better illustrated than in the divergent, binarily opposing views of Andrew Murray and James Stewart.

According to a 1899 *Kerkbode*[3] article, an English religious paper called *The Life of Faith* had brought the two missionary leaders' contrasting views to the surface by publishing extracts of Andrew Murray's letters and an extract of an interview that the editor of a New York newspaper had held with Stewart. The *Kerkbode* article evaluated the gist of the differences as follows: Revd Murray, who was among other things introduced as someone with much influence among the Afrikaners, Dutch and English, is reported as having spoken with 'intimate knowledge of conditions' [transl.]. He saw as a contributing factor in this war the natural desire by the Transvaal *volk* to fight for their freedom, even to the point of sacrificing their lives, if so needed. When he saw the destruction, the sin and the shame of the war, he pleaded with the British government to cease their campaign, and 'as messenger of peace' he demanded that all people should pray for peace.

Regarding the *Kerkbode* commentary on James Stewart, it is best to translate the paragraph in full:

> Dr Stewart to the contrary spoke as someone who wanted to know very little that is good about the Afrikaner boer. Paul Kruger is, according to him, the cause of all our troubles. The emigration of boers [Great Trek] was, according to him, one of slave holders, who could not do what they wanted in the colony, somewhat similar to the Mormon movement in America. He spoke with revulsion of the Transvaal government, and with disapproval 'of the attempts by the little Englanders and little patriots and many good pious people to make the peace'.[4]

Following this the *Kerkbode* article concludes by lamenting the fact that a follower of Jesus Christ such as Stewart would naysay the efforts of the peacemakers.

An important theme to keep in mind in relation to both Murray and Stewart is their Nyasaland/Malawi connection (see Chapter 4). Both were heavily invested in the complementary missionary efforts of their respective bodies there. Related to this in the case of Stewart is the mentorship he had received from David Livingstone, the well-known pioneer missionary and bane of the slave industry. Livingstone, to name one example regarding his efforts to end the slave trade in Central Africa, became intrinsically involved in negotiations between the slave trader Jumbe and Chewa chiefs at Nkhotakota on the shore of Lake Malawi in the early to mid- 1860s.[5]

The question of slavery also seems to lie at the heart of Livingstone's unsympathetic estimation of the Boers, as revealed in his mid-nineteenth-century writings. In fact, it was his first, traumatic, contact with Boers that set him off on his anti-slavery campaign. This incident occurred in 1852 in the kingdom of the Bakwena under Sechele, where Livingstone and his wife Mary had established a mission in 1847. Boer migrants, who had moved away from the Cape Colony in protest of British abolitionist policies, now entered this area in what is contemporary Botswana. They raided the village where the Livingstones were staying. David described it in a letter to a friend as follows: 'The Boers plundered my house, and carried off upwards of two hundred children after killing many of the adults . . . I felt it to be my duty to expose the slave-making deeds of the Boers in a letter to government.'[6]

James Stewart, as a next-generation church and missionary leader, was deeply influenced by Livingstone. Stewart, who is most typically remembered for his role as principal of Lovedale College in the Eastern Cape, served as moderator of the Free Church of Scotland in 1899–1900.[7] Shortly after the outbreak of the Anglo-Boer War, an article in the *Record* argued that Stewart's attitude towards the Boers 'seems to show that the opinion of Livingstone represents with very little alteration to the condition of affairs to-day' (December 1899).[8]

In a research article focusing on James Stewart's perspective on the war, the author G. C. Cuthbertson argues that Stewart's views were in line with most nonconformist missionaries at the start of the war. That the idea of slavery and the alleged Boer perpetuation of a form of it was a convincing narrative for Stewart is clear from statements such as this one:

> The native of South Africa, though he cannot be made a slave in the strict sense of the word – that is, bought and sold – may be and is within the area of the Transvaal treated as one who has no rights, political or other. These rights as a citizen of a civilized State he may fairly expect to possess. Substantially he is dealt with as an inferior creature, or he would have been had slavery continued.[9]

However, the typically missionary and certainly laudable concern for the just treatment of the indigenous population aside, there was at least one other important reason for Stewart to oppose the Boer position during the South African War. He thought that the Boers' dangerous '"dream or delusion" of Dutch supremacy superseding British rule throughout South Africa was "the mainspring of the (Republican) movement"'.[10]

Hence, for Stewart there was no doubt about who the real aggressors in South Africa were. With a war that in his view had been 'forced upon' the British, they had no choice but to resort to the 'final arbitration of the sword'.[11]

Despite the fact that Stewart's views were shared by perhaps the majority of his nonconformist peers, especially in South Africa, there was some opposition as well, and even influential pro-Boer sentiments in Britain, to take account of. According to Cuthbertson, such sentiments were based on the premise of 'Boer and Briton as kith and kin sharing a common "race" and common religion . . .' Moreover, 'British nonconformists were more likely than Anglicans to identify with Afrikaner Calvinists. However, this potential sense of common identity was over-ridden for South African nonconformists by the stronger ideological and national antagonisms which existed between Boer and Briton.'[12]

Yet for Stewart, not all Afrikaners were equal(ly bad). His special ire was reserved for Paul Kruger and the Transvaal Republic. Upon the British occupation of Pretoria in 1900, Stewart had among other utterances the following choice words regarding the toppling of the Kruger administration: '[S]ome more devout will thank God that the blast of war has driven off the earth one of the most rapacious, shamelessly dishonest, and infamous administrations that has ever been dignified with such a name. It touched nothing which it did not turn to vile uses.'[13]

On the other hand, when it came to the Cape Afrikaners, Stewart was much more conciliatory, which is perhaps ironic given that many Afrikaners in the Cape were in turn becoming increasingly sympathetic to the plight of Boers in the fallen northern republics. Stewart, at any rate, might be quoted as follows: '[T]here are many loyal Dutchmen in the Cape Colony. I must add that they are men whose good sense and unquestioned and splendid loyalty deserves all praise . . .'[14]

Cuthbertson finally mentions that in spite of Stewart's incisive understanding of the South African context during this era, he apparently had one glaring 'blind spot', and this concerned his silence regarding the so-called 'methods of barbarism',[15] including the 'scorched earth' policies employed by the British during the war. Cuthbertson concludes: 'Perhaps he preferred to remain uninformed.'[16]

Andrew Murray, on the other hand, had his own sympathies and blind spots, but they were very different from those of James Stewart. As an influential leader in the DRC, even though there tended to be important political differences between most Cape DRC members and their northern brethren, it is not surprising that Murray's views reflected the generally shifting, increasingly pro-Boer sentiments of the Cape Afrikaners as exemplified in the Cape DRC. Therefore, a noteworthy document to more closely consider is an undated thirty-eight-page pamphlet conspicuously entitled *The Truth about the Boer and his Church* and undersigned by nine influential ministers, including Andrew Murray. They were members of the *Moderamen* (church leadership) and of the synodical mission board and professors of the theological seminary.

The Truth laments the 'race feeling' that was being engendered between Dutch and English portions of society as a consequence of the war, and it asks how a united South Africa would ever be possible in its aftermath. 'The horrors of a war between two Christian races both of Teutonic extraction, intimately related to each other by kindred traditions, a kindred faith, and in many cases by the still closer bond of bloodrelationship, are now upon us.'[17] The pamphlet argues that if only 'a little more patience or a little more consideration for the rights and privileges of the two free and independent republics'[18] might have been exercised by the British authorities, this war could have been averted.

A strong attempt is made by *The Truth* to refute the much-publicised 'slander', to which much of the media and influential public figures like Dr Stewart allegedly subscribed, that the Boers were slaveholders and that they were 'a semi-barbarian race "with a dash of Hottentot-blood in their veins"'.[19] One way in which this refutation proceeded is by reference to the ways in which the Boers were actually related to the British, as argued by the historian George Theal, for example.[20] According to this more sympathetic view, the Boers were men of our own race, of that sturdy Nether Teuton stock which peopled England and Scotland as well as the delta of the Rhine . . . Their religion is that of the people of Scotland, of a large proportion of the people of England . . . There is in truth hardly any difference in sentiment between these men and a body of Englishmen or Scotchmen of equally limited education.[21]

The alleged perpetuation of Boer slavery and/or the notorious 'apprentice-system', which involved the taking of children whose parents had died in skirmishes and warfare, were strongly denied as a contemporary practice among the Boers. It was affirmed to be in contravention of both the laws of the Transvaal Republic and the polity of the DRC in the Transvaal.[22]

The Truth furthermore referred to the favourable contrast expressed by the Aborigines Protection Society in its journal the *Aborigines' Friend*, wherein it was argued that the treatment of blacks on Dutch farms in southern Africa was comparatively fairer than conditions found among other colonial structures, including those under British rule.[23] *The Truth* next gave an extended apologia about how the original Boer emigration out of the Cape Colony was not, as was the common assumption, a protest against the abolishment of slavery. Really, according to *The Truth*, the root cause of all the troubles was that the Boers were misunderstood and underappreciated in so many ways.

Almost the entire second half of the document concerns mission work,[24] including the DRC's own mission activities, as well as a description of the relationship between the Boers and other missionaries. It chiefly purports to show that they were in fact not at all anti-mission, despite having some disagreements with individual missionaries.

It is very likely that Andrew Murray was mainly responsible for this part of the document. His own writings, both unpublished and published in *De Kerkbode*, among other news outlets, show sentiments that resonate clearly with those expressed in *The Truth*. One Andrew Murray article published on 5 October 1899 is evocatively entitled 'An Appeal to the English People on Behalf of Peace'. Another, from the same month and year, is a multi-chapter series of writings under the general title 'A Plea for Peace'.

It is important to note that Murray is not merely writing here as a pastoral representative of the Afrikaner people, although that aspect of his role deserves emphasis. He is also personally entangled on the Boer side of the conflict through the actions of various family members, most prominently his son, John Neethling Murray, a Boer sympathiser, who became a POW in India after being nearly executed for high treason by the British authorities. More about this incident follows below.

The conflicted state of Andrew Murray's Afrikaner-Scottish 'hybridity' is illustrated in some of his own writings, as well as in what others had written to and about him. In 'An Appeal to the English People', Murray starts out acknowledging as much when he writes:

> As the oldest minister in the Dutch Reformed Church, as one known, and sometimes even misjudged by my own people, for my loyalty to British interests, as one not unknown in England, as a teacher and a worker in the service of God and humanity, I venture ... to make this appeal for peace.[25]

In this aptly titled article on the eve of war, Murray emphasises what he believes to be the Christian character of the English people, as well as their historical advocacy of the principle of liberty, and then he turns the rhetorical tables on his intended audience, asking how such a Christian nation could wage war on the 'youngest and smallest of its free States'? His appeal to the English pride in their advocacy of liberty obviously refers to their abolitionist history, but the theme of slavery and abolition is not directly mentioned. Instead, this theme features to criticise English insensitivity to the Boer desire for national liberty and independence.

Murray argues that 'British supremacy and paramountcy in South Africa are not the cause of the war'. Nor is any of the other typical answers that has been given, such as the controversy over the *Uitlander* 'franchise' (see below). Instead: 'The one cause of the war is the independence of the Republic. It refuses to be dictated to in internal affairs.'[26] England, according to Murray, had failed to understand this basic fact about the Boers. By doing so, the English had effectively rendered all their other laudable liberty-inspired efforts in the region ineffective.

Obviously not shy to flout his personal, divided, sentiments in the interest of averting war, Murray writes towards the end of the article,

> I believe with my whole heart that in many respects Britain is the noblest, the most Christian nation in the world, its greatest power for good or evil. I cannot believe that the English Cabinet, if it had not been misled by one-sided and false representations as to the necessity, the duration, the results of the war, would ever have threatened it.[27]

In Murray's first chapter of 'A Plea for Peace', many of the above sentiments are repeated, but a noteworthy addition is that Murray also here writes sympathetically about the 'great emigration from the Colony' as the foundation of the Boer sense of independence. This is important because his father, the original Andrew Murray in South Africa along with other first-generation Scottish immigrant ministers, was among those Cape DRC leaders who harboured strong sentiments against the motivations and aspirations of the emigrants. Yet, on these pages, Andrew Jr seems to fully buy into the budding discourse of Afrikaner national identity as emerging out of the 'Great Trek' and the concurrent military victories over African peoples, which were often interpreted on a popular religious level as signs of God's blessing and election. 'One can easily understand how the Transvaal Boer now prizes his liberty. He honestly believes, and who can say that he has no reason for it, that contrary to all human expectation, he won it from England in war, and gained it from God in prayer?'[28]

Murray's role as Boer apologist continues, even intensifies, as the writing develops. For example, in Chapter 3 of 'A Plea for Peace' Murray addresses and debunks the so-called *Uitlander* grievances. From a British point of view, unfair treatment of immigrants known among the Boers as *Uitlanders* (foreigners), at the hands of the Transvaal administration of Paul Kruger, was the primary cause of war. Yet Murray, in clear support of Kruger's policies, writes: 'In connection with this matter there are three expressions that have come into use latterly – "equal rights," "immediate relief" and "constitutional rights." I believe all three to be incorrect and impossible.'[29]

Murray, however, did not only write admonishing letters to the British. This becomes clear from the perusal of a handwritten letter[30] by F. W. Reitz, the last State Secretary of the Transvaal Republic, in which Reitz rather brusquely responds to a communication he had earlier received from Murray. In his letter dated 4 October 1899, Reitz refers to and quotes from Murray's earlier letter, in which the latter evidently pleaded for calm heads to prevail on both sides, for the 'disarmament of both sides' (transl.). Reitz comments on this that the Transvaal Republic had only sent troops to the border after the British had failed to withdraw theirs. Reitz furthermore argues that the word *Uitlanders* was being misused by politicians like Alfred Milner and Joseph Chamberlain to make it seem as if all foreigners supported the British occupation, whereas it was only 'English Jingoes and Jewish capitalists' [transl.] who did. Most of the others supported the Republic's independence, according to Reitz. Was this argument perhaps what inspired Murray's subsequent trivialisation of *Uitlander* grievances, as mentioned above?

Murray, as cited by Reitz, had also pleaded for 'noble-spiritedness and generosity'. Reitz writes in rebuttal that 'the man whom England currently has the dishonour of being represented by in South Africa' [transl.] has not shown any inclination to such a spirit in all the negotiations up to that point.

When war finally broke out, Murray's writing to his own people sought to interpret the calamity in a way that made theological sense. Now that God had sent the war, what are we to think about it, and moreover, how should we deal with it? Such concerns seemed to underpin the main thrust of his rhetoric. The general answer in *Kerkbode* articles such as 'De Zegen der Beproeving'[31] and in a pamphlet published shortly after the outbreak of war with the title *De Oorlogsklok* seems to be that God was testing his people and thereby strengthening them. It is not that God had forsaken them as some might assume given the circumstances. No, God should not be questioned, according to Murray. Rather, people should question themselves and their unmerited confidence in their own abilities.[32]

In *De Oorlogsklok*, Andrew Murray mentions the difficult situation of the Cape Afrikaners. As citizens of the British Empire they were trying to do right by God's Word and the demands of their conscience. 'Even so there is something in us that not only inculcates participation with the fate of our blood relatives in the Transvaal, but that our heart is filled with the hope that the freedom which we have enjoyed should not be taken from them' [transl.].[33]

As the conflict dragged on, Andrew Murray's sentiments, along with perhaps most of the Cape Afrikaners', continued to shift in support of the Boer cause. Many such families suffered personal tragedies during the war, and the wider Murray family had its fair share. It is known that a nephew of Andrew Murray, Willie Louw, was tried and executed for fighting on the side of the Boers, and hence a traitor to the British Crown, in Cradock on 23 November 1901.[34] I briefly mentioned the Murrays' son, John Neethling Murray, who nearly suffered a fate similar to that of his cousin Willie, but was instead sentenced to three months' hard labour followed by deportation as a POW. John committed, apparently, a much lighter offence than Willie, having not taken up arms against British forces, although he did serve for a time as chaplain to the Boer forces in the early stages of the war. As a 1901 letter[35] from his father to Lord Kitchener explains in appeal of a lighter sentence, John had been working as a missionary at Waterberg in the Transvaal when war broke out. Faced with the choice of either abandoning his mission station or becoming a citizen of the Transvaal, John, who as mentioned by his father was married to a niece of the Boer military commander General Louis Botha, chose the latter course of action. When the British took possession of Waterberg, John was interned in Pretoria. He was eventually granted 'parole' and after a sojourn through various parts of South Africa he ended up in his parental home in Wellington. It was from this location that he committed the crime, which got him into such deep trouble, which, according to Andrew, was to write in a postcard to a friend in the Transvaal encouraging him to 'keep up his courage, as the English were in a tight place'. For that he was arrested. Andrew, in the letter, asks Kitchener whether the sentence was not disproportionate to the crime committed, and pleads that the hard labour part of the sentence be commuted, since a portion of it had already been served by the time the letter was written. Murray adds that 'by showing mercy [Kitchener] would earn our heartfelt gratitude and that of many of the Africander people'. Whether or not Kitchener ever responded, I do not know, but it seems likely that John Neethling Murray's connection to Louis Botha was at least a contributing factor to the level of surveillance and the sentencing.

It is interesting to note that although Andrew Murray was a strong peace advocate before the war had broken out, once it was underway his sympathies did not apparently lie with those, from the Boer side, who had wanted to surrender. This much could be surmised from pages of the Lovedale publication, *The Christian Express*, which ran a story in June 1901 with the title 'Rev. Dr. Andrew Murray and the Peace Envoys'. Herein mention is made of large numbers of Boer fighters surrendering and working towards peace in the Orange Free State. Mention is also made of the Cape Afrikaners represented by the Afrikaner Bond and the DRC. In the case of the former, not much headway had been made in terms of peace negotiations, the paper laments, and in the case of the latter the curious case of Murray comes to the fore. It would be best to quote directly from *The Christian Express*. This is how Murray is introduced:

> The Rev. Dr. Andrew Murray's reply to the Peace Envoys has come as a painful disappointment to many who have a very high regard for Dr. Murray himself . . . We have always regarded him as one of the most remarkable men of his time, blending to an uncommon degree, as he does in himself, administrative ability with scholarliness and a deep, true piety. The reverence in which he is justly held, and his long tenure of office as Moderator of the Dutch Reformed Church, have endowed him with well nigh the authority of a pope among his brethren. They look to him for a lead.[36]

However, Murray's 'great love' and sympathy for the 'Dutch people' had blinded him to the way of peace, which is 'the way for the Africander people to a larger and more fruitful life and a wider influence within a world-wide Empire'.[37] Referring to a letter which Murray wrote in response to the 'Peace Envoys' and an interview 'Rev. Mr, Du Plessis' had with him, the article finds 'that Dr. Murray will lend his countenance to no peace which does not provide for the independence of the late Republics; and that he will encourage, by his prayers and his influence, those who are in the field to continue to fight until that is obtained.'[38]

Whether this estimation of Murray's seemingly increased hard-line stance as the war progressed was indeed justified is perhaps a question of interpretation. It is clear, though, from his writing that theologically he had come to see the war as perhaps a time of necessary divine testing for the Afrikaner people. Certainly, absent is any idea of God punishing the Afrikaner for sins committed. Nevertheless, an enduring theme, not only in the writing of Murray but in the works of Boer apologists more generally at the time, is that God was strengthening them or even calling them to a higher purpose. Such an understanding seems to support the rhetoric in a 1901 *Kerkbode* article with the title 'De Zegen der Beproeven', which might be translated as 'the blessing of the ordeal'.

The specific 'blessing' discussed here concerns a noteworthy series of revivals that led to an emerging mission consciousness in the camps housing Boer prisoners of war. More detail about specifically what had occurred in these camps, particularly on the so-called islands of exile where large numbers of Boer prisoners were held, mainly Ceylon and St Helena, will be discussed below. In this *Kerkbode* article, Murray refers to the conversions and revivals in the camps as examples of what God could also do for the people at home. He mentions that they, presumably the DRC, had been praying for two years that God would turn the ordeal of war into a rich blessing. What occurred was that, according to Murray's description, hundreds of people had been converted in the POW camps, but this same blessing had not yet affected the home front to a similar degree. Such a development is what now had to be prayed for.[39] Regarding spiritual developments on one of the islands of exile, Murray writes as follows: 'Wonderful are the ways of God, is it not; that the war and exile to St Helena had to occur for these prayers to be answered. And there are so many reports that, not only through conversion but through renewal and confirmation of life in God, the imprisonment has been a blessing for many' [transl.].[40] How that occurred will be discussed next.

A Developing Mission Consciousness among Boers

For safety and strategic reasons, the British authorities preferred to keep their prisoners of war outside South African borders, and given the ultimate locations they were kept in, it would seem as far offshore as possible. The vast majority of POWs were sent to camps in Ceylon, India, St Helena and the Bermuda Islands. Some ended up in Portugal. Revivalism and missionary enthusiasm blazed like wildfires in these POW camps, and Murray relatives were deeply involved in the generation of such spiritual trends. However, it would be useful to mention that missionary fervour did not emerge from nowhere in the camps. It was already present among Boer fighters in the field, as the following example illustrates.

Although perhaps not directly attributable to the Scots Afrikaners, there were indirect links to a unique missionary society formed by members of a Boer Commando under General C. F. J. Beyers. *De Commando's Dank Zendingvereeniging* (CDZV) was constituted in the aftermath of an intercultural experience that Commando members had had of life on a Swiss Romande missionary station in the northern Transvaal. The experience included participation at a Sunday morning worship service. According to a report in *De Vereeniging*, the visit to the mission station had caused these Boer fighters to feel ashamed of the fact that it had been left to 'foreigners' to go and preach the gospel to the indigenous population in the northern Transvaal. Why could they not themselves take on this responsibility, the Commando members reportedly asked themselves?[41]

This sequence was set in motion by an impromptu visit that three of the Commando members had initially made to the station. Two of those three would later become influential DRC ministers, but with widely divergent careers. Jozua Naudé would avoid capture during the course of the war. He fought until the 'bitter end', earning for himself the mythical Afrikaner accolade of *Bittereinder*. Eventually he would be one of the founders of the *Afrikaner Broederbond* in 1918.[42] He is also the father of the well-known anti-apartheid stalwart Beyers Naudé, who had started out as a DRC minister himself, before becoming full-time director of the eventually banned Christian Institute.

One of Jozua Naudé's companions in the scouting out of the mission station and another co-founder of the CDZV was J. A. (Kotie) Retief, originally from the Murray stronghold of Graaff Reinet in the Eastern Cape. He would subsequently be captured near the town of Ladysmith and found himself in danger of suffering a similar fate as the above-mentioned Willie Louw who was executed as Cape Rebel, as the disloyal colonial subjects fighting on the Boer side were often termed. Through a fortuitous series of events, including an outbreak of measles on the ship he was travelling on between Durban and the Cape, the Cape Town port authority disallowed any disembarkation of passengers. Hence, Retief was able to avoid facing trial and instead continued along with the other prisoners to the island of St Helena, where he was booked in as a POW.[43] In later years, Retief would become a leading missionary in Nyasaland (Malawi) (see Chapters 4 and 6), and he played a central role in ecumenical projects involving representatives of the Scottish missions there. More will be written about him in the subsequent pages, but it should be emphasised here that he was spiritually and eventually through marriage connected to the Scots Afrikaners. He originated from the area of Graaff Reinet, the Murray bastion in South Africa. There he grew up in a family of devout members of the DRC that at the time was pastored by Charles Murray, another of the sons of the original immigrant Andrew, who had himself been a lifelong minister of the Graaff Reinet DRC. Charles Murray's preaching early on instilled in the young Retief the kind of spirituality that would later help to make a missionary career seem like an attractive idea.[44] Much later, Retief would marry Helen Murray, a niece of both Charles and Andrew Jr, and a daughter of George Murray (see below).

Let us now turn attention to the prisoner of war camps. Arguably the most important religious organisation on the so-called islands of exile was not the DRC as such, but the para-church American-originated Christian Endeavour Society. This organisation was originally founded in Portland, Maine by a married couple, Clark, in 1881. The goal of the Endeavour society was broadly to advance the Christian life in the world. In 1887 it arrived in South Africa, and none other than Andrew Murray Jr became the first president of the local society.[45] Initially, the society had joint meetings between English- and Dutch/Afrikaans-speaking members, and the languages were used equally and interchangeably, but this amicable relationship did not endure, especially as the outbreak of war caused an increase in distrust and animosity between the two language groups. Ultimately, by the end of 1900 it was decided that an Afrikaans-speaking formation of the *Christelike Strewersunie*, or simply *Strewers*, as they were colloquially known, would be brought into direct connection with the DRC. Andrew Murray's name is notably absent among those mentioned as taking charge of this new development by an internal source.[46]

A well-researched Afrikaans text, *Sonderlinge Vrug*, describes the influence of the South African War on the mission work of the DRC. Here it is mentioned that Andrew Murray was one of a number of DRC ministers doing chaplaincy work among prisoners of war, in his case at the Cape Town-based camp, Groenpunt. Kok, the author of *Sonderlinge Vrug*, writes that branches of the *Christelike Jongeliedevereniging* (Christian Young People Society) and *Christelike Streversvereniging* (Christian Endeavour Society) were active in these camps in order to help the Boers keep themselves busy with spiritual matters. When the news broke that Boers would no longer be housed in POW camps on South African soil, but abroad in other areas under control of the British Empire, a delegation consisting of Revds Andrew Murray, J. H. Neethling, J. R. Albertyn and Prof. Hofmeyr of the Stellenbosch Seminary went to see the governor general to plead against such a move, but to no avail. Boers would now be sent into exile, as they saw it, and the DRC leadership made plans to minister to them in this new situation.[47]

An Islands Ministry: The Christian Endeavour Society with Specific Reference to Revds George Murray and A. F. Louw

The *Strevers/Strewers* had a massive impact on the social and religious life in Boer prisoner of war camps on the islands of exile. There are accounts of mass prayer meetings conducted by the *Strevers*, especially on the larger camps on the islands of Ceylon and St Helena. The *Strevers* furthermore conducted smaller Bible study groups and distributed literature to arouse a mission-minded consciousness among the prisoners. This strategy met with much success. An exile narrative found fertile soil in many a Boer prisoner heart. Many were keen to embrace their situation in religious terms, that is, they were being castigated by the Almighty in order to be tempered and thus readied for a higher calling upon their eventual return to Africa. For some, this even translated into a lifelong commitment to mission work that went beyond the borders of South Africa.

It furthermore seems that there existed a somewhat symbiotic relationship between the *Strevers* and the mission-minded contingent within the DRC, or to put it differently, they were one and the same influence group. DRC ministers who were friendly to and supportive of *Strevers'* causes accepted calls to serve as chaplains on the islands. For my purposes, two of the most prominent names in this regard were A. F. Louw, who served in St Helena, and George Murray in Ceylon. The latter was a younger brother of Andrew Murray, and Louw was a nephew, his mother being Jemima, one of the Murray sisters. A. F. Louw was also the older brother of the above-mentioned Willie Louw, who was executed as Cape Rebel. Another of their brothers, A. A. Louw, had by this time become the founding DRC missionary in Mashonaland (more on him in the following chapter).

George Murray was actually the person responsible for founding the *Streversvereniging* on Diyatalawa Camp in Ceylon. This was according to a journal published at the camp titled *De Strever: voor Christus en de Kerk*. In the introductory article describing the raison d'être for the journal's existence in service of the Christian Endeavour Society with its approximately seven hundred members among the POWs in the camp at that time, the following is mentioned: 'With all of this we intend to answer to the cause of what the Lord of our Society in Diyatalawa has made us found more than a year ago through that honourable servant of the Lord, Rev. George Murray' [transl.].[48]

When A. F. Louw reflected on his life in an autobiography he wrote when he was ninety years old, he recalled his chaplaincy on St Helena as particularly formative and spiritually moving. He described his decision to go there as a difficult but ultimately blessed one: 'For the rest of my life I was thankful to the Lord that I received on that day, 2 April 1901, the grace to push through and not turn back! Incredibly much poorer my life would have been without the experience that awaited on that remote, lonely piece of earth' [transl.].[49]

The ministries of Louw, Murray and others in the POW camps found a very fertile soil thanks to the activities of the *Strevers*. Kok describes in *Sonderlinge Vrug* how strongly mission-oriented the *Strevers* were. They held daily prayer meetings, and on St Helena every Wednesday's prayer session was set aside for mission.[50] On St Helena some members also started the *St Helena Christelijke Strewers Zending Handwerkers Genootskap*, which was a sub-formation of artisans who specialised in making ornaments from wood, bone and other materials. These were then shipped to be sold in South Africa, and the income derived was allocated for mission work.[51] In fact, the international trade in Boer POW curios occurred not only between the islands and South Africa. Under the heading *Naar Holland Gezonden Curios*, the Ceylon- based journal *De Strever* reported on curios sent from there to Holland in August 1901, the sales revenue of which was to be allocated to aid for the 'women's camps',[52] that is, the notorious concentration camps in South Africa holding Boer women and children during the latter stages of the war.

Kok further mentions that mission conferences were held in many of the POW camps, and he gives more detailed commentary about a large conference at St Helena on 22 November 1901 that was attended by three hundred POWs. Interestingly, Kok mentions that the watchword of this conference was 'The Evangelisation of the World in this Generation' [transl.],[53] which was the exact phrase chosen as watchword of the famous 1910 missionary conference in Edinburgh. The term originated with the American missionary 'statesman' John R. Mott, who played a leading role in Edinburgh in 1910 and also at the massive 1900 mission conference in New York city, which drew 2,500 official delegates and up to 200,000 attendees.[54] Mott published a book with the title *The Evangelization of the World in this Generation* in 1900.[55]

What the use of this phrase perhaps illustrates is that the Boer POW mission enthusiasts on their islands of exile such as St Helena were interconnected within a wider Protestant world of popular thought concerning similar missionary ideas and activities, much of which having originated in the English-speaking world.[56] No doubt the *Strevers* (Christian Endeavour Society) had much to do with providing or facilitating these linkages. This idea is further substantiated in the pages of *De Strever*, the journal that originated on Diyatalawa Camp, Ceylon. Although much of the writing in *De Strever* concerned the situation in the camps directly, including updates from Strewer activities in other POW locations like St Helena, Portugal and Bermuda, there were also occasionally included devotional writings from well-known international Christian leaders, for example a Dutch translation of a short piece by Dwight L. Moody on the theme of 'the privilege of freedom' [transl.].[57]

There also occurs a detailed report regarding life on a mission station by a DRC woman missionary teacher, Miss Zondagh from Kongwe, Nyasaland. This was apparently excerpted from a letter she had written to friends at Diyatalawa Camp, 'Hut 36'. Zondagh mentioned the names of her three co-workers. One of them, Miss Hofmeyr, had recently taken ill with blackwater fever, a serious complication associated with malaria. Consequently, Miss Hofmeyr would either return home or to the original DRC mission station of Mvera, leaving Miss Zondagh with full responsibility for the girls in the mission school.

Miss Zondagh further imagined that the men in the camp might be wondering what the Nyasaland missionaries were doing on a daily basis, and so she proceeded to relate the activities from rising at 5:30 a.m. to Bible class with teachers an hour later, to breakfast, and then school from 9 till 11. During school they taught more than three hundred children, and it seemed they mostly concentrated on Bible studies. She mentioned the Psalms and the fact that the founding DRC missionary, A. C. Murray, had translated a number of these, and she conveyed the joy of the children to have something like that in their own language. 'Rev. A. C. M. has also translated the gospel of Matthew. It is highly prized by the people among whom we are working' [transl.].[58]

Other school activities continued through the morning and afternoon, and she specifically mentioned in the concluding paragraph the afternoon school from 2 p.m. for the teachers. 'These teachers, ah! They know so little, that is why we teach them to read, write, count, and calculation . . . It is yet so delightful to know that on Ceylon, specifically for us – Nyasaland workers – prayers are being said' [transl.].[59]

In the same issue of *De Strever* there appears a page-long call to mission, replete with biblical references and a general theological argumentation that being Christian means being missionary, entitled 'The Missionary Awakens'.[60] This is attributed to William Carey, the Englishman who has often been called the 'father of modern missions'.[61]

From Exile through Imprisonment to the Self-imposed Exile of the Mission Field

The missionary interest awakened by the Christian Endeavour Society and the ministers associated with it had repercussions. One direct consequence was that 175 young men among the POWs in the various camps decided to dedicate the remainder of their lives to mission work. This presented a new challenge to the Cape DRC. Its ministers, through the activities of the Christian Endeavour Society, among other influences, had inspired this movement after all, and of course this development fully corresponded with the mission-minded vision of the church leadership that was still strongly influenced by Andrew Murray and his protégés. A special commission was called to take charge of the next steps, which would include the founding of an institute for the training of these prospective missionaries who had various levels of primary and secondary schooling. As written in the Report of the Commission for the Training of Mission Workers, the commission was initiated after a decision taken at a ministers' conference on mission at Stellenbosch on 16 September 1902, with the purpose of looking into the founding of an institution that could accommodate such candidates who had not or could not attend any of the other existing institutions, and to train such candidates for mission work.[62] Further organisation went apace, funds were raised and a site was purchased. The official opening of this institution was on 12 February 1903 at Worcester.[63]

In the aftermath of the war, the above-mentioned A. F. Louw played a leading role at *Het Boeren Zending Instituut*, as this missionary-training institution was named, where he served as principal from its founding until December 1905.[64]

The kind of schooling offered by *Het Boeren Zending Instituut* was a basic education for many former POWs who did not have much in the way of official schooling background. The focus was on artisanal skills, in order to develop candidates for agricultural and so-called industrial mission. A number of these men ended up in the DRC's foreign missionary enterprise, including in Nyasaland.[65] However, there was at least one example of a POW with a post-secondary degree who upon his return to South Africa enrolled at the theological seminary in Stellenbosch. The above-mentioned J. A. Retief was profoundly influenced by the ministry of A. F. Louw on St Helena.[66] Although he had previously trained to be a teacher, and taught at a primary school near Paarl in the late 1890s, on St Helena he came to the decision to prepare for the ministry and then to become a missionary. This planned course of action first took him to study theology in Stellenbosch, followed by a short medical course for prospective missionaries at Livingstone College in London in 1907, and this overseas adventure culminated in a period of study at Princeton Theological Seminary in the USA.[67] In 1909 he was ordained in Paarl, South Africa, and then set off to join the DRC mission in Nyasaland. In 1910 at Mvera, he would marry Helen Murray, daughter of the above-mentioned George Murray, founder of the Christian Endeavour Society branch on Diyatalawa Camp, Ceylon. Helen Murray was a teacher and graduate of Huguenot College in Wellington, where Pietjie de Beer, a fellow missionary and the author of Helen's memorial, met her in 1903 during the time when 'the pious Dr. Ferguson was our principal' [transl.].[68] This is a reference to Abbie Park Ferguson (mentioned in Chapter 4), one of the Mount Holyoke Seminary graduates who co-founded Huguenot College.[69]

Conclusion

Andrew Murray and the wider Murray family were the central actors in this chapter. The second South African War/Anglo-Boer War was a formative experience in this family's ongoing self-identification. On the one hand, the Murrays became more closely aligned with the Afrikaans people, among whom a number of them ministered. At the same time, they continued to cultivate international networks, most notably through the Christian Endeavour Society. The war and the prisoner of war camps provided an unorthodox milieu for the furthering of a perennial Scottish–Afrikaner interest, and the cultivation of strong missionary enthusiasm among the Afrikaner people. Not only was this achieved through a stirring-up of missionary consciousness, but through the implementation of programmes and structures to channel this consciousness once awakened. The activities of the Christian Endeavour Society on the POW camps and the founding of *Het Boeren Zending Instituut* after the war were of primary importance in this respect. The consequences and complexities flowing from this engendering of a missionary impetus among a people with generally conservative, even intolerant racial views will be the subject of the next chapter.

Notes

1. John M. MacKenzie and Nigel R. Dalziel (2014) *The Scots in South Africa: Ethnicity, identity, gender and race, 1772–1914*. Oxford: Manchester University Press.
2. *The Truth about the Boer and his Church* (n.d.). DRC Archive, Stellenbosch, B1250. The letter was signed by J. H. Hofmeyr, A. Moorrees, J. P. van Heerden, A. Murray, J. H. Neethling, N. J. Hofmeyr, J. I. Marais, P. G. J. de Vos and C. F. J. Muller.
3. 'Ds. A. Murray, D.D. en Dr James Stewart, over de Transvaalsche kwestie' (30 November 1899) *De Kerkbode*, p. 755.
4. Ibid.
5. See https://whc.unesco.org/en/tentativelists/5603/
6. Maurice Boucher (ed.) (1985) *Livingstone Letters, 1843–1872: David Livingstone correspondence in the Brenthurst Library*. Johannesburg (Houghton), South Africa: The Brenthurst Press, p. 69.
7. G. C. Cuthbertson (1982) 'James Stewart and the Anglo-Boer War, 1899–1902:

a nonconformist missionary perspective', *South African Historical Journal*, 14:1, p. 68.
8. *Record* (1 December 1899), quoted in Cuthbertson, 'James Stewart and the Anglo-Boer War', p. 69.
9. James Stewart (1 November 1899) *Mission World*.
10. Cuthbertson, 'James Stewart and the Anglo-Boer War', p. 70.
11. *Christian Express* (1 February 1906), p. 28.
12. Cuthbertson 'James Stewart and the Anglo-Boer War', pp. 80–1.
13. Stewart Papers, BC 106 L3: 'The Abuse of Mr Chamberlain: A Remonstrance', p. 4, quoted in Cuthbertson, 'James Stewart and the Anglo-Boer War'.
14. *Christian Express* (1 December 1899), p. 179.
15. See S. B. Spies (1977) *Methods of Barbarism? Roberts and Kitchener and Civilians in the Boer Republics January 1900–May 1902*. Cape Town: Human & Rousseau.
16. Cuthbertson, 'James Stewart and the Anglo-Boer War' p. 82.
17. *The Truth about the Boer and his Church*, pp. 2–3.
18. Ibid., p. 5.
19. Ibid., p. 8.
20. See George McCall Theal (1888) *History of the Emigrant Boers in South Africa*. London: S. Sonnenschein, Lowrey.
21. *The Truth about the Boer and his Church*, p. 8.
22. Ibid., p. 9ff.
23. Ibid., p. 10.
24. Ibid., pp. 18–32.
25. Andrew Murray (5 October 1899) 'An Appeal to the English People on Behalf of Peace', *South African News*. DRC Archive: PPV 1460/4.
26. Ibid.
27. Ibid.
28. Andrew Murray (13 October 1899) 'A Plea for Peace: Chapter 1', *South African News*. DRC Archive: PPV 1460/4.
29. A. Murray (16 October 1899) 'A Plea for Peace: Chapter 3', *South African News*. DRC Archive: PPV 1460/4.
30. Personal correspondence by F. W. Reitz to Andrew Murray (4 October 1899), Pretoria. DRC Archive: PPV 1451.
31. Andrew Murray (19 September 1901) 'De Zegen der Beproeven', *De Kerkbode*, No. 37, Part 18, pp. 523–6.
32. Andrew Murray (1900) 'Oorlogs Gedachten', *De Kerkbode*, p. 133.
33. Andrew Murray (1899) *In tijd van oorlog: de oorlogsklok: Gods roepstem naar de binnenkamer*. Kaapstad: Townshend, Taylor en Snashall, pp. 9–10.
34. See https://www.executedtoday.com/2017/11/23/1901-willie-louw-boer-commando/
35. Personal correspondence of Andrew Murray to Kitchener (September 1901). DRC Archive: PPV 1451.
36. 'Rev. Dr. Andrew Murray and the Peace Envoys' (1 June 1901) *The Christian Express*, Vol. 31, No. 369, pp. 81–2.
37. Ibid., p. 82.
38. Ibid.
39. Andrew Murray (19 September 1901) 'De Zegen der Beproeven', *Kerkbode*, No. 37, Part 18, pp. 523–6.
40. Ibid., p. 523.

41. *De Vereeniging* (30 December 1903), p. 6.
42. See Official minutes of the founders' meeting quoted in J. H. P. Serfontein (1978) *Brotherhood of Power: An Exposé of the Secret Afrikaner Broederbond*. Bloomington and London: Indiana University Press, p. 32.
43. See Jeanette Ferreira (2012) *Boereoorlogstories 2: 32 verhale oor die oorlog van 1899–1902*. Kaapstad: Tafelberg.
44. J. A. Retief (1951) *Ontdekkings in Midde-Afrika*. Stellenbosch: C. S. V. Boekhandel, p. 11.
45. *Strewerskonferensieboek: verslag van die 22ste Algemene Vergadering van die Christelike Strewersunie in verband met Die Ned. Geref. Kerke in Suid-Afrika, gehou 3–6 Julie 1941 te Riversdal*, p. 20.
46. Ibid., p. 21.
47. J. W. Kok (1971) *Sonderlinge vrug; die invloed van die Tweede Vryheidsoorlog op die sendingaksie van die Nederduitse Gereformeerde Kerk in Suid-Afrika*. Pretoria: N. G. Kerkboekhandel, p. 33.
48. *De Strever: voor Christus en de Kerk. Orgaan der C. S. V. onder de Krijgsgevangenen* (19 December 1901) No. 1, Diyatalawa Kamp, Ceylon. NGK Argief.
49. A. F. Louw, quoted in Kok, *Sonderlinge Vrug*, p. 34.
50. Kok, *Sonderlinge Vrug*, p. 36.
51. Ibid.
52. *De Strever* (11 January 1902) No. 4.
53. Kok, *Sonderlinge Vrug*, p. 37.
54. See Thomas A. Askew (October 2000) 'The New York 1900 Ecumenical Missionary Conference: A Centennial Reflection', *International Bulletin of Missionary Research*, pp. 146–54, p. 147.
55. John R. Mott (1900) *The Evangelization of the World in this Generation*. New York: Student Volunteer Movement for Foreign Missions.
56. This would further support and extend the argument by S. E. Duff regarding the nineteenth-century international linkages of the DRC's revivals. See S. E. Duff (2018) 'The Dutch Reformed Church and the Protestant Atlantic: Revivalism and Evangelicalism in the Nineteenth-Century Cape Colony', *South African Historical Journal*, 70:2, pp. 324–47.
57. D. L. Moody (29 March 1902) 'Het Voorrecht der Vrijheid', *De Strever*, No. 15.
58. Miss Zondagh quoted in *De Strever* (18 January 1902) No. 5.
59. *De Strever* (18 January 1902) No. 5.
60. *De Strever*, (18 January 1902) No. 5, 'De Zendeling Ontwaakt'.
61. See Galen B. Royer (1915) 'William Carey: The Father of Modern Missions', in Galen B. Royer, *Christian Heroism in Heathen Lands*. Elgin, IL: Brethren Publishing House.
62. *Notulen der Commissie voor de Opleiding van Zendeling Arbeiders* (16 September 1902). DRC Archive, Stellenbosch.
63. Kok, *Sonderlinge Vrug*, p. 50.
64. Gys R. Hofmeyr en C Gie Murray (1906) *Zuid Afrikaansche Jaarboek en Algemeene Gids 1907 (3de jaar)*. Kaapstad: Cape Times, p. 329.
65. See Janet Wagner Parsons (1998) 'Scots and Afrikaners in Central Africa: Andrew Charles Murray and the Dutch Reformed Church Mission in Malawi', *The Society of Malawi Journal*, 51:1; and Retief Müller (2018) 'War, Exilic Pilgrimage and Mission: South Africa's Dutch Reformed Church in the Early Twentieth Century', *Studies in World Christianity*, 21:4, pp. 66–81.

66. Retief, *Ontdekkings*, p. 19.
67. See Bernard Retief (19 April 2000) 'Ds. Kotie Retief, Rebel van Graaff-Reinet se Sneeuberge', *Die Burger*.
68. Pietjie de Beer (15 February 1928) 'Helen Murray Retief', *De Kerkbode*.
69. See Dana L. Robert (1993) 'Mount Holyoke Women and the Dutch Reformed Missionary Movement, 1874–1904', *Missionalia*, 21, pp. 103–23.

CHAPTER SIX

Other(ing) Identity Formations: From Mission Field Ecumenism to Home Church Controversy

Let me transition into this chapter by referencing once more the massive impact of the South African War on identity formation in South Africa and beyond. Among other things, it drove a wedge between the English- and Afrikaans-speaking portions of the settler population. This precipitated a crisis of identity for the Scots Afrikaners, but also for the wider population of Scottish immigrants in South Africa. In Chapters 1 and 2, I referred to John MacKenzie, who suggested that nineteenth-century Scots in South Africa tended to rely on their common Presbyterian identity as a primary reference group. This identity came in handy for differentiating themselves from the English in South Africa, and such reference group identification also tended to draw them closer to the Dutch Calvinists at the Cape.[1]

Yet this familiarity among Calvinists of different provenance was destabilised in the aftermath of the South African War, with Scots apparently now thrown more definitively in the English camp over against the Afrikaners. In this regard the Pretoria-based newspaper of the Transvaal DRC, *De Vereeniging*, carried a noteworthy article in 1903 on 'Onze Kerk en de Schotsche Kerken'. Herein mention is made of a visit to South Africa by representatives of the 'Scottish church' in July 1902, in order to attempt repairing the good relations that had existed between 'our' and 'their' churches, but which had become disrupted by the war. The Afrikaner perspective is then related at length. The first part of the letter appears to be conciliatory, thanking the Scots for reaching out, and emphasising everything that had bound the two Calvinist churches to each other in the past. Then, however, the tone changes, asking in effect: why do you seek reconciliation now? Why didn't you speak up and come to our aid during the war when everything was going up in flames? The letter conveys a deep resentment on the part of the Boer church that their Scottish spiritual kin had shunned them and painted them 'black' during the war years. Among several complaints raised, one theme tying in with what I discussed in the previous chapter concerns the divergent opinions of James Stewart and Andrew Murray. The letter berates the Scots church for listening to a 'man' like James Stewart, in contrast to a 'father in Christ, such as Andrew Murray', renowned around the world as a Christian leader, who was born in Africa and who had been busy with his ministry for sixty years. Murray had been revered by the Scottish churches before the war, but since and after the war he had been completely sidelined by them. The *De Vereeniging* article even seems to attribute prophet status to Murray, stating that 'his voice was in your ears like that of one calling in the desert . . .' [transl.].[2] Hence the letter, which subsequently tones down to more friendly lines of Christian well-wishing for the Scots' ministry, first makes the following statement, which concerns the actual decision regarding where things stood. It also happened to be a portent of things to come: 'Brothers, is it so surprising that we have to leave this sincerely sought reconciliation between your church and ours up to the next generations!' [transl.].[3]

Of course, the South African War and its repercussions also brought an amount of tension between DRC missionaries and the colonial authorities in places such as Mashonaland and Nyasaland. Some of the missionaries, furthermore, had family members killed or executed for fighting on either side of the conflict. Something of a family scandal might even be thought to apply to the slaying of W. H. (Willie) Murray's (see Chapter 4) younger brother, Robert, at the hands of Boer forces, while fighting for the British.[4] In a letter, dated a few months ahead of his death, which Robert had written to his missionary brother, he acknowledged that Willie would likely not approve of his decision to join the British side in the war, but Robert justified himself by stating that his band of soldiers was a great service to the community, because among other things they were hard at work 'catching a good few of the armed rebels, who were the cause of great distress in this district to many of our Dutch people'.[5] Scarcely three and a half months later Robert would be dead, having been ambushed and shot by Boers during a reconnaissance operation.

Imagine the underlying interfamilial dynamics when one considers the fact that Robert's cousin, Willie Louw (see Chapter 5), the son of Jemima (Murray) Louw, who was a sister of Robert and Willie Murray's father William, was among this category of 'armed rebels' that Robert had been intent on catching. Willie Louw, who was a younger brother of A. F. Louw, the previously mentioned Boer chaplain among the POWs on St Helena, also had, like Robert Murray, another brother in the mission field. This was the pioneer Mashonaland missionary, A. A. Louw, founder of the Môrgenster mission station, situated in the south-eastern part of contemporary Zimbabwe. Willie Louw joined a Boer commando near the start of the war at Colesberg and travelled and fought with them until he was captured by British forces in mid-1901. On 23 November 1901, he was executed at Colesberg for high treason due to his armed involvement on the side of the Boers.[6]

Chapter 5 also mentioned John Neethling Murray, son of Andrew Murray Jr, who nearly suffered a similar fate for his alleged Boer sympathies, and it focused much on Andrew Murray's own shifting loyalties as the tensions grew and the eventual war escalated. However, the above two tragedies neatly encapsulate the conflicting mixture of push and pull that all Scots Afrikaners must have experienced to some degree during this time, vis-à-vis the British Empire.

One area in which the chicks of these divided loyalties came home to roost was in the newly expanded foreign mission field of the DRC, which in all cases continued to be in areas controlled by the Empire. Although the war also brought positive spin-offs for the DRC missions in Nyasaland and elsewhere, due to the strengthening of personnel through recruitment that had taken place in POW camps, as discussed in Chapter 5, war and its repercussions must have been a psychological blow of some magnitude to the formerly easy colloquial relations that had existed between Scots and Afrikaners in Nyasaland. Although not venturing into specifics, A. C. Murray intimates as much when he writes: 'In so far as the Boer war affected mission work in Nyasaland it is difficult to say. Our missionaries, because they are belonging to the "Boer church", were constantly under suspicion, and also the natives had heard about it' [transl.].[7]

An incident in Nyasaland, the so-called Kasungu controversy, is perhaps one example of how the more strained relationships between Scots and Afrikaners also affected the Livingstonia and DRC missions. I shall describe this situation, which concerned the transfer of a mission station of the Livingstonia mission to the DRC's Nkhoma mission, in some detail below.

An Ecumenical Missionary Conference at Mvera (1910)

On the ground, ecumenism continued strongly in Nyasaland in the early twentieth century, a development not entirely out of sync with post-South African War political developments in South Africa, where the former Boer generals Smuts and Botha moved swiftly to reconstitute the country under the British flag, culminating in the formation of the Union of South Africa in 1910.[8]

Hence, an important marker of ecumenicity in Nyasaland was the general mission conference of August 1910, which was held at what was at the time the DRC head station, Mvera. All of the Protestant missions were represented with the exception of the Universities' Mission to Central Africa. This was not the first or only such conference. It was in fact pre-dated by similar, albeit smaller, events in 1900 and 1904. However, 1910 is an auspicious year in mission and ecumenical history, with the Mvera conference following in the wake of the more famous conference in Edinburgh scarcely two months earlier. In its report of the Mvera conference, *De Koningsbode* makes an explicit connection between the two conferences and calls up the image of a 'mission war council' to describe the significance of both. After all, these conferences discussed the best ways not only to overcome an enemy, but also to turn that enemy into a soldier on the side of God, the argument went.[9]

The way A. C. Murray lists in his memoir the churches and mission societies that attended, followed by the number of their representatives, is somewhat interesting. I quote him directly, translating only the few Afrikaans terms in the list: 'Dutch Reformed Church, Livingstonia-mission 6; Church of Scotland (Blantyre) 6; Zambesi Industrial Mission; S. A. General Mission; London Missionary Society; Nyasa Industrial Mission and Baptist Ind. Mission.'[10] Perhaps one should not always read too much into punctuation, but is the fact that only a comma separates the DRC and Livingstonia rather than a semicolon, as is the case between all the other listed entities, perhaps indicative that Murray understood these first two as part of the same enterprise, as had in fact been the case when he started his career in 1888? This might, of course, simply be a typo.

Donald Fraser, the South African Boers and the Mvera Conference

Donald Fraser was another Scottish missionary who had great influence in Nyasaland, and he also had good contact with the DRC missions. Fraser had much experience of the DRC in South Africa as well. In fact, on the way to start his missionary work in the late 1890s in Nyasaland, he had first spent some time on evangelistic endeavours in the Cape Colony. J. A. Retief wrote in his autobiography that he remembered being present upon the occasion when Donald Fraser co-founded with Luther Wishart[11] the 'CSV' (*Christelijke Studentenvereniging*) in Stellenbosch.[12] It might be that Retief had an overblown sense of the role Fraser played in all of this. Fraser was certainly present, but his wife, who was also his biographer, presents a somewhat different perspective, although she did emphasise the work he did among students in 1896:

> When, after disembarking at Capetown, he travelled to Stellenbosch to attend the first South African Student Conference, convened because Luther Wishart was visiting there from America, such pressure was put upon the ex-Travelling Secretary [Fraser] to go round the colleges and schools of the Colony that he felt he could not refuse . . . He found the students very impressionable and responsive, and the wonderful work he did then and the permanent effect produced were often alluded to when, almost thirty years later, he was again touring South Africa and meeting many proofs of how he had so won the hearts of the Dutch that not even the Boer War, so soon to follow with its aftermath of bitterness, could affect their attitude to him personally.[13]

By way of elaborating the theme of Fraser's Dutch sympathy, it is worth mentioning that in Agnes Fraser's biography, she recalls the following incident that occurred while the South African War was ongoing. The Fraser couple had attended, in London, what turned out to be a propagandistic film, which purported to portray Boer atrocities:

> Within a brief time three instances of dastardly treachery on the part of the Boers were shown. The war was going on at that time, and feel-

ings were running very high, and to my dismay Donald's voice, raised to an audible pitch, remarked emphatically, 'They have *no* right to give that impression of the Boers. It's unfair! It's untrue!'[14]

Such were the disagreeing sentiments of the audience around them that the Frasers decided to leave the theatre.

It is not known whether they would have been privy to this story, but with that as background it is scarcely any wonder that such a character would have been respected, even admired, by DRC missionaries. Evidence of this is an article glowingly filled with admiration for Fraser and his work, written by A. A. Louw, founder of the DRC's Mashonaland mission and brother of the executed Willie Louw, mentioned above. A. A. Louw and his wife Cinie had travelled to Mvera to attend the 1910 conference, and afterwards visited Fraser's Nyasaland station, Loudon. There they attended a church service that had a rousing effect similar to what must have occurred on the day of Pentecost, according to Louw. Louw ascribed the revivalist nature of this service to Fraser and the apparently highly charismatic influence he had over his people.[15] These spiritual manifestations were described in similar terms by Agnes Fraser in a chapter entitled 'African Pentecost'.[16] Not only did it occur among 'Europeans' who had gathered for prayer, but also separately among the Africans who had met at the same time as 'we Europeans'. It appears that an important inspiration for this was the Keswick Convention represented at Loudon. Also prior to that there were revivalist manifestations at the Mvera conference as conducted by 'Mr. Inwood', who was there at the invitation of Fraser.

Regarding the Mvera conference itself, Agnes Fraser writes that Donald had a disastrous journey there, due to a motorcycle that broke down, which forced him to walk to Kasungu without food or water. By the time he reached Mvera he was still not recovered from the ordeal. Hence, he was 'unable to enjoy, as he should have done, the meeting with so many friends, for his earlier student work in the Cape had brought him into touch with many now in the Dutch Reformed mission field'.[17]

Donald Fraser's own commentary after the conference (published in the *Glasgow Herald*), or at least parts of it, is conveyed by A. C. Murray. This is significant for the view of the other expressed by Fraser, but also for the fact that one or two aspects perhaps intended as critical by Fraser are not taken as such by Murray, who devotes a page and a half of his book to relaying Fraser's views.[18]

According to Murray's presentation of Fraser's commentary, the Dutch mission had a cautious attitude in their relationship with the Africans, but this is portrayed as quite a healthy addition to the situation in the Nyasaland Federation. Generally, Fraser's quoted commentary does indeed seem positive about the Dutch in these quoted sections, complimenting them for their work with women and girls, and the fact that they greatly cooperated with both Blantyre and Livingstonia. However, he also states that in terms of education the Dutch were not prepared to give such an advanced level of it as the Scottish missions were. The Dutch were basically satisfied when their converts could read the Bible.[19] Evidently, Murray did not interpret this last bit of commentary as negative, as he repeated it verbatim in his book.

It is interesting to compare Murray's selection of Fraser's commentary with the latter's original writing in the *Glasgow Herald*. The 12 April 1913 article, entitled 'Boers and Missions', gives an informative overview of this subject, which, Fraser writes, has been 'greatly misunderstood by most people in Britain'.[20] Fraser goes on to acknowledge that the Boers have in many cases exhibited racist attitudes in religious matters, including a notorious notice seen on a church door, 'Dogs and Hottentotte not admitted'. However, he states that there were also other situations where Dutch masters and slaves attended the same church service, although 'this was not a general condition'. On the frontier especially, removed from religious influences, greed for land ruled the day. Fraser specifically mentions the opposition David Livingstone experienced at the hands of frontier Boers, a situation which necessitated Livingstone to conduct further 'explorations which finally revealed Nyasaland to us'. At the same time, 'the Dutch Church was awakening to her responsibilities' and started a missionary movement.

Fraser specifically mentioned A. C. Murray as the DRC's pioneer missionary to Nyasaland, and he also emphasised Andrew Murray Jr's role in the Ministers' Missionary Union as follows:

> Dr Andrew Murray, the veteran leader of the Dutch Reformed Church, was the inspirer of this enterprise. He is of Scottish parentage, and, with his distinguished brothers, has exercised a unique influence upon the work and spirit of his church. When the ministers' union began operations they sought the advice of Dr Stewart, of Lovedale, and Mr John Stephen, of Glasgow, and were advised to cooperate with the Livingstonia Mission in Nyasaland.[21]

Fraser described the state of the DRC missionary enterprise, including the by now familiar story of its significant expansion in the aftermath of the Anglo-Boer War, the role of the chaplains in Ceylon and on St Helena, and so forth. Fraser mentions that by the time of his writing, the DRC's was the largest mission in Nyasaland. Andrew Murray's role in achieving this is again emphasised:

> Two years ago, in furtherance of the laymen's missionary movement, Dr Andrew Murray, although well over 80 years of age, forgot the infirmities of his years and started out on an apostolic tour of the churches, preaching with extraordinary vigour and rousing everywhere a great interest in foreign missions. Huge sums of money were promised by the Dutch farmers . . .[22]

Then Fraser zoomed in on the distinctive aspects of the DRC mission, which A. C. Murray also related in his book. Fraser's description followed under the heading, 'A Great Mission'. He mentioned the work they were doing among women in the villages, their emphasis on basket and chair weaving, that is, the kind of work sometimes described as industrial mission, as well as their wonderful gardens abundant with fruit and vegetables. Yes, they were 'slow to devolve authority to the natives', but as Murray intimates in his own account, Fraser seemed overwhelmingly positive rather than critical in his estimation. This was simply a different approach from a unique perspective, and a valid one in Fraser's estimation. 'In this way these men, who have been accustomed from youth to deal with native peoples, are bringing their contribution to the general science of mission work.'[23]

All of this was described in the aftermath of the 1910 conference at Mvera, so let us return to that subject. From the DRC side, this was undoubtedly seen as a wonderful success. Nyasaland missionary Revd Attie Hofmeyr concluded his part of the report for *De Koningsbode* as follows:

> Between mission and mission a brotherly bond has been created during this week, which, in the following years, will reveal itself in much intercessory prayer and thoughts of goodwill towards those with whom we had spent such a happy, blessed week there at Mvera. [transl.][24]

Writing in *De Kerkbode*, one DRC attendee at the conference, Revd P. H. Roux, described how everything proceeded in a generally harmonious way, although there were differences of opinion on a couple of aspects. He briefly referred to the issue of the educational level aimed for in terms of African converts, without elaborating on the specifics of differences, except to mention that the DRC emphasised the Word of God and proclamation of the gospel. He furthermore stated that nearly everyone expressed themselves in favour of higher education. The more contentious issue from Roux's point of view was the question of ordination of native Christians. Roux understood, interestingly, that the conference held to the general conviction that the black African in 'his current state of development [was] only a child and not able to stand at the helm of affairs, but should rather work under the supervision of whites'.[25] To apparently substantiate this sentiment of supposedly shared prejudice, Roux pointed out that after thirty-five years of mission work, the Livingstonia mission did not have a single ordained African worker.[26]

An important point regarding growing ecumenicity was that the conference accepted a decision to become a federation. Five ground rules were drawn up, and all missions that subscribed to the rules then became part of this federation without giving up any of their own autonomy.[27] This, one would imagine, was a necessary first step towards the greater church unity that would follow.

A Rocky Road towards Unification

W. H. Murray's biographer, M. W. Retief, wrote that the two Scottish missions, Livingstonia and Blantyre, had already started to discuss the possibility of amalgamation as early as 1903. In fact, Robert Laws and Alexander Hetherwick had discussed it as early as 1893, but perhaps without DRC missionaries being aware of it.[28] Detailed discussions occurred at the 1904 general mission council in Blantyre, and the question was whether the DRC mission would also consider joining in the prospective union. Murray could not at the time express any opinion about the idea without sanction from his home church, but he wrote about the suggested union to the general mission secretary in the Cape. There he argued that church unification was biblically sound, and ideal. Yet would it ever be practically possible, he asked rhetorically?[29]

Church unification might have been inadvertently aided by government actions and attitudes towards the respective missions. At times there was much strife and suspicion between colonial administration and the missions in Nyasaland.[30] An example of this could be seen in the wake of the Chilembwe rising in 1915, when a number of 'Europeans' lost their lives. The colonial authority suspected the missions of facilitating black discontent through their educational work. The commission of enquiry that followed laid bare much interracial strife. Both Murray and Hetherwick were called in to testify, much to the former's discomfort. Hetherwick's fighting spirit, however, was properly kindled, according to his perhaps not entirely unbiased biographer.[31] Apparently, Hetherwick's unintimidated testimony had made a great impression on Murray. W. P. Livingstone quotes Murray on Hetherwick at a time when Murray served as chair of the 1924 meeting of the federated missions at Livingstonia:

> His ability, his determination, his fearlessness made him the trusted champion of mission interests. He belonged to us all and not merely to the Blantyre Mission. If he was feared by the Government officials we knew the reason why – he knew too much of Nyasaland's history. In any case, they could not but respect him.[32]

Another contributing aspect to missionary–colonial tension, on the one hand, and a growing affinity among the various missionary formations, on the other, was the detrimental effects of the First World War on mission. It was detrimental for several reasons, among which was the fact that missionaries, including DRC missionaries, were called up to serve as overseers of military transportation regiments in German East Africa.[33] Missionary knowledge of indigenous languages made them valuable to the imperial campaign, which relied heavily on African recruits. The result was that mission stations were often understaffed during these years. In an article entitled 'Onze Zendelingen in het Oorlogsterrein', *de Koningsbode* reported that ten of the Nyasaland missionaries, including all the lay male personnel, had been called up to serve in East Africa. Although this was a source of real grief to the DRC's mission commission, this article also argues that some positive results were forthcoming as a result of the unfortunate situation. The unauthored article, but probably from the pen of A. C. Murray in his capacity of general editor, refers to the testimony of an incompletely named Scottish missionary. This 'Rev. N.', quite likely Robert Napier, claimed that missionaries, unlike regular soldiers, were trusted by African carriers and the governing forces alike. Missionaries also had a positive spiritual impact on the behaviour of both whites and blacks. The article further claimed the testimony of a recruiting officer in Zomba during the signing up of three DRC missionaries. According to this paraphrased testimony, 'missionaries are the most trustworthy men in our service . . .'[34]

The First World War had also perhaps delayed the founding of the CCAP. According to W. H. Murray's biographer, negotiations had progressed to such an extent that church union, including the incorporation of the DRC congregations, might already have been possible in 1914 had it not been for the logistical challenges caused by the war.[35]

It seems that W. H. Murray not only had to contend with negotiations involving the Scottish missions. He also hoped to negotiate different, at the time still regionally independent, South African factions of the DRC and their respective missions abroad into a unified body. Thus, although he was theoretically in favour of church union involving the Scottish missions, he wrote in a 1916 letter that his hope was for the Cape (Nyasaland), Transvaal (Portuguese East Africa) and Free State (northern Rhodesia) missions of the DRC to first amalgamate into one unified church and synod. 'And concerning the union with Blantyre and Livingstonia, I reckon it should wait until this other step has been taken, and the Cape, Free State and Transvaal missions are formed into one church and synod' [transl.].[36] Contrary to Murray's wish, the unification of the different DRC missions proved to be an insurmountable challenge at the time, whereas the Nkhoma synod's joining with the Scottish missions would be realised in the following decade.

The relationship with authorities shifted over time. For example, A. C. Murray, in his second book on the subject, published in 1931, declared that the relationship with the colonial authority had much improved in 'recent times', with the government cooperating especially in terms of medical and educational services. He also mentioned the fact that since the founding of the protectorate in 1891, its executive council included a representative of the missions. Laws, Hetherwick and W. H. Murray all had on different occasions served on this council.[37] Therefore, the implication is that in this council, missionary leaders were quite literally expected to randomly represent the *other* in mission.

An important step towards closer cooperation and perhaps trust building between missions occurred when the Livingstonia mission offered the DRC the opportunity to take over their operations at the Kasungu mission station. This was a controversial step, because there are strong indications that the locals opposed this proposed transferral (see below). Apparently, the DRC mission had already decided in 1900 to start work under chief Mwasi's people at Kasungu. Formerly Dr Laws was said to be of the opinion that Kasungu fell within the field of Livingstonia, but in this year their mission council decided to ask the DRC missionaries to take over work at that station due to the fact that the same dialect was spoken there as in the rest of the DRC mission field. DRC evangelist teachers were sent to start the work there, but when the case of the transferral of Kasungu was brought to the mission commission of the Free Church in Scotland, they refused to go along with the idea. The DRC had no choice but to recall their teachers. For the following two decades Kasungu continued to resort under Livingstonia, until the commission in Scotland came to the conclusion that the work belonged more properly to the DRC, with the effect that the station together with all its buildings was offered and accepted by the DRC synod and mission commission in 1923.[38] This was, perhaps not insignificantly, a year prior to the DRC's decision to allow its Nkhoma synod to join the CCAP.

As is so often the case, the indigenous voice is muted in the missionary literature discussed here, but indications of indigenous sentiment regarding these negotiations and how they themselves were being negotiated do present themselves here and there. A recent PhD thesis by Mapala highlights this subject of the discussions surrounding Kasungu in particular.[39] A. C. Murray's 1924 visit to Kasungu, shortly after the handover, uncovered that all was not rosy from the indigenous point of view. There were 'unique' troubles at the station. Murray did not specify exactly what, but he stated that this had to do with the people being used to the ways of Dr Prentice, who had operated there as sole missionary for many years. Now they had to get used to 'our South African methods'.[40] Murray wrote that the introduction of such 'methods' had to proceed with much caution, but perhaps this was easier said than done. In fact, McCracken points out that indigenous resistance to the takeover originated from alarm about 'the paternalistic attitudes of the Dutch and the low standards of education that prevailed in their schools'.[41]

There appears to have been a general lack of enthusiasm about the plan at every level of engagement. The Nkhoma mission council was also not immediately inclined to accept the offer due to lack of funds, primarily. However, they seemed to hope that their general mission commission would react favourably to the request, perhaps with a pledge of additional funds and personnel.[42] An issue of the *Koningsbode* in 1923 reported on a telegram that the mission commission had received from W. H. Murray, which conveyed the news that Livingstonia had again enquired regarding the DRC taking over not only Kasungu but also another station, Tamanda. Regarding the former, the commission's response was favourable, provided that the Nyasa sub-commission, that is, the Nkhoma missionaries, could negotiate to have it under the best conditions possible. Should money become an issue, they should first re-establish contact with their own synod's finance commission for guidance. Tamanda would be offered to the DRC in the Orange Free State as an option, if they could afford it. The response closed with the telling remark that Murray should make it clear to the Livingstonia mission that this commission, that is, the general mission commission of the Cape DRC, did not have the power to authorise its Nyasa mission to join up with the planned General Presbyterian Church in Nyasaland. Only the synod could make this decision.[43]

The minutes of the Nkhoma executive council provide detail about its deliberations in 1923, both regarding the Kasungu and Tamanda offers, and the possibility to be part of the CCAP, and who was responsible for the various negotiations. J. A. Retief of Nkhoma was the only name on both the commissions that would negotiate regarding Kasungu/Tamanda with Livingstonia, on the one hand, and with the presbyteries of Blantyre and Livingstonia as well as the DRC general mission commission regarding possibly joining the CCAP, on the other.[44]

'A New Spirit at Work'

It seems the spiritual depression resulting from the First World War did not last very long in the mission field. *Koningsbode* articles from 1922 struck an upbeat note, also with respect to the other in mission. There is for example a detailed article on recent revivals in Scotland. That this featured in a DRC mission journal perhaps illustrates the ongoing value and interest given by some Afrikaner mission enthusiasts to Scotland as a spiritual beacon. Particularly auspicious is the fact that this article is immediately followed, on the same page, by a short note from Nyasaland, with W. H. Murray now reporting: 'There is a new spirit at work among the people, a spirit of harmony, of interest in the religion . . . God's Spirit is at work . . .' [transl.].[45] One logical conclusion from such a juxtaposition of writings that one could make is that revival starting in Scotland had spilled over into the Nyasaland mission context to the blessing of all it encountered. The reason why this might be a logical deduction has much to do with Dr Donald Fraser.

Although the above article did not mention Fraser or indeed anyone by name for involvement in the Scottish revival, a Cape DRC general mission commission report of the following year mentioned the fact that Donald Fraser was in attendance at their meeting, on his way to the mission field. Fraser, the report states, had been on furlough in Scotland, during which time he was elected moderator of his church. According to the report, Fraser had undertaken an 'important and successful mission campaign in Scotland'. As a result, 150 young people had offered themselves to the mission field. It is likely that the charismatic Fraser was not only able to achieve such results in his own country, but that he was also able to soften hearts within the Cape DRC mission commission, enabling it to become steadily more amenable to the idea of greater ecumenicity in Nyasaland. He was given the opportunity to address the commission's meeting, where he assured it of the Free Church's appreciation for the work of the DRC Nyasa missionaries, especially their emphasis on the 'spiritual life'. Fraser spoke of the planned union between the Livingstonia and Blantyre missions, and expressed the strong hope that the Nkhoma mission would also join them in this venture.[46]

As indicated above, Fraser had a long-standing interest in South Africa and had earlier undertaken a 'South African Campaign', as a chapter title in Agnes Fraser's biography describes it.[47] Agnes Fraser relates the motivation for the campaign as follows:

> Fraser understood the difficulties and complications of the question of race relationships, and realised that the supreme task for South Africa was to work out to its solution the problem of a stable ethical civilisation. It had been suggested, when we passed through Capetown in 1919, that he might be able after his return to help the South African Churches to get a clearer view of the Christian responsibility and attitude . . .[48]

Agnes Fraser went on to write that the idea for the campaign was warmly received by all church leaders, except the Roman Catholics, of course, and that the other church leaders 'appointed a Day of Prayer' to prepare for it:

> Many apart from the Church welcomed the idea. General Smuts sent a message, telling of his interest and pleasure that they should have the guidance of an expert like Dr Fraser, coming to speak, with the authority and experience of a lifetime spent in African work, on the subject that most concerned the future of the country.[49]

Fraser and a colleague on the campaign, 'Arnold Bryson from China',[50] toured much of South Africa during this time. Apparently they were not equally enthusiastically received everywhere, with only sparse attendance at some of the churches where they spoke.[51] On one occasion, Fraser had to rebuke a group of students who had conducted all the affairs of a service in Afrikaans right up to the moment of his speaking. Fraser then told them that 'they had done their best to make him feel an 'Uitlander' by not enabling him to worship along with them. He spoke plainly about Church division and the absurdity of bringing their historic prejudices out to Africa.'[52]

The language issue was no small matter, as the following situation also indicates. It seems that a DRC in Johannesburg invited Fraser to preach at a regular Sunday service:

> [I]t was felt to be a matter of some moment, considering the state of racial feeling . . . Driving to the Dutch Reformed Church Fraser was told that he would, of course, be interpreted into Afrikaans, not, it was admitted, because they would fail to follow him in English, but

because of their sensitiveness about their own language. To his glad surprise when he entered the Session room, where the Kirk Raad were assembled, one of the old men announced that they had decided that he should speak without interpretation.[53]

Such contradictory discourses indicate an ongoing ideological tug of war between an affirmation of a shared evangelical Christian identity across linguistic and national barriers, on the one hand, and on the other, the growing imposition of an ethnic pride among the Afrikaner populace in the interwar period. Undoubtedly it was an increasingly sensitive time to attempt church unity with Scots missions in Nyasaland.

The CCAP and the 'Weakness of Some' Rebooted?

Nineteen twenty-four was the year in which this ecumenical venture would finally come to fruition. A conference for the purpose of church founding was held at Livingstonia, with the Blantyre and Nkhoma missions in attendance. A. C. Murray, pioneer missionary and contemporary editor of *De Koningsbode* and general mission secretary of the Cape DRC, travelled to Nyasaland for this momentous occasion. Most *De Koningsbode* issues of that year concerned Nyasaland and the new indigenous church there. Also seen among its pages is a running travelogue by A. C. Murray recounting his journey into Central Africa, which entailed a bout of illness (probably malaria)[54] and an overnight visit to Dr Hetherwick's manse at Blantyre.[55] The February issue of *De Koningsbode* contains an article authored by his cousin, W. H. Murray, wherein the latter recalls an inscription from A. C. Murray's 1895 diary. This concerns a leopard attack that A. C. Murray survived, which from a human point of view, according to W. H. Murray, would not have been possible were it not for the medical administrations of the Scottish Dr Prentice.[56] Was this incident perhaps recalled here to ramp up sentiments of gratitude and indebtedness towards the Free Church of Scotland and its mission? This is not unlikely given that both Murrays and the Nyasaland missionaries in general were strongly in favour of unification. It was their synod back in the Cape that had to be convinced.

Another ray of light regarding Scottish Afrikaner relations concerns the above-mentioned issue of Kasungu. A. C. Murray visited this station during his 1924 journey to Livingstonia and held a conference attended by 450 people. A *De Koningsbode* article reports extensively on various aspects of the newly acquired station, including the fact that the United Free Church of Scotland had donated the station and all its buildings free of charge to the DRC.[57] It seems the above-mentioned 'best possible' terms that the DRC mission commission wanted for the transfer had become reality.

An article by an anonymous DRC missionary on the way to the Livingstonia conference contains interesting opinions regarding the Universities' Mission at Likoma island on Lake Nyasa, which the DRC delegation visited. Particularly interesting are the views expressed regarding another colonial European other, the Portuguese. The author asserted that Africans preferred staying on this barren island rather than on the Portuguese-controlled mainland on the eastern side of the lake, in order to escape Portuguese injustices. Such injustices were the consequences of the fact that the Portuguese did not regard the 'kaffir as a person, but as a "thing"' [transl.].[58]

The Livingstonia conference was regarded as a success and experienced as very interesting by this unnamed missionary. The founding of the CCAP had taken place there, but whether 'our mission classis of Nkhoma' would participate still remained unclear and subject to the decision of the 'Mother Synod . . . Us missionaries in Nyasaland feel that it is highly desirable, and that it will be to the benefit of the great cause of the Lord in Nyasaland' [transl.].[59]

More details about what exactly had transpired at Livingstonia are presented among others in M. W. Retief's biographical account of W. H. Murray, and by DRC missionaries J. A. Retief, A. C. Murray and Robert Laws of Livingstonia. M. W. Retief, a nephew of J. A. Retief, was not a missionary, but an author and editor of missionary narratives. He served for a time as executive editor of the DRC mission journal, *Op die Horison*, and he was also an important policy shaper of DRC mission policy, which, as Richard Elphick most recently demonstrated, served as a blueprint for the emerging apartheid policy of the National Party in South Africa.[60] What makes this information important for the present discussion is that M. W. Retief made some extraordinary claims regarding events that transpired at the 1924 Livingstonia conference. It is furthermore significant, I think, that the following narrative is only recounted in the original Afrikaans version of his book on W. H. Murray, and not at all in the very slightly abridged English translation. Virtually every other aspect of the 1924 conference discussion is related in both versions, but not this following narrative, which I translate thus:

> During these negotiations something happened that nearly derailed the amalgamation of our church with the CCAP. Dr Laws arranged a room where whites and natives had to eat together. One of our representatives had not known about this arrangement. And when they were brought in for the meal, they found that the spaces along the table were so arranged that whites and natives had to sit next to each other. Dr [W. H.] Murray could not condone this. While he was eating he did not speak one word. Immediately afterwards he confronted Dr Donald Fraser and protested strongly against the communal meal. Dr Fraser said to him that he is not a consistent Christian, because the Bible says that we are all one. Dr Murray asked Dr Fraser if he would allow the marriage of his daughter to a native. Dr Fraser said: 'No.' Then Dr Murray said: 'Then you are not consistent either.' Dr Murray further said that if the Scots could not make a different arrangement

regarding meals, then our delegates are going home straight away. A different arrangement was consequently implemented.[61]

True to form for an apartheid apologist, M. W. Retief added to this a justifying perspective, which is also recounted but with less embellishment of content in A. C. Murray's diary, that 'the natives of our mission were also unhappy with the eating arrangement . . . They say they don't even eat together with their own chiefs, and how could they then eat with the white missionaries with their much higher standing than their chiefs?'[62]

M. W. Retief concludes his deliberations regarding this embarrassing episode by stating that if the Scots had not made the concession regarding the eating arrangements, the DRC amalgamation with the CCAP would in all probability have derailed. To this he adds: 'Here it might be said that the Scots have since realised their error, and that they no longer eat together with natives. They have also now accepted our standpoint on this issue.'[63]

This was written during a highly optimistic phase in Afrikaner politics and religiosity. Apartheid ideologues genuinely believed they could convince others of the reasonableness and desirability of non-equalisation. An interesting side-note is that most of the other published sources did not mention this sordid affair at all. Pauw, in his dissertation on DRC mission work in Malawi, mentioned it though,[64] and he referred to the diary entries of A. C. Murray as his source.

Back at Nkhoma, as they reviewed their experiences of the Livingstonia conference, A. C. Murray urged his fellow representatives not to make too much of this issue when writing home.[65] In all likelihood he had in mind the negative ramifications for negotiations with his church back in the Cape, and their possible rejection of the proposal based on racial prejudice and fear of Scottish mixing tendencies.

Although M. W. Retief did not cite any sources, it seems probable that he also relied on A. C. Murray's diary, but he had likely also been informed by oral sources, that is, his uncle J. A. Retief, and his biographical subject, W. H. Murray. A. C. Murray's diary does bear testimony not only to this incident, but also to a drawn-out series of often contentious negotiations during the Livingstonia conference. It mentions the 'commotion' among 'our missionaries' over the eating with Africans, which was discontinued after breakfast and lunch on 12 September.[66] That it really was a sticking point is evident from the next day's entry, when Murray relates how 'hot' the discussions had been at times when they were at Dr Laws' home to discuss church union. Part of the problem seemed to be that the terms of union had already been decided in advance. This put the ball in the DRC's court, but without much wiggle room for entering their own stipulations. Then follows this sentence, evidently highlighting the central sticking point: '[Livingstonia missionary] Mcalpine is much surprised when I tell him how strongly our men feel about the native ministers eating with us at the same table, thinks our position is unchristian.'[67]

DRC missionary J. A. Retief in his autobiography also described the 1924 meeting in detail, but without mentioning the specifics regarding this incident.[68] However, he did suggest that the DRC was able to negotiate the Scots away from their former policy directions, and towards the adoption of ones more in line with the DRC positions. He specifically mentioned African beer, the consumption of which was formerly allowed by Blantyre but subsequently halted, because both Nkhoma and Livingstonia were against it. Livingstonia, on the other hand, allowed children to be baptised when the mother was a Christian but the father not. The other two missions were against it. Subsequently, Livingstonia adapted its policy to be in line with the stricter views held by Nkhoma and Blantyre.[69] Thus the intimation seems to be that the DRC was the moderating force in the centre keeping everyone together, and all the while exercising a correcting influence on the divergent Scots and their somewhat strange ideas.

This is not at all how these relationships were described by the Scottish sources, of course. From reading Laws and the biography of Hetherwick, it rather seems that Nkhoma was more of an afterthought to what was essentially a negotiated settlement between the two Scottish missions. Regarding negotiations with the DRC representatives, including the ultimately unsuccessful talks with the Orange Free State DRC's mission in Northern Rhodesia, Laws mentions the following:

> Both of these churches approached the Church of Africa Presbyterian [sic] with a view to further union. The [DRC of the Cape] made certain stipulations with regard to training their own native ministers and teachers: these were agreed to. The [DRC of the Orange Free State], however, raised points which, if conceded, would have given them the right to dictate the policy of the Missions of our Scottish Churches.[70]

The Free State DRC's stand could of course not be agreed to. Hence, *Madzi Moyo*, as the DRC mission in Northern Rhodesia was known, under the control of the Free State synod, did not become part of the CCAP, to the disappointment of many.[71] Laws did not specify what the contents of the policy demands might have been, but DRC sources elaborated on the topic. There was a specific fear inherent in DRC circles, even more deeply felt in the conservative Free State, but nonetheless a dominant factor also in the Cape. This was the so-called threat of modernism, which some believed to be a contaminating theological influence in certain Scottish Presbyterian circles. A. C. Murray wrote to Laws:

> There is another question which may arise, and that is, whether there will be any guarantees that modernist teaching will not be allowed in the Central African Church. As you know, our standpoint with regard to the Inspiration, the Virgin Birth, and other doctrines regarding our Lord, is a conservative one, and if there is any danger of the Central

African Church being open to teaching which conflicts with these views there will be difficulty.[72]

It seems Laws was able to placate Murray's fears by emphasising the importance and usefulness of 'a simple statement of faith' within the Malawian context over against an unproductive insistence on confessional adherence.[73] This does not attest to any kind of 'modernism' on Laws' part, but rather about what he considered to be fit, proper and necessary for the indigenous church to be founded, and he was primarily driven by pragmatic rather than doctrinal considerations. To quote from Livingstone's biography of Laws: 'The creed of any future Presbyterian Church of Africa, he maintained, should be of the simplest nature and divested of all European elements not consonant with the needs of the natives.'[74]

Murray and the DRC negotiators were eventually prepared to accept this statement, a decision that would create some difficulty in later years. Laws was no doubt a convincing negotiator. J. A. Retief mentions how during one instance of particularly difficult talks during the 1924 conference, Laws led everyone in an impromptu prayer session, which smoothed the way for further discussion to proceed.[75] One might suggest that in addition to testifying to the personal piety of Laws, the act of apparent spontaneous praying at the Livingstonia conference might also have served as a shrewd diplomatic move on his part.

Despite differences of opinion regarding the protocol of relations with Africans, Donald Fraser seems to have been overall sympathetic to the Boers, as indicated above. Apart from any warmth he might have felt towards the DRC missionaries, his sympathetic attitude could partly be explained by his distrust of denominationalism. Agnes Fraser wrote: 'When the three Presbyteries of the Livingstonia, Blantyre and Dutch Reformed Missions joined to form "The Church of Christ (Presbyterian) in Central Africa", Fraser was only partially satisfied. He would have omitted "Presbyterian" . . .'[76] This did not actually have anything to do with accommodating the DRC specifically, since Fraser might have considered them as fellow Presbyterians in any case, even if not in name. Rather, the idea of omitting 'Presbyterian' from the new church's name was in view of a hoped for still greater ecumenicity involving other Protestant missions in the region. Ironically, such greater ecumenicity and the dropping of the term 'Presbyterian' would have made DRC participation in this indigenous church all but impossible. Although not officially part of the Presbyterian tradition, but rather Dutch Calvinist, once they joined the CCAP, the term Presbyterian with its connotations to Reformed identity might have become dearer to the DRC missionaries than it might have been even to their Scots colleagues (more on this below).

At the end of 1925, W. H. Murray could report to the members of the Nkhoma executive committee that their 'Mother', the Cape DRC synod, had given its approval for all congregations belonging to the Nkhoma mission council to join the congregations of the Livingstonia and Blantyre missions in a Central African Indigenous Church.[77] Being on furlough in the Cape at the time, J. A. Retief, who had served on the commission that negotiated the merger with the Scottish missions and the DRC general mission commission, was able to attend the 1924 synod in order to make the case for this ecumenical venture. Following much doctrinal handwringing, the DRC synod had indeed come to the above decision, but it was a decision that carried with it the provision, or threat, that they could at any point withdraw from the amalgamation if their general mission commission (GMC) was no longer satisfied with the arrangement.[78] Such a conditional decision, followed by the difficulties thereafter, which I shall elaborate on below, I think helps to explain the self-censorship DRC missionaries seemed to exhibit regarding their reporting on the 1924 Livingstonia conference, with their conspicuous silence surrounding the mixed-eating incident. Not one of the DRC missionaries who published books about their experiences mentioned it during a period of history when apartheid was becoming increasingly entrenched as normative and eventually enshrined in South African law.

What is furthermore significant is the commentary by Pauw about the above condition relating to the GMC.[79] Pauw makes the case that the CCAP was never fully aware of the stated condition of withdrawal inserted by the DRC synod. Pauw states that it was in fact in conflict with the terms of union, which did not allow for an outside body to potentially jeopardise church unity after it had occurred, except if the agreed-upon terms of union themselves were changed. As it turns out, the DRC synod of 1945 did indeed seek to enforce this condition in order to break away from the CCAP, a move described by senior Nkhoma missionary J. A. Retief as 'illegal' and 'unchristian', among other things (see below). The fact that such an attempt was made could be ascribed to a strengthening of Afrikaner nationalist sentiments within Cape DRC circles during these years, as well as a doctrinal hardening against the perceived threat of theological modernism. This hard-line spirit particularly showed its hand in the 1930 expulsion from the theological seminary of Stellenbosch of a former general mission secretary of the DRC, Prof. Johannes du Plessis, who was a close friend of W. H. Murray and the Nkhoma mission in Nyasaland, and someone with a 'predilection for Scottish theology'.[80] In these controversies the perceived liberalism of the Scots Presbyterians in Central Africa and their influence on the DRC missions was a serious bone of contention.

Before moving on to the next section, let me briefly note the irony of the above-mentioned 'mixed-eating' incident, and the way in which the DRC missionaries such as W. H. and A. C. Murray, both grandchildren of Andrew Murray Sr, had to be accommodated in their proverbial 'weakness' by the Africans and Scots comprising the other parties in this church union. The pragmatic mission strategy underpinning the 1857 decision to accommodate the 'weakness of some' resurfaced in full force, only this time the spiritual and physical Scots Afrikaner descendants of the original architects of racist accommodation were the ones who in this instance had to be accommodated themselves. Once more, Scots missionaries were the primary if protesting enablers of racist accommodation. I shall return to this theme in the concluding chapter.

Afrikaner Opposition to the Ecumenical Project

De Koningsbode reported the contents of a private letter from Nyasaland in 1919 in which an anonymous author lamented the state of the missionary enterprise. Church and school buildings had been destroyed in many places, and the spiritual condition of the converts reflected the dilapidated state of the buildings. This was a common complaint in the missionary literature during and shortly after the First World War. Apparently there was a strong resurgence of pre-Christian ways, interpreted as backsliding by discouraged missionaries, as a 1920 report by W. H. Murray also makes clear.[81] The above-mentioned letter did not go into any such details, but it still paints a picture of doom and gloom that could only be alleviated by renewed prayer. Interestingly, the letter closes with the question of who or what was to blame for the poor current state of affairs, and then answers this with a counter question: 'Does the blame not lie with the mother church in its coldness and powerlessness?'[82]

That many people in the DRC mother church were not exactly enthralled by the existence of their foreign missionary enterprise by this stage in Afrikaner history is indeed a fact. In the first decades of the twentieth century, the so-called poor white question would influence politics and public discourse in various ways. It would over time become an important factor in the rise of Afrikaner nationalism. There were many causes for the phenomenon of poor whites in urban and rural areas. Industrialisation and an increasingly skilled African workforce certainly played a role, and for this reason the theme of poor whites was often tied in with white nationalist, anti-black sentiment.

It is also evident from different writings that there was a tendency to cast suspicion on mission enthusiasts for being unduly concerned with black lives; and for possibly neglecting the needs of their so-called 'own' people, that is, those of similar language and skin tone. Mission enthusiasts of course rejected such polarisation between the two themes. Johannes du Plessis was one outspoken critic of this as a false dichotomy, and he contradicted no less a figure than Jan Smuts in 1917 for having, falsely according to du Plessis, argued that the DRC did nothing for the poor whites.[83] In the same year another mission advocate, Revd J. R. Albertyn, made a very similar yet more concise sort of argument to that of du Plessis in *De Koningsbode*. Albertyn effectively deconstructed the legitimacy of any comparison between the two themes of mission to black Africans and concern for white poverty, stating that unlike the millions of (black) heathens, poor whites had been relatively well taken care of. Moreover, the poor white's need was not a spiritual need for the gospel, but merely improved education and the development of a self-respecting work ethic.[84] One could imagine that these sentiments would not have gone down well with the propagators of Afrikaner victimhood narratives.

Crude racism, of the non-accommodating kind, was ever-present among sectors of the Afrikaner population. This was often the real driving factor behind anti-missionary sentiment. In a 1921 *De Koningsbode* article intended for a young readership, the theme of racism is directly addressed. The article, entitled 'Het 'n Kaffer 'n siel?' (Does a Kaffir have a soul?), seeks to debunk what was a common assertion among contemporary Afrikaners, that is, that unlike whites, the black person was not in possession of a soul that could be saved. Hence, missionary work was a waste of time and resources. The author, the principal of an orphanage and a brother of A. F. Louw and A. A. Louw of Môrgenster, first sets out to educate his readers about the derogatory nature of the term 'kaffir', and then goes on to narrate a true-life story of how a supposedly soulless black person from his brother's mission station in Mashonaland had donated money to his own orphanage where children from white Afrikaner families, ascribing to exactly such crudely racist views, resided. Having aired already one generally unpopular opinion among an Afrikaans audience, the author also took the opportunity to criticise, or at least question, the legitimacy of different salary scales for different racial groups, as enshrined in contemporary legislation.[85]

This article predictably led to an objection from at least one correspondent, to which the editor of *De Koningsbode* wrote a short yet accommodating response, which affirmed the generally accepted DRC missionary theory that blacks were at a lower level of development and morality compared to whites who originated from numerous past generations of Christian ancestry. The subtext thus fully subscribed to the view that Christianity and 'civilisation' were inexorably tied to one another, with the former predicting the course of the latter. However, the editor also affirmed the original article's main contention that no distinction was to be made between the value of souls belonging to either white or black people, and that blacks could and often did attain higher states of spiritual development than their white counterparts.[86]

Challenging though general anti-missionary sentiment in the DRC undoubtedly was to Scottish Afrikaner relations in Central Africa, a far more serious threat to the ecumenical project in Nyasaland arose when an influential missionary insider from the Orange Free State (OFS) began to discredit the CCAP's foundations and to object to the desirability of DRC participation in it. Pauw mentions the role of the controversial mission secretary of the DRC in the OFS, J. G. Strydom. This controversy is related to an ongoing tussle between the missionaries in Northern Rhodesia who wanted their mission of *Madzi Moyo* to join the CCAP, on the one hand,

and their sending church, on the other, which resisted this initiative. Such a proposal was served at the 1928 Free State synod, where it was initially approved. However, the synod subsequently took the unusual step of appointing a delegation led by Strydom to further investigate missionary conditions in Northern Rhodesia and Nyasaland.[87]

Strydom, a former missionary to contemporary Nigeria, was a staunch Afrikaner nationalist and a biblical fundamentalist. He did perhaps more than anyone to implement a mission policy based on strict segregationist principles, which would over time come to influence the National Party's political programme of apartheid. It was under this policy that the National Party was victorious in the general elections of 1948.[88] Two decades prior to this development, Strydom's 1928 visit to Central Africa served to convince him beyond a shadow of a doubt of the horrors of ecumenical cooperation on the mission field:

> So perturbed was he by what he observed concerning the theologically liberal views held by Scottish missionaries that the delegation upon its return requested the OFS Synodical Committee to suspend the decision of the 1928 Synod and submit the matter once again to the next Synod which was due to meet in 1931.[89]

Pauw furthermore points out that in addition to doctrinal concerns, Strydom had a strong aversion to the cultural otherness of English-speaking missions and their ways. When one compares such views with the personal closeness between Nyasaland missionaries such as the Murrays and their Scottish counterparts, as well as taking into consideration the supposedly Scottish-leaning theological views of Strydom's antagonist in chief, the former Cape mission secretary and Stellenbosch theology professor, Johannes du Plessis, it becomes very clear why the Nkhoma affiliation to the CCAP was deeply suspect to Strydom and those of his ilk.[90]

Strydom's was no lone Christian nationalist voice crying out in the proverbial wilderness. He had plenty of support among the Afrikaner community. One may point to the example of an anti-CCAP salvo that was fired by C. F. Kies, a former missionary to Zambia and supporter of Strydom. This occurred during Kies' inaugural address as professor at the Missionary Institute in Wellington in 1933. Kies used the occasion to lambast the 'so-called' CCAP for being basically entirely Scottish in character, and for bearing virtually 'no trace of any qualities of the DRC'.[91] This critique drew strongly worded responses from senior Nkhoma missionaries W. H. Murray and J. A. Retief.[92] Yet suspicion had by now been sown widely about Nkhoma and the CCAP, even in the Boland area of Wellington, which was very much in the nerve centre of the Cape DRC.

This growing tension and even antagonism came especially to the fore in a series of *Kerkbode* articles and rebuttals involving Strydom and J. A. Retief in 1940. As already seen with the above-described mixed-eating incident, the DRC missionaries, and J. A. Retief was no exception, were always careful to express themselves as in agreement with their home church's mission policy. This policy continued to emphasise the theme of *geen gelykstelling* (no equalisation), which effectively meant no social mixing between whites and blacks. This had already nearly derailed the Nkhoma synod's amalgamation with the CCAP, and, if anything, the policy had hardened by 1940. In the *Kerkbode* debate between Retief and Strydom, this issue arose, as did the theme of modernism.

The controversy was unwittingly initiated with an article by Retief explaining the relationship between church and mission, in which the author strongly emphasised the positive aspects of the church union in Nyasaland. Herein he relied among other things on the previously mentioned argument of the supposedly positive ways in which the DRC missionaries were influencing their Scottish partners, specifically regarding questions of African beer drinking and baptismal requirements.[93] Strydom responded with an article that attacked every argument advanced by Retief, and fundamentally made the claim that while the DRC, on the one hand, was a Calvinistic and Reformed church, the Scottish missionaries, on the other, were increasingly modernist freethinkers. Strydom, rhetorically, asked what had evidently been for him the fundamental question: 'How could an orthodox Church or Mission unite itself with a liberal church?'[94] He furthermore spelled out the above-mentioned mission policy of the DRC, which was strictly one of '*total social apartheid* between whites and coloured races of Africa' [transl.; his italics]. The Scots had the 'absolute opposite policy'.[95]

Retief responded with a rebuttal in which he defended the orthodoxy of the Scots. As supporting evidence, he mentioned the participation of a couple of conservative DRC representatives at joint conferences involving the Scots, for example, the 1924 Livingstonia conference where D. G. Malan (later professor) was present. Malan was a key opponent of the above-mentioned Johannes du Plessis, whose heresy trial raged in South Africa during the mid- to late 1920s. Yet, Retief pointed out, Malan was in favour of union with the CCAP and had never made any criticism of Scottish so-called liberalism.[96]

Regarding equalisation, Retief argued rather counterintuitively that the Scots were coming around to the DRC point of view of refraining from social mixing. As evidence of this, he gave the example of his own attendance at a recent synod meeting in Blantyre where he had spent a week among the Scots, and there he found no sign of social mixing. '*Here* we cannot accuse them of equalisation', he asserts. If there had been tendencies in this direction in the earlier days of the Scottish missions, this was no longer the case, 'partly as a result of our influence'.[97]

It seems that notwithstanding Retief's apologia regarding Scottish orthodoxy and non-equalising tendencies, the detractors remained unconvinced. In fact, a serious attack was launched against ecumenicity during the 1945 synod of the DRC,[98] which drew a blistering response from Retief in the form of an unpublished essay, found in the DRC archive in Stellenbosch. This concerned a motion introduced by Revd J. F. Mentz, who was according to Pauw a strong supporter of the Free State's Strydom, which was subsequently adopted by the synod.[99] According to Retief's missive, the synodical decision effectively demanded that the CCAP should institute a change in its Statement of Faith; if this was not complied with, then the Nkhoma missionaries had to withdraw from the church.[100] Retief called the directive, which demanded the CCAP's subscription to an explicit statement affirming that the Bible *is* the Word of God rather than that it *contained* the Word of God, not only illegal, because it amounted to the breaking of a contract, but also unchristian because it sought to initiate a schism in a church that was established without a doubt in the spirit of Christ. He recalled that moment at Livingstonia in 1924 when talks for unification had hit an impasse, and when Dr Laws had halted proceedings in order to pray to God for guidance. Retief related how a light then went up for everyone, how the tensions eased out and the path towards union became passable. Was this not under the guidance of the Lord, as they had all so keenly felt it at the time? Now they were confronted with this plan of the DRC synod, which Retief compared to a 'vicious bomb' that was aimed at destroying this beautiful church.

Here, then, we have the interesting, almost ironic, reversal of sorts of a DRC missionary, who was among those that had been called out by the Scots for their unchristian refusal to eat with black colleagues in 1924 at Livingstonia, now calling his own sending church unchristian for seeking to destroy the church which had been formed on the foundations of those rocky beginnings. The implication seems to be that the DRC had by now become more *other* to this Afrikaner missionary than either the Scots or the indigenous Malawians in the CCAP.

Fortunately for the Nkhoma missionaries, the bomb button was never pushed from the side of the DRC synod. Furthermore, the pragmatically diplomatic spirit prevailed in the CCAP. The Blantyre and Livingstonia synods of the CCAP subsequently all but bent over backwards to accommodate Nkhoma with an amendment to the Statement of Faith. Nkhoma missionaries of course remained under DRC jurisdiction, even if the church they served in Malawi paradoxically was not.[101]

In the increasingly *volk*-centred, nationalist and parochial religious climate of Afrikanerdom, the thorny issue of the DRC's participation in the CCAP, which was an anomaly from the beginning, became not so much resolved as marginalised within the broader DRC culture in South Africa. Nonetheless, the experiment with the Scots and the Malawians in the CCAP remained in place, if precariously so. Perhaps this narrative of Nkhoma's participation in the CCAP, problematic though it is on so many levels, should be read as a kind of virtual historical monument symbolising an alternative reality for the DRC and perhaps South Africa. That is, if one could imagine an alternative history where the ecumenical spirit, rather than the parochial nationalist elements in the DRC, had the upper hand around the middle of the twentieth century.

Conclusion

The early twentieth century was a critical moment in the formation of Afrikaner nationalism. The remembered tragedy of the turn-of-the-century war became useful ideological fodder for stoking this fire in which anti-British sentiment was rife. The DRC's participation in the CCAP was ultimately out of step with the developing Afrikaner culture and its ideological underpinnings. As this new reality became more mainstream, it was not only ecumenical endeavours on the mission field that became suspect. The hybrid identity of the Scots Afrikaners was itself identified as a contaminating influence in a hardened perspective of what it was supposed to mean to be an Afrikaner and a Calvinist. Chapter 7 will trace this narrative of growing suspicion as the Scottish legacy became problematic in Afrikaner history.

Notes

1. See, for example, John M. MacKenzie and Nigel R. Dalziel (2007) *The Scots in South Africa: Ethnicity, identity, gender and race, 1772–1914*. Oxford: Manchester University Press, p. 17.
2. 'Onze Kerk en de Scotsche Kerken', *De Vereeniging* (7 October 1903), p. 5.
3. Ibid.
4. See letter by Robert Murray's cousin, Haldane Murray, to Robert's mother (3 May 1902). DRC Archive, Stellenbosch.
5. Robert Murray to Willie Murray (18 January 1902). DRC Archive, Stellenbosch.
6. 'De Kerk en de Bijbel op Commando', *De Vereeniging* (7 October 1903), p. 7.
7. A. C. Murray (1931) *Ons Nyasa-Akker: geskiedenis van die Nyasa sending van die Nederd. Geref. Kerk in Suid-Afrika*. Stellenbosch: Pro Ecclesia, p. 130.
8. Stephen Leacock (1910) 'The Union of South Africa', *American Political Science Review*, 4:4, pp. 498–507.
9. *De Koningsbode* (January 1911), p. 156.
10. Murray, *Ons Nyasa-Akker*, p. 205.
11. See David Brown Lowry (1951) 'Luther D. Wishard (1854–1925): Pioneer of the Student Christian Movement (1877–1888)'. Princeton University senior thesis, http://arks.princeton.edu/ark:/88435/dsp018910jv758.
12. J. A. Retief (1951) *Ontdekkings in Middle-Afrika*. Stellenbosch: C. S. V., p. 11.
13. Agnes R. Fraser (1934) *Donald Fraser of Livingstonia*. London: Hodder and Stoughton, p. 39.
14. Ibid., p. 78.
15. *De Kerkbode* (6 October 1910), pp. 219–20.
16. Fraser, *Donald Fraser of Livingstonia*, pp. 206–11.
17. Ibid., p. 207.
18. Murray, *Ons Nyasa-Akker*, pp. 210–11.
19. Ibid., p. 211.
20. Donald Fraser (12 April 1913) 'Boers and Missions', *The Glasgow Herald*.

21. Ibid.
22. Ibid.
23. Ibid.
24. *De Koningsbode* (January 1911), p. 157.
25. *De Kerkbode* (29 September 1910), p. 207.
26. Ibid.
27. Ibid.
28. John McCracken (1977) *Politics and Christianity in Malawi 1875–1940: The Impact of the Livingstonia Mission in the Northern Province*. Cambridge: Cambridge University Press, p. 247.
29. Malcolm Wilhelm Retief (1948) *Verowerings Vir Christus*. Stellenbosch: C. S. V. Boekhandel, p. 231.
30. See W. H. Murray (9 March 1895) 'To Father – Mvera'. DRC Archive, Stellenbosch, k-div 1144.
31. W. P. Livingstone (1931) *A Prince of Missionaries: The Rev. Alexander Hetherwick C.B.E, D.D., M.A. of Blantyre, Central Africa*. London: James Clarke, pp. 156–9.
32. Ibid., pp. 183–4.
33. See *De Koningsbode* (November–December 1917), p. 218.
34. *De Koningsbode* (January 1918), p. 11.
35. Retief, *Verowerings*, p. 232.
36. Ibid.
37. Murray, *Ons Nyasa-Akker*, p. 36.
38. Ibid., pp. 135–6.
39. C. W. Mapala (2016) 'Ethnicity and Christianity: A Historical Study of the Border Dispute Between the Livingstonia and Nkhoma Synods of the Church of Central Africa Presbyterian'. PhD thesis, University of Kwazulu-Natal, Pietermaritzburg.
40. *De Koningsbode* (October 1924), p. 235.
41. McCracken, *Politics and Christianity in Malawi*, p. 230.
42. *De Koningsbode* (March 1922), p. 53.
43. *De Koningsbode* (October 1923), p. 257.
44. *Die 43ste Vergadering van die Uitvoerende Raad van die Ned. Geref. Kerk Sending na Midde Afrika, gehou te Mkhoma, vanaf 17 tot 25 September, 1923* (1923), p. 313. DRC Archive, Stellenbosch.
45. *De Koningsbode* (April 1922), p. 72.
46. *De Koningsbode* (October 1923), p. 257.
47. Fraser, *Donald Fraser of Livingstonia*, pp. 258–66.
48. Ibid., p. 258.
49. Ibid., p. 259.
50. Ibid., p. 260.
51. Ibid., p. 262.
52. Ibid., p. 260.
53. Ibid., p. 264.
54. *De Koningsbode* (September 1924), p. 205.
55. *De Koningsbode* (August 1924), p. 186.
56. *De Koningsbode* (February 1924), p. 7.
57. *De Koningsbode* (October 1924), p. 235.
58. *De Koningsbode* (November–December 1924), p. 362.

59. Ibid., p. 363.
60. Richard Elphick (2012) *The Equality of Believers: Protestant Missionaries and the Racial Politics of South Africa*. Charlottesville, VA: University of Virginia Press, pp. 222–37.
61. Retief, *Verowerings*, p. 234.
62. Ibid.
63. Ibid.
64. C. M. Pauw (1980) 'Mission and Church in Malawi: The History of the Nkhoma Synod of the Church of Central Africa, Presbyterian', DTh thesis, University of Stellenbosch, p. 274.
65. A. C. Murray diary (24 September 1924) DRC Archive, Stellenbosch.
66. A. C. Murray diary (12 September 1924) DRC Archive, Stellenbosch.
67. A. C. Murray diary (13 September 1924) DRC Archive, Stellenbosch.
68. J. A. Retief did mention an unnamed stumbling block that nearly jeopardised the proceedings. He also seems to indicate that Revd (later Prof.) D. G. Malan, 'who was conservative in his views', was among the delegates and played a leading role in the negotiations. This is mentioned just prior to the comment about the unnamed trouble, interestingly (Retief, *Ontdekkings*, p. 199). Even more interestingly, he elsewhere provides an anecdote that seems to indicate a much more common culture of social equalisation in the Nyasa mission field compared to the state of affairs in South Africa. In a section on the different types of socialisation that mission children were acculturated to, often with supposedly humorous consequences, he mentions an incident where he and his family visited friends in Pretoria. His young son, Hoffie, upon finding a black servant eating alone in the kitchen, was deeply perturbed by the sight, asking 'Father, why is that Uncle eating in the kitchen?' (Retief, *Ontdekkings*, p. 160).
69. Retief, *Ontdekkings*, p. 205.
70. Robert Laws (1934) *Reminiscences of Livingstonia*. Edinburgh: Oliver and Boyd, p. 144.
71. Retief, *Verowerings*, p. 244.
72. A. C. Murray to R. Laws, as quoted in Pauw, 'Mission and Church in Malawi', p. 274. From P. Bolink (1967) *Towards Church union in Zambia: A study of missionary co-operation and church-union efforts in Central-Africa*. Franeker: T. Wever, pp. 197–9.
73. R. Laws quoted in Pauw, 'Mission and Church in Malawi', p. 274. From Bolink, *Towards Church union in Zambia*.
74. W. P. Livingstone (1921) *Laws of Livingstonia: A Narrative of Missionary Adventure and Achievement*. London: Hodder and Stoughton, p. 308.
75. Retief, *Ontdekkings*, pp. 199–200.
76. Fraser, *Donald Fraser of Livingstonia*, p. 167.
77. *Die 45ste Vergadering van die Uitvoerende Raad van die Ned. Ger. Kerk Sending na Midde Afrika, gehou te Mkhoma, vanaf 25 Nov. tot 4 Desember, 1925* (1925), p. 345. DRC Archive, Stellenbosch.
78. Ned. Geref. Kerk Synod Acta (1924), pp. 31–2. DRC Archive, Stellenbosch.
79. See Pauw, 'Mission and Church in Malawi', pp. 278–80.
80. Ibid., p. 280.
81. 'Jaarverslag N.G. Kerk, Zending, Nyasaland, 1920', *De Koningsbode* (June 1921), pp. 109–10.

82. *De Koningsbode* (September 1919), p. 172.
83. J. du Plessis (1917) *De Arme Blanke en de Heiden-Zending*. Kaapstad: Z. A. Bijbel Vereeniging, p. 8.
84. *De Koningsbode* (February 1917), p. 28.
85. *De Koningsbode* (August 1921), pp. 167–8.
86. *De Koningsbode* (October 1921), p. 203.
87. Pauw, 'Mission and Church in Malawi', p. 280.
88. See Elphick, *The Equality of Believers*, p. 226ff.
89. Pauw, 'Mission and Church in Malawi', p. 280.
90. Ibid.
91. Pauw, 'Mission and Church in Malawi', p. 341; see *Die Gereformeerde Vaandel* (June 1933), pp. 227–31.
92. J. A. Retief (12 August 1933), 'Die Kerk van Midde-Afrika: 'n Skewe Voorstelling', *Die Kerkbode*, pp. 200–1.
93. *Die Kerkbode* (10 July 1940), pp. 66–9.
94. *Die Kerkbode* (7 August 1940), p. 240.
95. Ibid.
96. *Die Kerkbode* (25 September 1940), p. 566.
97. Ibid., p. 567.
98. See Pauw, 'Mission and Church in Malawi', pp. 278–9.
99. Ibid., p. 348.
100. J. A. Retief (8 February 1946) Kaapstad. Unpublished letter. DR Church Archive, Stellenbosch.
101. See Pauw, 'Mission and Church in Malawi', p. 346ff.

CHAPTER SEVEN

Afrikaner *Volkskerk* Ideologues and the Scots Afrikaners

As the twentieth century progressed, variegated and mounting challenges were posed to the endurance of the Scottish legacy in the DRC and Afrikanerdom more generally. This chapter constructs a narrative in illumination of this theme in reference to selected texts and episodes from the late nineteenth to the mid-twentieth century. In *The Equality of Believers*, Richard Elphick shows how apartheid was 'invented' by evangelical mission enthusiasts in the DRC before the programme became adopted and fine-tuned by a subsequent generation of neo-Calvinists.[1] Although this is indeed a convincing narrative, there is another way in which that story could be told. This is through the lens of a progressive loss of influence of an irenic Scottish ecumenical and evangelical tradition to an Afrikaner nationalistic religiosity. Afrikaner Christian nationalism initially received inspiration from elements of the older evangelicalism, but this was soon overshadowed by explicitly ethnocentric ideas. This occurred in the milieu of a developing Afrikaner identity formation for which church and theology provided a ready if defective moral compass.

Although the term 'Scottish–Afrikaner hybridity' might, from the outside, be usefully employed as an interpretive lens for the trials and travails of the Murrays and other Scottish descendants in South African religious history, there is a basic and serious problem with the term. This is the fact that Afrikanerdom, as conceived through the Afrikaner nationalism of the early twentieth century, had an abhorrence of any kind of mixing. Of course, the most problematic mixing pertained particularly to occurrences across the so-called colour line, but even intimate relations, including marriages, between white Afrikaners and white so-called 'English' people were suspect in the eyes of nationalists. Such ethnocentric exclusivism was of course not unique to South Africa, but the point I wish to make here is that while hybridity, though not described as such of course, was certainly a possibility, even a necessity from the Scottish side in the encounter, from the Afrikaner side there was, for a time at least, much resistance to what might have been seen as imperialism under a different guise.

Andrew Murray and his biographer, Johannes du Plessis, were important figures in this narrative as representatives of the maligned Scottish legacy, as were Afrikaner nationalist figures like D. F. Malan and the father-and-son pair of S. J. and J. D. du Toit, who in different yet complementary ways represented the opposition.

Let me acknowledge that a division of these characters into two opposing camps is a precariously constructed contrast in many ways. Stark binary divisions of historical figures often hide more than they reveal. As Brian Stanley writes in the introduction to *Missions, Nationalism, and the End of Empire*: 'The local and the universal, the national and the international, are hence more often to be found in ambiguous and subtle combination than in simple binary opposition.'[2] Moreover, among the figures I am discussing, J. D. du Toit (Totius) never belonged to the DRC, but to the smaller Gereformeerde Kerke in Suid Afrika (GKSA), the so-called *Doppers*. Nevertheless, there were streams of influence and schools of thought in Afrikanerdom. The discourses of nationalism and ethnocentricity were coloured by various shades of racism. The particular feature that this chapter wishes to highlight is that the more overtly nationalist Afrikaner Christian intellectuals, in addition to being generally xenophobic, developed a distinctly anti-Scottish, anti-Murray bias, which would over time prove to be quite convincing to the mainstream of Afrikaner theological discourse.

Andrew Murray, who 'Poisons the Wells with his English Poison'

This chapter is set within the context of a Scottish legacy, as particularly personified by Andrew Murray Jr, which became steadily more unpopular as the rising tide of Afrikaner nationalism grew and reached its crescendo by sweeping apartheid ideologues into power in different sectors of society in 1948 and beyond. So this is primarily a twentieth-century narrative. However, strong resistance to and suspicion of Murray et al. was already evident in the later nineteenth century, and not only from the side of the so-called 'liberals' in the DRC. In Chapter 2 I mentioned Murray's deeply controversial, not to mention unsuccessful, attempt to halt Britain's relinquishment of the Orange River Sovereignty. That planted the seed of suspicion against his loyalty to the Afrikaner people, a suspicion which was somewhat alleviated by his subsequently pro-Boer stance during the South African War. However, once tainted by anti-nationalist, anti-republican sentiments, Afrikaner South Africa in the twentieth century was not the easiest place to shake off the distrust of one's detractors. Therefore it is important to begin this part of the discussion by pointing to a particularly virulent volley of attacks that came early in 1893, when *Di Afrikaanse Patriot*, a journal started by Totius' father S. J. du Toit, published a couple of rather defamatory articles about Murray. S. J.'s older brother, D. F. du Toit ('Oom Lokomotief'), was officially the editor, although Giliomee, for example, makes it clear that S. J. du Toit was the real driving force behind the paper.[3]

The titles of the two articles say it all in a way, being respectively entitled, according to my translation, *Rev. A. Murray the greatest enemy of our nationality* and *Rev. A. Murray the greatest enemy of our reformed doctrine*. The author of these articles was given under the pseudonym of *Streng Gereformeerde Patriot* (Strictly Reformed Patriot). According to Johannes du Plessis, whose commentary on these articles features below, the author was none other than the editor, S. J. du Toit, journalist, theologian, *taalstryder* (promoter of the Afrikaans language) and political figure of note, especially for his role in the early nationalist *Genootskap vir Regte Afrikaners* (Society for Real Afrikaners).[4] He and his son, Totius, represent excellent contrasting cases to the Scots Afrikaners within broader Afrikanerdom. First, a bit of background on S. J. du Toit and his contentious relationship with the Cape DRC,[5] which had been a long time coming, as Hermann Giliomee explains in relation to du Toit's newspaper:

> The church hierarchy watched the *Patriot* with growing concern. For many, du Toit had been a thorn in the flesh; he opposed many things for which the Reformed Church stood: revivals, special prayer meetings, English in schools, meek submission to the colonial and imperial government, and, in a pamphlet on the prophecies of the apocalypse, he criticized certain aspects of the church itself. Now he was openly encouraging resistance in the Transvaal to the God-given authorities. The 1880 Cape synod discussed the paper over three days, one speaker after the other denouncing its 'pernicious' influence as casting suspicion on the government, the church, and its office bearers. Du Toit defended himself and the paper at the synod, but the die was cast. In a vote of 114 to 2 the synod condemned the paper.[6]

In the later attacks against Murray, Strictly Reformed Patriot (SRP) started off by writing that although Mr Murray was a man of much talent and drive, he had not been using these qualities to build up but rather to destroy 'our nationality', and to undermine 'our pure Reformed doctrine'. SRP further alleged that Murray had attempted to undermine Afrikaner nationalism in various structures, first in the state, then in the church, then in the school, and finally in the family unit. 'Thus he ever approached with finer deviousness, until he now arrived at the source itself, to poison it with his English poison' [transl.].[7]

SRP argued that Murray was able to exert such influence because he was considered by many to be infallible, even more infallible than the Pope in the Roman Catholic Church. The latter is considered infallible due to his office, but Murray was considered infallible in his *person*. Hence, SRP foresaw that there would be strong opposition to his writing of these notes of detraction. As could perhaps be expected, the first evidence SRP brought forth about Murray's English (note not Scottish or British) leanings concerns the previously mentioned plea (see Chapter 2) to the imperial government to keep control of the Orange River Sovereignty. SRP rejoiced at the memory of Murray's failure: 'The God of our fathers was against Rev. Murray's work of destroying our nationality; his attack was defeated.'[8] According to SRP, this was the last time Murray had tried to break down 'our nationality' by using the state. Since then his tactic and that of his followers had shifted in a different direction. Whenever a minister attempted to do something for the 'building up of our *volk*', such ideas were completely shot down by Murray and his ilk. SRP struck a sarcastic tone as he agitated over the stance of the Murray supporters:

> 'It is a mortal sin for a minister to involve himself in politics!' But that Rev. Murray went to England in order to murder our nationality in the existence of the youthful Free State, oh no that was no evil, but a service to God, because for Rev. Murray and his followers an expansion of the British Empire and the Kingdom of God is one and the same thing.[9]

Hence, with Murray and friends eschewing direct involvement in politics, they instead used the church to propagate their imperialistic agenda, which was to uproot the developing Afrikaner nationalism. Murray did this by first importing English preaching into 'our Dutch Church' in the Cape. This was followed by English confirmation, English baptism, English communion. In fact, soon everything became English. True to form, Murray's followers followed suit, so that at Stellenbosch it became a requirement that students conducted their trial sermons in both English and Dutch. SRP comments that the close, and to his mind positive, links between language and nationalism had been well demonstrated in publications such as the *Patriot*, especially. Now Murray and his followers came and propagated English in the Dutch church, which had always been the strongest pillar for the preservation of 'our language'. Clearly this strategy was nothing short of a Trojan horse in the interest of British imperialism. Although SRP did not use that specific phrase, that was the implication of his agitation. SRP further accused Murray of undermining the attempts by Revd Van der Lingen of Paarl and others to safeguard Christian schooling. To the contrary, Murray actively propagated the new School law, which was also supported by government schools that 'imported English language, English history, English literature, and with that English books, English magazines, English teachers, English morals and customs!'.[10]

Still Murray remained unsatisfied. He also wanted to make sure that English was spoken in households so that it could thereby supplant the place of 'our mother tongue', in the same way as in his household and those of his followers. In this way Murray wanted to destroy the *landstaal* (national language), root and all. Thus, he now infiltrated the households 'to poison the wells with his English poison'. How did he do this? Through 'his English-American girls' schools' initiated in Wellington, Cape Town, Worcester and elsewhere. 'What is the purpose of these girls' schools? To Anglicise our daughters, hence our future mothers, so that the mother tongue of their children in a following generation should no longer be Afrikaans, but English.'[11]

For SRP, the bitterest pill to swallow about these schools was the fact that they were called by the title *Hugenoteskool* when everything about them was not to foster and strengthen the good legacy of the French Huguenots, regarding whom Afrikaner nationalists tended to have legendary views (see Chapter 1). 'No, here our future mothers are trained to be murderers of our language and nationality, just like the Egyptian midwives were for the [biblical] Israelites.'[12] It is perhaps not incidental to this specific indignity that the du Toit family, to which SRP most likely belonged, had been one of the most prominent French Huguenot families in South Africa.

Finally, SRP accused Murray of initially showing no interest in an initiative to provide education for poor white Afrikaners. When John X. Merriman, *Onze* Jan Hofmeyr and others connected to the ruling political party in the Cape became interested in instilling a national spirit, they tried to get Murray interested, but eventually proceeded without his support on the project. Then, afterwards, Murray tried to take control of the project by initiating a ministers' conference in Wellington to discuss the matter. SRP suggested that the aim of this conference would be to hijack the process so that the 'ruling church party' of Murray and his followers could receive government funding to implement an education that would turn these poor children into 'bastard English'. SRP concluded his accusation by acknowledging that although all of this commentary might sound harsh, it cannot be helped because: 'The enemy of our nationality and language and doctrine is our enemy.'[13]

In his follow-up article, SRP made his case for why Andrew Murray was also the greatest enemy of the reformed doctrine, thus making him a heretic against both nation and true religion, a true devil in other words. This seemed to be a more difficult argument to make, because SRP announced in the preamble that he would focus not on what Murray had done to counteract reformed doctrine, but instead on what he had not done to promote it. In the mind of the author there was certainly a logical connection between non-patriotism/non-nationalism and heresy. He quoted a sermon by Revd (S. J.) du Toit to that effect, or put differently, he quoted himself. Du Toit apparently preached that 'true love of the fatherland and real religion could not be separated from one another'. Reflecting on this, SRP asked rhetorically, 'which true biblical saint had ever committed treason against his country, or undermined his language and nationality? Yes, which true saint in the bible and in church history was not at the same time a patriot?'[14] For SRP, the answers to these questions were self-evident, and since it was already demonstrated, in the mind of the author, that Murray was no patriot, he was, according to the circular logic of the author's argumentation, disqualified from being a true saint as well.

It was furthermore clear to SRP that Murray did not do anything to promote the pure doctrines of Dordt at the seminary in Stellenbosch, which he could and should have done in his capacity as moderator of the church and curator of the seminary. No, he did not actively promote these doctrines, and instead he spread around his own 'Scots-Methodist little books!'. Therefore, in SRP's estimation, Murray was already under God's judgement, because the Bible did not only judge those who spread a false doctrine, but also those who did not teach the right doctrine.

Instead of teaching orthodox reformed doctrine, Murray did the following, according to SRP:

> ... he imported a Scots-Wesleyan revivalist spirit; he promoted the unbiblical Faith healing; he advocated the unscriptural Prohibition; he promoted the unchristian Salvation Army; in one word in all things new he is the leader, and with Pope-like tyranny he rules it over the consciences not only of his congregation members, but of the whole church.[15]

Regarding the Salvation Army, it seems the assertion that one of Murray's daughters belonged to this group, coupled with the fact that Andrew Murray did not actively speak out against it, was enough evidence for SRP that Murray promoted the Salvation Army. The allegation of Murray's support of prohibition stood on firmer foundations. SRP complained that Murray actively promoted it until he realised the stance would lead to a schism in his Wellington congregation. Then he started a more subtle campaign of promoting prohibitionist thinking through his Huguenot girls' school and the missionary training institute in Wellington. Mr Ferguson, in charge of training the missionaries, even went as far as to introduce communion services with unfermented wine, and then offered this communion to young members of the various institutes and from the congregation in Wellington. To add insult to injury, this unbiblical, unreformed communion service then proceeded in the English language! Additionally, prohibition is promoted in various ways in these schools. 'And that occurs while Rev. A. Murray has his whole income as a result of the honest labour of the wine farmers.'[16]

SRP seemed particularly preoccupied with the girls' schools and the way they functioned. According to him, they were akin to convents for nuns, as evidenced by the crosses on walls, prayer sessions and confessionals. All of these constituted a Roman yeast spreading through everything the schools did. Even worse was the conversion rhetoric prevalent in these circles: 'And then Rev. A. Murray openly promotes the *preaching of women*, which Paul certainly judged negatively' [my transl./SRP's emphasis].[17]

SRP further accused Murray of nepotistic behaviour in his church council, when it came to the selection of his successor. Finally, SRP asked, again rhetorically, if there had ever been a new thing or idea or movement or heresy that Murray did not seek to promote? The answer was no. But when it came to the reformed doctrine, all he did was to undermine it. SRP's concluding lines seem rather ominous in retrospect:

> What should we, according to God's Word, think of teachers that are blown along with every wind of doctrine? What of a man that has

broken his oath of honour to the doctrine of his church? Who undermines the doctrine of his church, and the language and nationalism of our *volk*?[18]

Dutch Calvinism versus Scots 'Methodism'

Despite the unconvincing attempt at anonymity with the pseudonym SRP, it is obvious that whether or not S. J. du Toit was the author, he and his brother, 'Oom Lokomotief', would not have published these articles in *Di Patriot* had their general tone of argumentation not carried their blessing. Moreover, the central ideas expressed by SRP regarding the inseparable connections between nationality, language and religiosity were repeated by S. J. du Toit at a conference in Paarl in 1897. The *Tweede Samenkomst van Geloovigen aan de Paarl*, 29–31 January 1897 directly followed the *Di Twede Afrikaanse Taalkongres gehou an di Paarl*, 27–8 January 1897, and a joint report was subsequently published. S. J. du Toit played a leading role in both conferences. A foremost concern set out in the report was the perceived crisis of a diminishing adherence to Reformed (*Gereformeerde*) principles in South Africa.[19]

The linkages between a re-establishment of Reformed principles and Afrikaans language and nationalism were then outlined. Of relevance here is an argument made by S. J. du Toit, according to whom there existed a general consensus that politics, religion and language should not be separated among the participants of these conferences. This led one participant, N. Badenhorst Jr, to enquire from du Toit, who was obviously taken as the expert on these matters, why it had come to pass that such a separation had indeed occurred in South Africa, in contradistinction to the formerly properly connected state among these forces?

Du Toit replied by setting out a historical sketch of Dutch Calvinism in which the Bible that arrived with the DEIC at the Cape (*de Staten Bijbel*) was indeed a bible commissioned by the Dutch state. Hence politics and religion were connected in the early colony. So, du Toit repeating Badenhorst's question, further asked: where did the separation come from? To this he posed a rhetorical counter-question: 'Is it not possible that the foreign ministers and school masters had anything to do with it?' Yes, the places of the 'sons of country' had been taken up by foreigners. Everyone knows how things were earlier, du Toit asserted. 'There was a shortage of ministers, and then ministers were imported from Scotland, men who could not feel or sympathise regarding our language and nationality, since they were from a different nationality, and they did not know the morals, customs and especially the language of our people.'[20] Du Toit was quick to add that he did not have anything against these Scots, but it was simply impossible for them to promote 'our national feeling and our language' like 'real sons of the land' in the same way that it would have been impossible for du Toit himself, if called to preach the gospel in Scotland at that very moment, to 'promote the Scottish nationality and language'. Fortunately, stated du Toit, the tide had turned in the church and 'sons of the land' were now taking up the positions formerly occupied by the Scottish ministers. However, the Scottish/English influence had subsequently shifted to education. Du Toit estimated that three-quarters of the teachers were Scottish or English. 'Is it any wonder that our nationality is dying and that love for the mother tongue is no longer to be found?' Then in an apparent exegetical appropriation of the biblical Ruth's words to her future mother-in-law, Naomi, du Toit stated, 'the Scot can say: "your God is my God," but he cannot say: "your *volk* is my *volk*."' This must not continue, du Toit concluded. The 'sons of the land' should occupy their rightful roles. 'We stand on dangerous territory, and the time has come that we should open our eyes.'[21]

As formulated by S. J. du Toit, the meeting made a resolution, the first part of which, when translated, would read as follows:

> This Gathering proclaims its sincere conviction that Language, Nationality, and Religion constitute a three-part cord that could not be broken without damage to each one of the three, and [the gathering] announces its heartfelt wish that the three should be practised ever more closely together by our Afrikaans *volk*.[22]

However, in the case of religion there was nothing generic in its characterisation, and for the Afrikaner *volk* there was a particular type of religion that du Toit had in mind, summarised by the following question: 'To what an extent is the Reformed principle in our country going forwards or backwards, and to what an extent is it connected to our national progression or regression?'[23]

Du Toit again mentioned the contrasts between 'on the one side the pure doctrine of Dordt, and on the other side that of the Armenian and Scottish Methodist, and ... that we have completely turned away from the former and come to stand on common ground with the latter'.[24]

This, it seems, was the root cause of all the problems the Afrikaner were experiencing, as du Toit then proceeded to explicate with the help of additional testimonies regarding the neglected state of pure Calvinist theology. This situation was attested to by various conference representatives from around the country. The crucial difference between the two theological positions in the minds of du Toit and company was that pure Calvinism necessarily involved itself with a *volk*'s nationalism, language and politics, whereas Scots 'Methodism', in South Africa, eschewed such involvements. This point of difference, in the view of S. J. du Toit at least, had perhaps less to do with theological reasons, and more with the foreignness (Englishness) of the Scottish ministers.

Later anti-Methodists would de-emphasise the xenophobic element in their attack, focusing instead on theological themes, as will be discussed below. However, the issue of the relationship between church and nation, or religion and politics, remained the central underlying thread in the defamation of the Scottish legacy. While this chapter focuses primarily on detractors of the Scottish position, it is important to have a Scottish perspective, and who better to provide that than Andrew Murray, regarding this point of contention. This is available in the form of a commentary by Murray on a speech given, not by any of his direct opponents, but by D. F. Malan, who would later become the apartheid-inaugurating prime minister of South Africa. However, prior to setting out on a political career, Malan was a DRC minister and subsequently a newspaper editor in the Cape. He was also a man with connections to the Murray family. His older sister, Cinie, was married to Mashonaland missionary A. A. Louw (see Chapter 6). Malan was also ideologically rooted in the broad missionary-minded tradition of the DRC. Yet Malan would, over time, virtually switch sides, but without exactly becoming a dyed-in-the-wool neo-Calvinist.

Murray versus Malan

In a publicised disagreement between Murray and Malan, Murray responded critically in the form of a pamphlet to a speech delivered in mid-1915 by D. F. Malan at Somerset West, which also repeated a number of the themes addressed by Malan on the occasion of his farewell address delivered to the congregation of Graaff Reinet, where he had served for a couple of years until 13 June 1915, the date of the address.

Malan fits directly into the larger narrative of a rising Afrikaner nationalism coinciding with strong anti-imperial sentiment that I have already alluded to above. Malan was a pivotal figure[25] who, in addition to enunciating the theological connections between Afrikaner religion and nationality, also took the discourse a step further than early nationalists, such as S. J. du Toit, by expounding on the Afrikaner's God-ordained position with respect to the racial other in southern Africa, that is, black Africans specifically. Best known as the leader of the (Purified) National Party that was unexpectedly victorious in the 1948 elections against Jan Smuts' United Party, Malan became the first prime minister to rule South Africa on an explicitly apartheid agenda. However, prior to the advent of his political career, in which he successfully harnessed a rising wave of Afrikaner nationalism, Malan was a prominent DRC minister with postings in important rural Cape congregations, especially Graaff Reinet, the South African ancestral home of the Murrays, where he concluded his ministry in 1915. Malan had strong mission interests, with a social gospel impetus, and as Elphick points out, this provided the inspiration for his eventual emphasis on the alleviation of white poverty.[26] When he was minister at Montagu between 1906 and 1912,[27] Malan's congregation provided the full financial support of a missionary to the western Sudan, present-day Nigeria. This, perhaps not insignificantly, was Revd J. G. Strydom, who subsequent to his missionary career, which had to be cut short for health reasons, became mission secretary of the Free State DRC.[28] In this capacity, Strydom was one of the most vociferous early apartheid ideologues (see Chapter 6). Malan also undertook a tour into the proverbial dark depths of Africa, recounted in his 1913 travelogue *Naar Congoland*, on which he visited mission stations, most importantly that of his older sister Cinie and her husband A. A. Louw at Morgenstêr in Mashonaland.[29] Louw's mother, as previously mentioned, was a Murray and a sister of Andrew Murray.

During his sojourn into deeper Africa, Malan commented widely on matters pertaining to mission, 'civilisation', nation and nationality, among other things. He had some interesting things to say about what he considered to be typical Afrikaner behaviour, which, no doubt intended to be complimentary, might on at least one level be read as rather patronising and classist. Commenting on his experiences during the northbound train journey, he contrasted what he understood to be the typical nature of the English-speaking passenger with that of the Afrikaner. The latter, he writes, is always ready to strike up a conversation with you with a 'good day cousin', and before the end of it, your conversation partner might discover that there were more extended members in his family than he had formerly imagined. 'Childlike innocence, product of our unique national history, mother of numerous virtues!' [transl.].[30]

Following such allusions to the simplicity and perhaps shallow gene pool of his own childlike *volk*, Malan further pondered their tendency for northerly expansion, which he states was present since the days of Jan van Riebeeck. According to his observation, there was a continuous flow from the various regions of South Africa, and even from South-West Africa, of Afrikaners either settling or scouting out the situation for potentially settling in Rhodesia. He concluded his musings on these migrations with a rhetorical question, followed by what seems a hypothesis:

> Where will the Afrikaner stop with these northbound migrations? One should almost want to believe that we are the lost ten tribes, that therefore the 'wandering Jew' is personified in our nation, and that we will find rest only in Canaan. It goes well with the migrants! [transl.].[31]

For someone who would become the primary advocate of apartheid in subsequent years, Malan's commentary on indigenous Africans seems surprisingly sympathetic on some occasions, particularly regarding Christian ones such as the Tswana king Kgama, who is described as both a devout Christian and a man of character.[32] Malan also commented positively on the marital practices encountered in Rhodesia, which he judged as less barbaric than 'Kaffir marriages' elsewhere. Indeed, the Rhodesian native marital practices were more protective of *het romantische* (the romantic side of things) than was the case with the marriages of whites. Regarding their sacrifices and non-Christian worship, Malan asserted that these practices were so heartfelt that they occasionally make a deep impression even on a white person such as himself: 'Has, even here, not been established an altar for the unknown God?' [transl.].[33] Malan elsewhere in the travelogue also shows himself inclined to a romanticised primordial view of Africa, for example when in reference to the fertility of the soil and the abundance of game, he comments, 'North-Rhodesia is one Nimrod's paradise' [transl.].[34]

Malan was a complex figure, as Lindie (Korf) Koorts showed in her research.[35] As indicated in this African travelogue, he seemed to posit a unique paternalist relationship not between whites and blacks, generally, but specifically between blacks and white Afrikaners. Malan apparently, naively or disingenuously, believed that black Africans had far greater respect for Afrikaners than for any other nation: 'It is for this reason that they elevate "Paul" [Kruger] as a much greater man than even Rhodes. And it is for this reason that even in the Congo, where the Afrikaners have never been, that as a rule they address the white man as "baas" [boss]' [transl.].[36]

Furthermore, the existence of such esteem for the Afrikaner among the natives was no accident, as Malan continued to expound. This was indeed a God-given role that the Afrikaner occupied in Africa: 'The Afrikaner wields power over the Kaffir. But truly, we would not have had this power had it not been given from above. Would God not have put aside therein for our *volk* a high and holy calling?' [transl.].[37] This line of thinking underscores Lindie Koorts' contention that for Malan, Afrikaner nationalism was not merely an ideology but a 'belief-system'.[38]

Malan commented on the comparative ease with which the colonisation of Northern Rhodesia occurred, with hardly any bloodshed. Considering the great cost in lives at which the provinces of the South African union were settled, this more recent development was remarkably peaceful for Malan. He expressed certainty over the fact that this was due to the earlier victories of the Boers over Africans in South Africa, news of which had in the intervening years travelled north:

> In this way, the authority of the white races were established for good, not only in South- but also in Central Africa . . . Dingaan's Day may well be celebrated as far as Congoland. And yet, today, in both Rhodesias, and even in Natal, the language and with it the nationality of these same Afrikaners should be satisfied with the lowest place, if they are not completely trod upon under feet. Weeping injustice! [transl.][39]

In a similar vein, Malan agitated over the neglect of '*Hollandsch*' language in the imperial Rhodesian school system. Such neglect of the language loosened not only the national ties of Afrikaners but also their church affiliation, because confirmation in the DRC effectively presupposed a competence in reading Dutch.[40]

Malan's Rhodesian sojourn apparently exposed him to the realities of interracial unions between blacks and whites. Such practices, which he described as shocking and shameful, led Malan to devote a section to the 'native question' and how that should be negotiated back in South Africa, so that it would not lead either to a liberalisation of interracial relations or to outright revolution. He appeared to acknowledge that programmes to inhibit black political participation and educational achievement could not lead to a peaceful resolution, because blacks would resist such measures and continue to strive upward. Malan's solution to the 'problem' hinged on the idea of 'respect' as the only way in which the situation could be resolved, that is, that blacks should have respect for whites. The only way in which that could be a realistic expectation would be when whites lived so excellently on the spiritual and moral level that they were in fact the most educated and morally admirable nation in the world:

> Should the lower race have respect for the higher one because the higher race is worthy of that respect, then there would no longer be any native question of any consequence ... Seen from this perspective, the solution to the poor white question is also the solution to the native question. [transl.][41]

That there should be legal measures to protect the white race from 'lowering' itself made total sense to Malan, because the way in which certain whites lived not only implied a personal degradation, 'an animalisation of their humanity, but it is also a serious offence against the entire white race of South Africa' [transl.].[42]

As a clergyman, for Malan there was a natural role for the church in all of this. Perhaps interestingly, he did not seek out the opinions of theologians in this regard, but instead took the testimony of the former president of the Orange Free State, M. T. Steyn, as authoritative. Malan stated that some years past he had asked Steyn's opinion on the reasons why 'our *volk* has remained so pure'.[43] Steyn's answer was simply that it was all due to the church, which protected morality and maintained the division between Christendom and heathendom, 'and has therefore naturally drawn the colour line, and saved the white race from mixing and decay' [transl.].[44]

Rather than disputing the racialised logic of heathen and Christian, as one might expect from an evangelically minded scholar, Malan, showing again his nationalistic a priori colours, confirmed that indeed the answer to the native question was not a political one but a spiritual and moral one, and therefore a churchly (religious) one. For this reason, the Christian churches had to be encouraged to execute their spiritual and moral influence as strongly as possible on the white race. As was the case in South Africa, this would also save Rhodesia, in Malan's estimation.[45] It is perhaps ironic that Malan, on an African tour involving missionary institutions, would choose to reflect so strongly on the ways in which the church could be harnessed essentially in service of the white race.

Malan's emphasis on his own *volk* and their well-being does not mean that he had become anti-missionary, though. In a chapter focusing on Morgenstêr, the oldest DRC station in Rhodesia, where Malan's older sister Cinie and her husband Andrew Louw were based, Malan writes in the role of a mission apologist. He makes an interesting argument that Africans, through their contact with whites who did not believe in spirits and witchcraft, were bound to lose their religion anyway. His point seems to be that the younger Africans basically followed white ways in all respects once they came into contact with 'civilisation'. Would the enemies of mission now want to deny them the salvation of Christ, the only thing that could replace this void? Malan remarked that by opposing mission, those members of his *volk* with such attitudes were endangering the future of South Africa, opening it up to the whims of an uncontrolled heathendom.[46] In any case, contrary to their argument that the 'mission kaffirs' showed little respect for white people, Malan maintained that in so far as this might be true for other mission organisations, on 'our stations' the converse was rather true: 'To the contrary, we must honestly admit that we have never in our lives encountered such politeness elsewhere' [transl.].[47]

Regarding mission work and education, Malan made some telling remarks: 'Even if for the sake of the majority of the white race a hostile attitude to the education of the Kaffir might be justified, there, where the natives unquestionably strive upwards, such opposition is in either case futile' [transl.].[48] In other words, it would be pointless trying to prevent Africans from acquiring the education they strive for. Malan's solution to avert this threatening equalisation was to ensure 'more and especially better education' for whites so that they could maintain their supremacy without resorting to violence.[49]

Hence Malan was, generally speaking, in favour of education for Africans, but he asserted his dislike for the type of education that was normally given, and which the Africans also thought they needed, which, according to Malan, amounted to little more than a bit of English: 'It is an education that is calculated to dislodge the native from his nature and his *volk*.'[50] With this Malan then makes his case for what would become known as '*volkseie*' education, that is, education for the purpose of strengthening the supposedly innate characteristics of each *volk*. 'No *volk* can ever truly be educated, that is, spiritually and morally, made strong by the disregard of its natural capacity and of its national idiosyncrasies and traditions' [transl.].[51] This does indeed sound like the type of argument someone like S. J. du Toit, with his unity of nationality, language and religion idea, could make. Evidently, Malan thought of education in similar, shall we call them organic, terms.

In the conclusion of *Naar Congoland*, Malan repeated a recurring sentiment throughout the book, and this is that Africans admired Europeans: 'He even addresses him by the same name he uses for the Supreme Being.'[52] If only the Afrikaners in Rhodesia would not mess up this image by breaking down what 'our missionaries are trying to build up' then this sentiment of admiration would doubtless continue to be the order of the day.[53]

The themes of race and nation interested Malan greatly, so much so that his commentary on mission and religion in some cases cast them in the light of supporting acts to his principle discourse of white Afrikanerdom and the maintenance of its supremacy. It is perhaps not surprising that Malan resigned his position as minister of the DRC in Graaff Reinet in 1915 in order to take up a journalistic and political career. His farewell address to the congregation is especially revealing in terms of his philosophy on the relationship between church and state/*volk*, etc.

Malan used this opportunity to good effect to assure his church members that his decision to leave behind the full-time ministry did not entail any break with his calling. To the contrary, this decision marked an expansion of his calling into hitherto unfamiliar terrain. Malan argued that he was going to serve 'our *volk* and our Church' along the way of what had thus far been an untried route.[54]

Malan was clearly aware of the criticism his decision was bound to provoke among church members. Hence he pleaded for a recognition of Christian conscience, and a non-legalistic approach to the theme of calling. He summarised his main points as follows:

> The first is that not only the churchly religious life of a *volk*, but also the broader, national and political life, should be subjected to the reign of God. The second is that there are extraordinary circumstances that may call us to serve God outside the life of the church. And the third, which must always be kept within sight, and which has just now come into play for us at the most fundamental level, is the honour of God in our national life. [transl.][55]

Malan seems to be making the case here for the idea of national calling, but he also advocated a slight blurring of the boundaries between the secular and the sacred, which would make sense if one thinks of him as influenced by social gospel ideas, as Elphick argues,[56] but it is also virtually synonymous with S. J. du Toit's above-mentioned portrayal of the Calvinist principle. Malan argued that in the past, too stark a line had been drawn between religion and politics, between the church and the wider national life.[57] In other words, he might as well be making an anti-'Methodist' argument, without actually doing so in any direct way, of course.

It is perhaps significant that he did not attempt to argue here that this was an exceptional situation for the Afrikaner. He mentioned several individuals from Europe and Britain who chose other career paths to strengthen the Christianisation of their nations. For example, the Welsh preacher William Rees used journalism as a vehicle for bringing about the 'national rebirth of Wales'. Malan proceeded to mention more names in this vein, from Germany, England and the Netherlands, including the well-known Abraham Kuyper.[58]

Malan referred to a great crisis of his time, which was the growing rift among the Afrikaner *volk*, presumably between those favouring a republic and the rest. This rift endangered, according to Malan, the one ideal of the Afrikaner *volk*, which was to have one Reformed, united, national and evangelical church. However, if the current political division persisted or even worsened, such an ideal was doomed to failure: 'The clock of our *volkskerk* has been set years back' [transl.].[59]

At the root of this turmoil, according to Malan, was the question of the future existence or 'suicide' of the Afrikaner *volk*. Malan undoubtedly saw himself as an advocate of Afrikaner life, and he made the case that a unified vision of Afrikaner life was also crucial for the unity of the church, because a stark political divide might lead to a rift in the church. Therefore, and here Malan made an interesting conceptual leap: 'Every well-meaning attempt to repair our broken national unity is therefore an attempt, not only in the interest of our *volk*, but also in the interest of the gospel and the church of our fathers, that we all love so dearly' [transl.].[60]

Malan, however, wanted to take this theme to a deeper level. Is Afrikaner history – the fact that the Afrikaner became a *volk* over time – the result of human actions, or is it the work of God? The answer to this question was of crucial importance, because a *volk* that acknowledged God as responsible for its coming into being, also took its future existence very seriously. Such a *volk* will bow down before the will of God, but, and here Malan contradicted the melting-pot idea of nationhood as an evolving phenomenon, if you ask such a *volk* to lose itself within some existing or not yet existing *volk*, then the answer is 'for the sake of God's honour definitely no . . . But if you ask them to bow down before God who had made them and to resign themselves to his sovereignty then the whole Christian Afrikaner *volk* will answer: for the sake of God's honour, wholeheartedly, yes' [transl.].[61]

This seems like a plea for what might be described as Christian nationalism before the term itself was in common parlance in South Africa. If God created a nation, then that nation had a calling and a purpose. Indeed, it had a certain if unspoken sacral status. To attempt to pour such a nation into any kind of national melting pot, to immerse it in hybridity in other words, would be going against the will of God, who wanted this nation to be distinct. The melting-pot ideal is thus a heretical idea as expressed in Malan's farewell address, and no doubt equally so understood by many of his listeners. Crucially, it should be noted that the silent opponents were not pleading for a hybridity across the so-called colour line, but for a South African nation encompassing English and Afrikaans whites. This is the type of hybridity that Malan and his supporters feared so much in 1915, and for which he had to leave the ministry in order to ensure the apparently God-willed future existence of Afrikanerdom.

Scarcely a month after the delivery of this address, Malan reiterated many of these sentiments in a speech given at Somerset West. He particularly emphasised the theme of the threat that a politically divided *volk* posed for the unity of the church. According to Malan's view of ecclesiology, as quoted in Andrew Murray's response, there should always be an impetus among members of the same church to be not only a unity in terms of confession and faith, but also in their political sentiment.[62] Again, this is an idea not very different from the religious/national/linguistic unity advocated by S. J. du Toit (see above).

That Andrew Murray in his old age deemed it necessary to pen his utter disagreement with this understanding of ecclesiology is important for several reasons, but let me try to capture the main bones of contention. I shall start by translating Murray's introductory lines on the subject:

> I do not know how I can express the difference between these ideas and my feeling more clearly than by saying that I utterly could not understand why a schism in the church should be necessary, even if there exist two parties with differing political ideas. The Church is after all a spiritual body, created intentionally by God in order to make one in the power of his supernatural love, all members, even from nations, which hate and despise each other, through the church's power in her unity with the Lord Jesus through the Holy Spirit.[63]

Murray wrote that differences in political opinion were inevitable given the long history of the church, and that such differences were not necessarily the result of sin, but could be ascribed to different temperaments, education and environment. Moreover, Murray zoomed in his criticism particularly to the point where Malan made the case, also suggested in his farewell address, regarding the natural tendency of members in a church to want to be one in faith as well as in political ideals. Where does this 'natural tendency' originate from? 'From the Spirit of God, or from sinful nature, from the flesh? I am deeply convinced that the tendency is an attempt by human nature to let itself be counted in the things of God's Kingdom and to mix spiritual and fleshly things' [transl.].[64]

Murray denied that his position entailed a rejection of religious engagement in political affairs. To the contrary, the church should teach its members to live out their calling as 'citizens of the state'. They should obey God's will in all things and live in 'love not for themselves but for their fellow humans'. If this kind of Christian love, which is tolerant of the other, reigns in the church, there would be no question of schisms occurring along political lines. Hence the church should not be disengaged from politics, but: 'There is a big difference between the suggestion that the church should directly teach her members which political opinions are the right ones, and if they should be helped to apply for themselves the big principles of God's Word in their life' [transl.].[65]

Murray used the final page of the pamphlet to elaborate on a suggestion he had made to a Revd Botha, chair of the 'Bloemfontein Konferentie', regarding how the disunity in the church could be resolved. Part of the suggestion was that the different parties, the National Party and the South African Party, expressed their views on how the future of the Afrikaner should look. However, what was clearly of a deeper-lying concern for Murray is expressed in his wish 'that God may give to all the deep feeling that the unity of the church and the unity of all believers should stand higher with us than any temporal separation or disagreement' [transl.].⁶⁶

I am not aware that Malan ever responded to this reprimand from the aged Murray, but perhaps the above paragraphs will suffice in terms of exposing the hermeneutical gulf between the two individuals regarding church and nation and their relative value. For Murray, a nation was made up of individuals with diverse backgrounds and inevitable differences of political opinion. As far as any unity that is to be striven for was concerned, the primary union was a Christian union that obviously cut across these dividing lines, and moreover transcended national boundaries. Murray did not state outright that Christian union trumped national union in his philosophy, but this was clearly the implication of this pamphlet, in which he also referenced a well-known Pauline passage in the New Testament regarding the new person in whom there exists neither Greek nor Jew, circumcised nor uncircumcised, and so on, but Christ as everything in all.⁶⁷ I am not sure how Malan would explain a passage such as Galatians 3:28, which Murray alluded to here, but, as indicated above, for Malan the Afrikaner *volk* was a God-willed entity and Malan's God very much had a stake in nationhood. Fortunately for him, he no longer needed to apply his intellect to theological complexities, or shall we call them inconveniences. All of that belonged to the old Malan. The new Malan had a political career ahead of him in which he could devote himself fully to his nationalistic passions.

A final note about Malan, before I move on to other more directly explicit opponents of the Scottish legacy, concerns the fact that, as reported by Charles Bloomberg, less than three years after quitting the church ministry, Malan had accrued for himself the dubious credit of providing the catalyst for the formation of the *Afrikaner Broederbond* by giving a speech in Johannesburg that led to a riot among members of the white urban working class:

> The street fight followed a stormy Nationalist meeting in the Johannesburg City Hall on 13 April 1918. The main speaker was 34-year-old Dr D. F. Malan, who had recently abandoned the pulpit to assume the leadership of the Cape NP. Young Malan (who was also editor of *Die Burger*) had travelled the 1000 miles from Cape Town to bring the gospel of Republicanism to the Rand, the traditional focus of industrial and political power in South Africa, and stronghold of the pro-Empire SAP.⁶⁸

In his speech, Malan, among other things, denounced the Union Jack as a symbol of oppression and expressed strong sentiments against South African participation in the Great War:

> ... Malan called on Afrikaners to rally to the Republican banner, and for a concerted effort to abolish the Monarchy and convert the

Union into an independent Republic outside the Empire. He hit out at British 'injustices' against the Boers and demanded the restoration of their 'violated rights'.[69]

So riled up were the nationalist crowd by Malan's speech that the Union Jack was pulled down from its platform and torn to shreds, which in turn angered some English-speaking onlookers. A street brawl ensued.

The fracas touched off consequences which were ultimately to reshape South Africa. A group of angry young militants who had watched the riot from the Selbourne Hall balcony, including W. H. van der Merwe, H. J. Klopper and D. H. C. du Plessis, got together secretly afterwards to decide what could be done to promote the Nationalist cause. A month later 14 of them formed a Nationalist society called Young South Africa, which shortly afterwards became the *Afrikaner Broederbond*.[70]

Dopper Opposition to Scottish 'Methodism' and the *Strewers* under Attack

Malan was perhaps too astute, politically, to open the can of worms that would have been opened had he gone into debate with the hugely influential Murray regarding the above-mentioned disagreement on the relationship between *volk* and church. The twentieth-century attacks on Murray and what he was portrayed as standing for – broadly defined as Methodism – came from a different quarter of Afrikanerdom rooted in Dordt-enthused Calvinism. Already early on, in correspondence reported by Johannes du Plessis, Andrew Murray expressed the sentiment to his brother John, lamented in fact, that they had not been able to have any influence on the ultra-orthodox Dutch Calvinists. Andrew Murray stated that if it was up to him he would have had the Cape Church accommodate congregations that exclusively sang the Psalms – the hallmark of the *Doppers* – but this was nullified with the founding of the *Gereformeerde Kerke*, which commenced in 1859. Regarding this, Andrew remarked to John:

> We have never been able, even when willing, to reach the real, stiff *Dopper* mind. Our language was strange to it: these new ministrations, possessing their confidence, may reach hearts that appear to us quite closed against the gospel . . . I look upon the whole thing as a direct work of Providence, and though I would have been anxious to open our church for psalm-singing congregations and ministers, yet as no opportunity for acting in the matter was afforded, I am content.[71]

Whether one wants to call Murray's attitude to a rival religious grouping wise or naive, what he perhaps could not foresee was that from this group the strongest challenge to his legacy would emerge. This challenge mainly occurred indirectly, but also directly with some strong sentiments expressed against 'Methodism' generally, mainly in academic publications, but also against Andrew Murray personally in populist news outlets. Strictly Reformed Patriot (SRP), discussed above, represents an extreme point of view. S. J. du Toit, under his own name, also discussed above, represents the more typical opposition, but it now becomes important to move on to S. J.'s son, the most important early twentieth-century theologian of the *Gereformeerde Kerke* in South Africa, J. D. du Toit, and his school of thought as established at Potchefstroom.

J. D. du Toit, popularly known by his nom de plume 'Totius', was also an Afrikaans poet with a not so unique yet still remarkable ability to romanticise the Great Trek and other aspects of the Afrikaner tradition. In this respect he served the budding Afrikaner nationalist discourse exceedingly well. Du Toit became heavily involved in the construction of Afrikaans as a codified language distinct from the Dutch out of which it emerged. His father, S. J. du Toit, was among the primary drivers to initiate the Afrikaans language movement in the late nineteenth century,[72] and Totius, among others, would resume this initiative in the early twentieth century. By this time, the political climate was much more conducive to every strategy in the pursuit of legitimising the Afrikaner *volk* as a distinct nation with a unique history and, moreover, a God-willed destiny.

J.D. du Toit is significant for being among the most dedicated Afrikaner theologians in the attempt to create a biblical justification for the policy of apartheid as nothing short of a God-ordained state of being. This rather radical biblical reinterpretation occurred in the context of the South African variant of Dutch neo-Calvinism that was introduced to this country by the disciples of Abraham Kuyper, and among others, those of his son H. H. Kuyper, who supervised du Toit's doctoral dissertation, simply entitled *Het Methodisme*.[73] Neo-Calvinism concerned itself with the working out of a comprehensive philosophy of life for every aspect of society. The church as institution played a central role in this scheme, and in fact every institution or 'sphere' had a distinct God-ordained role to play under a broadly Calvinist umbrella of a people elected under the reign of a sovereign God. Scripture was creatively, if hermeneutically problematically, employed by neo-Calvinist theologians, such as J. D. du Toit in particular. Historians such as Kinghorn and more recently Elphick have articulated the implications that this theology had when transplanted to the South African context.[74] Most important about this development was that *volk* became an essential cornerstone, a cardinal sphere endowed with sovereignty. In this context, du Toit's dissertation was not so much a direct attempt to anathematise Methodism as heterodox. Rather it very carefully elaborated the intricacies of its essential differences from Calvinism, while maintaining a self-acknowledged appreciation for Methodism's founders and the important role this movement played in various contexts, especially in its formative years. The point the dissertation makes, however, is that Methodism is totally distinct from Calvinism and by implication irreconcilable with it. It is of crucial importance that du Toit gave a very broad definition of Methodism, not only identifying the term with church groups and individuals that described themselves as Methodist. Instead, Methodist characteristics and trends were identified, which could then serve to organise and categorise various movements, organisations, individuals and so forth. This more deliberate categorisation was started by Totius himself and carried further by his spiritual heirs at the University of Potchefstroom, but also elsewhere into broader Afrikanerdom.

As mentioned in Chapter 5, the Christian Endeavour Society (*De Jongelieden Vereeniging voor Christelijk Streven*) played a major role in terms of facilitating revivals and engendering mission fervour among Boer POWs during the South African War. The Murrays and their wider network were instrumental in this. In fact, in 1894 Andrew Murray had become the first president of the South African Christian Endeavour Society. And, as claimed by an internal *Strevers* source, the first South African branch started in 1892 in the Murray stronghold of Graaff Reinet.[75]

In an apparent homage to the old adage of the apple not falling far from the tree, J. D. du Toit, son of S. J. du Toit and author of *Het Methodisme*, wrote a rather polemical pamphlet in 1905, scarcely three years after the above-mentioned war, in which he specifically zoomed in on the *Strevers*, evaluating them from a 'Gereformeerd' point of view. This pamphlet perhaps more than anything provided the groundwork for a subsequent process of *methodisation*, that is, the vilification of the Scottish-influenced tradition as heterodoxic and 'Methodist'. This term would come to signify the broadly evangelical, missionary-minded camp, or put differently, the non-neo-Calvinists in the DRC.

Du Toit started off by giving a brief introduction of Wesley and his movement, emphasising the fact that Methodism began as a society within the Church of England, rather than as a new church as such. Then he posed the question regarding whether Methodism had anything to do with the *Streversvereeniging*, which was immediately answered in the affirmative. Indeed, in du Toit's view, the Christian Endeavour Society was nothing less than a continuation of Wesley's society. Several apparent correspondences between the movements were highlighted, such as the parachurch nature of both, the fact that both reacted against dead orthodoxy in their churches of origin, and the emphasis on the Christian life and revival as ways of counteracting such problems.[76]

Du Toit's main gripe with the Endeavour society was that it allegedly broke down the church rather than built it up due to its parachurch nature. Rather than reforming the church, it placed itself in its stead.[77] All these Christian organisations, according to du Toit, were unnecessary because the church itself was the institution called into life by God.[78] Hence, by not being a church yet by placing itself in the position of the church, the Endeavour society had become a pseudo-church in du Toit's eyes, although he put it more colourfully: '*the Endeavour society is a bastard church and therefore the Endeavourers' work is a bastard ministry*. God's Word demands that we distinguish between genuine and false . . .' [transl.].[79]

Furthermore, du Toit accused the Endeavour society of neglecting the biblical Covenant, and the doctrine of divine election. Over and against such universal Calvinist tenets, the Endeavour society emphasised the Christian life, but inadequately so, according to du Toit.[80] Perhaps most fundamentally, the society's emphasis on soul winning was contrary to the Calvinist doctrine of limited atonement, that is, the notions of particular grace and particular election. Du Toit argued that gospel proclamation belonged only to the ordained office-bearers and was not the responsibility of every believer, as the Endeavour society implied through its emphasis on soul winning. In this vein, du Toit critically cited the motto of the 'Streversvereeniging der krijgsgevangenenen te St Helena' [Endeavour society for Prisoners of War at St Helena], which was '*De wereld voor Christus in dit geslacht*' (The world for Christ in this generation).[81] Interestingly, this virtually mirrors what would be the theme of the 1910 World Missionary Conference in Edinburgh, 'The Evangelisation of the World in this Generation'.

Du Toit was either oblivious to this wider ecumenism into which the Endeavour society was tapping, or, more likely, he was aware of it, but for him this was precisely the underlying problem, especially since much of that early ecumenism was driven by the English-speaking Protestant world. Whatever the case, such a sentiment would accord well with the evolving attitude of anti-ecumenism as especially typified a few decades later in J. G. Strydom and the Free State synod of the DRC, as discussed in Chapter 6. Ultimately, though, all this boiled down to for du Toit was a choice that his Afrikaner reformed fellows had to make, which is extremely ironic given his theological proclivities that generally precluded the idea of human choice in religious matters. Yet for du Toit, the Afrikaner had to make a choice between Calvinism or Methodism.[82]

Du Toit received some pushback in the form of publications defending the *Chr. Strevers-Vereeniging* (CSV), including from Revd D. J. le R. Marchand, the chair of the 'CSV in relation to the DRCSA'. This prompted du Toit to reiterate his position in a follow-up pamphlet published in 1906. The foreword averred that Marchand resented the fact that du Toit, a minister in the Gereformeerde Kerke (GK), would meddle in the affairs of other churches. Du Toit's response was that he addressed himself primarily to people in his own church, but could he help it if members of the other two Afrikaans churches read his work enthusiastically?[83] Yet this was indeed the crux of the matter, because increasingly the theological line pushed by du Toit, with its overtly anti-Methodist and covertly anti-ecumenical overtures, would become the dominant line in Afrikaner religious discourse, including within the DRC, as illustrated by the writings of Vorster and Hanekom, to which I shall turn shortly.

Scots Afrikaners as Liberal Methodists

Before moving on to the heirs of Totius and neo-Calvinist nationalism at Potchefstroom and elsewhere, it is important to mention that Totius played a major role in the Johannes du Plessis heresy trial as a witness for the prosecution. Totius was an outspoken critic of modernism in theological matters. He abhorred higher criticism and endorsed a literalist interpretation of the Bible, in contradistinction to du Plessis. This is important background information for a 1932 piece in du Plessis' journal, *Het Zoeklicht*, in which du Plessis, in the aftermath of his concluded trial and excommunication from the Theological Seminary at Stellenbosch, recalled the nearly forty years earlier attack on Andrew Murray by *Streng Gereformeerde Patriot* (Strictly Reformed Patriot: SRP) in S. J. du Toit's journal, *Di Patriot*. In fact, du Plessis republished the two articles by SRP word for word. In his introduction, du Plessis mentioned the connection between S. J. du Toit and his own more recent tormenter, Totius, as well as the fact that the latter in the biography he wrote of his father[84] neglected to mention this particular episode where Andrew Murray was accused of unorthodoxy.[85] Du Plessis furthermore claimed that there could be no doubt that SRP was S. J. du Toit himself.[86]

Although du Plessis, in his capacity as editor of *Het Zoeklicht*, did not elaborate further on these articles, the intention of reminding his readership of them here in 1932 is obvious. Just like Andrew Murray was unfairly accused of heresy by the father, so he, du Plessis, the spiritual heir of Murray, was now attacked by the son. The point du Plessis wanted to make was that the du Toit pair of father and son were equally untrustworthy in their theological opinion, and that neither he nor Murray was heretical, but quite the contrary. Nonetheless, the like-for-like argument did not convince the majority of an Afrikanerdom in which Andrew Murray remained by and large revered, for the time being, while du Plessis was quickly anathematised. However, subsequent heirs to the du Toit/neo-Calvinist tradition would be only too happy to go along with this idea of linking Murray and du Plessis. Not to exonerate either of them, but to provide as firm a connection as possible between the unlikely bedfellows of Methodism and liberalism, as we shall shortly see.

Barring anonymous authors like SRP, the tendency to discredit the Scottish Evangelical tradition proceeded without the need to resort to ad hominem attacks against the Murrays or anyone else associated with them. One important aspect in strengthening the arsenal of the attack against Methodism[87] would be to tie the proverbial knot between 'Methodism' and liberalism. Christian nationalist thinkers strove hard, if in retrospect only halfway convincingly, to construct this union. Of course, the taking of imaginative flights of fancy in pursuit of an ideological point is hardly a new invention, and one should keep in mind that these were the Afrikaner intellectuals who had also been able to come up with the notion of biblical apartheid, an endeavour which relied on some rather inventive hermeneutical acrobatics.

The *Koers in die Krisis* series of publications between 1935 and 1941 might generally be considered as the bedrock of Afrikaner neo-Calvinist apologetics for Christian nationalism. Although the Potchefstroom Gereformeerde influence sits heavy in these works, included were the writings of representatives of all three main Afrikaner reformed churches, as well as some voices from the Netherlands. One of the editors of *Koers in die Krisis*, J. D. (Koot) Vorster, would in later years play a formidable role in Stellenbosch as chair of the DRC Curatorium, the ecclesiastical body charged with oversight of theological education at the seminary. Vorster's essay in volume three of *Koers in die Krisis* is of special interest for this chapter, its title being '*Die Metodistiese Invloed in ons Volkslewe*' (The Methodist Influence in the Life of our *Volk*). Let me highlight some of its central tenets.

Vorster started off by singing the praises of the formative influences of Calvinism in the religious and social life of the Cape Colony. Regarding the latter, he wrote:

> Thus was the social life ordered according to the principles of the Word of God. This gave the South African life its own advanced style not only in the intimate family circle, but also in relation to our own *volks*-members and the surrounding coloured population. The family life was patriarchal in organisation. [transl.][88]

Vorster's commentary on the issue of race is particularly striking. As closely translated as possible, it reads:

> Especially in its contact with the coloured races, [the Afrikaner *volk*'s] Calvinistic faith have led it to come to the viewpoint and tradition of absolute colour-line veneration and the protection of the purity of own blood. However, this also exempted it from acting in oppression and brutality. Thus have the South African Calvinism enriched the world with its policy of segregation and Christian guardianship – an original, from Scripture developed, solution to the Colour question.[89]

However, there soon appeared dangerous agents threatening this racially determined Calvinistic bliss, doing their destructive work under protection of the colonial government. Vorster mentions firstly and not surprisingly that perennially favourite devil of Afrikaner Christian nationalists, liberalism, which infiltrated all sectors of society, including the church. However, and here the reasoning becomes rather unique, liberalism's ostensible nemesis, the revivalist spirit (see Chapter 3) also known as 'Methodism', is now argued to be closely related to liberalism, and hence a secondary danger to Calvinistic Afrikanerdom:

> As in Europe, liberalism had a deadening influence on the churchly-religious life. So, the conditions were made favourable for the recep-

tion of the second stream, Methodism, which was welcomed as a means to revival out of the deadness. This second spiritual stream, which is closely related to liberalism [the first stream] due to its humanist tendencies, influenced our *volks*-life more and more effectively, because it had initially, and only apparently, stood against liberalism. [transl.][90]

It is particularly that last sentence that contains the stinger. It shows how a specific type of fake news was created and perpetrated by combining two widely divergent streams of thought, discourses that were in fact representative of opposing world views. The combination is constructed in broad categories and without naming individuals. The naming of individuals would have necessitated an actual historical grounding for what was being alleged, so the anonymity is not surprising here. The proverbial dog-whistle is used instead. The broad categories were liberalism and Methodism, with the latter serving as code for the nineteenth-century revivalist tradition in the Cape DRC, which, as we saw, was closely associated with Scottish first- and second-generation immigrants. The author knew that this would be a plausible connection among his readership in the 1940s, with anything British understood as the enemy of Afrikaner identity, in which so-called Calvinism and nationalism featured equally prominently.

Yet apart from its connection to the 'English' world, how exactly is 'Methodism' brought into connection with liberalism? Methodism's alleged humanism/anthropocentrism is one key factor. Vorster argued that 'Methodism betrays the free sovereign grace of God and makes salvation dependent on the free will of humanity'.[91] He furthermore portrayed Methodism as a stooge of imperialism. 'Indeed, Methodism, apart from its doctrine that is strongly humanistic and anthropocentric, was superficial, pleasantly warm and opportunistic, pliable and supple, a wonderful export article' [transl.].[92]

Vorster, however, denied the existence of any direct connection between the early nineteenth-century DRC and Methodism. He stated:

The English government certainly did import Scottish ministers to anglicise the *volk*, but generally speaking the Scots were Calvinists. In character and thinking they differed from the Boer, but in doctrine there was between the Scottish Calvinist and the Calvinistic Boer not much of a difference. [transl.][93]

Vorster argued, somewhat ambiguously, that it was through general anglicisation that Methodism prospered. He described this incipient process as follows:

In doctrine the Church and its ministers were Calvinistic; but with Dr. Faure as its head, supported by the Scots ministers, they came under the hypnosis of the English spirit. More and more they sought connections with the English churchly-religious and social life; although officially still belonging with the Scots-Calvinistic Church. In practice they came more into contact with the English state church and the Methodists. Along this indirect route Methodism gained its grip on our *volkslewe*, and it could still easier accomplish this, because imperialism could use Methodism so deliciously to pull the religious Afrikaner off the track of his Christian-Nationalist path. [transl.][94]

Therefore, Methodism infiltrated the church on a cultural level, which had very little to do with theology. The Scots ministers, being tainted by their linguistic and social proximity to the English, were perhaps predestined, to misappropriate a Calvinist term, to be sucked into the orbit of both imperialism and Methodism. A major part of the problem identified by Vorster is the dissolution of borders. He identified a specific moment in South African church history as being more responsible than anything else for giving Methodism an entrance into '*ons kerklike- en volkslewe*' (the life of our church and volk). This event occurred in 1842 with the founding of '*Het Zuid-Afrikaansch Evangelisch Verbond*' (South African Evangelical Alliance), which 'closely and intimately' connected the DRC with the English, Scottish, Independent and Wesleyan churches. Vorster disapprovingly quoted *De Kerkbode* of January 1858 in this regard, which I translate as follows: 'Today they [the Methodists] are in our midst. The dividing walls have collapsed. The brotherly love that springs from God has broken the rusted chains.'[95] Vorster commented further: 'This removal of boundaries and negation of dogmatic differences has blunted the people's feeling and love for the own and the pure, and the main emphasis was shifted to the "life" and on experience and feeling. With this the groundwork was prepared for Methodism' [transl.].[96]

A further step towards Methodisation occurred with various calls for revival in 1859, first by '*Het Z.A. Evangelische Verbond*' in the *Kerkbode* of August and then the call to prayer for revival published in October and undersigned by fifteen DRC ministers, of which nine were of Scottish descent:

> Along this route we had come under the influence of Methodism. So much smoother it found its entrance when liberalism raised its head during this same period in the Cape church. Against liberalism, Methodism was welcomed as fighter. Undoubtedly it played no unimportant role in the victory against liberalism. Still it remains a pity that the *Calvinistic principle was not strongly and purely* employed against the liberal principle, because the alliance with Methodism cost the Church dearly ... especially when in the twentieth century liberalism again launched an assault on our churchly life, it found an ally in Methodism against Calvinism. Only these streams were not called by their names, but unjustly there was talk of evangelical and Kuyperian streams. [his emphasis, my transl.][97]

That this allegation of a twentieth-century alliance between Methodism and liberalism unambiguously had Johannes du Plessis in mind is indicated by the fact that Vorster cites the sympathetic portrayal of du Plessis in F. S. Malan's book on the DRC's heresy trial of Prof. du Plessis as responsible for confusing the proper terminology by referring to the opposing evangelical and Kuyperian streams.[98] Even though not of Scottish descent himself, du Plessis was certainly firmly placed within this tradition. A graduate of the University of Edinburgh, not only was he a missionary statesman of no lesser stature than Andrew Murray himself, he was also a personal friend of a number of Murray family members, and of course the author of Andrew Murray's massively extensive and commissioned biography, which I rely on heavily in this book.[99]

During the course of his career, du Plessis wrote a lot, and consequently managed to offend a number of powerful people. For periods of time he was editor of *De Kerkbode* and later *Het Zoeklicht*, where he expounded his views on higher criticism and the Bible. Despite being highly sympathetic to the Boer cause in the South African War, during which he served as chaplain at internment camps in the interior of the country, du Plessis, who had an English-speaking mother with whom he was very close, expressed himself on occasion against nationalism and language movements of whatever sort, precisely when such movements were becoming increasingly popular among the mainstream of Afrikaners in the early twentieth century.[100]

After the heresy trial, du Plessis and his brand of intellectual biblical scholarship became anathematised in Afrikaner reformed Christianity. It is well known that fundamentalists and Kuyperians then took control of the DRC's ideological direction, as seen for example in the prominent role someone like Koot Vorster would come to play. Vorster himself acknowledged this shift, as he concluded his *Koers in die Krisis* article in a more upbeat tone with respect to general Afrikaner sensibilities, which, according to his judgement, had come to occupy a more proper line in every respect:

> Methodism could not totally supplant Calvinism, and imperialism could indeed rob the *volk* of its land and freedom, from key positions and language, but not from its God. God willed it so that the Afrikaner should live; therefore there came according to his ordinance a National revival after the Boer war. The *volk* again yearned after the old paths ... With their going back to the past, the Afrikaner again returned to the tracks of Calvinism; ... Thus the Afrikaner regained its once lost direction and jubilantly we see today that the Afrikaner is not dead and that the Calvinist faith is not dead in them. There are on all terrains the welcome signs of Christian-National life. [transl.][101]

So the duel threats of liberalism and Methodism were in the end vanquished. Yet the way in which the narrative as sketched by Vorster unfolds leaves a few questions unanswered. On the one hand, it seems clear that Methodism became a kind of suitcase term for religious sentiments that were aligned in opposition to the developing cosy relationship between *volk* and church, as particularly well facilitated in the neo-Calvinist conception of these categories of life. Although the connection between Johannes du Plessis and the nineteenth-century revivalist tradition, in which Scottish-descended ministers were so active, is indeed a justifiable connection, as I indicated above, it is also rather ironic that the Murrays and other Scottish-descended ministers would be implicated in liberalism. This leads one to an inevitable question: were du Plessis and his legacy the actual targets of this neo-Calvinist opposition, and were the steadily less influential Scottish connection in the DRC merely drawn in as handy tinder to an already blazing fire composed of all things outside the new norm? Given the fallout of the du Plessis heresy trial, it is tempting to think so, and indeed there are some justifiable grounds for making this case. On the other hand, the fact is that the Scottish legacy (that is, 'Methodism'), independent of any direct connection to du Plessis, is also cast in a negative light by Afrikaner theological writers during the course of the early to middle twentieth century. I shall discuss texts exhibiting this latter perspective after highlighting aspects of the work by long-time Stellenbosch DRC minister and professor of church history, Tobie Hanekom (1906–85). The book in question is titled *Die Liberale Rigting in Suid-Afrika* (The Liberal Direction in South Africa). It is a detailed treatise of liberal influences in church and society over time. Although villains by name are rather absent in these pages, among the heroes countering liberalism are certainly counted the father-and-son pair S. J. and J. D. du Toit. One of S. J. du Toit's notable contributions, according to Hanekom, was the 'powerful action' taken in 1881 of instituting the 'Vrije Christelijke School' as a countering institution to the liberal tendencies in the state-run schools. The NGK (Cape Church) had the official view that the latter should be somehow Christianised, but du Toit's newly founded Christian schools had the support of the Gereformeerde Kerke, and Hanekom approved in retrospect.[102]

Like Koot Vorster, Hanekom identified Methodism as complicit in introducing liberalism into South Africa. Hanekom rather sweepingly referred to a connection between Wesleyans, Armenians, Pietism and semi-Pelagianism. 'Methodist influence in South Africa was then also to a certain extent a strengthening force for liberalism where via an indirect route it contributed to the undermining of the reformed doctrine' [transl.].[103]

Regarding the specific route through which Methodism and liberalism entered the country, Hanekom posited a caricature of the overseas nineteenth-century theological student from South Africa, and this hypothetical student's exposure to suspect currents abroad as a definite culprit. 'They came under the influence of Dutch culture and Dutch liberalism!'[104] Among other things, Hanekom mentioned the Utrecht student society *Secor Dabar* (see Chapter 2), to which Andrew and John Murray, as well as Nicolaas Hofmeyr and J. H. Neethling, belonged. Some of the society's characteristics were its emphasis on the *life of faith* in the spirit of the Réveil, as well as the fact that they were referred to as the 'Chocolade-club' by other

Utrecht students, which according to Hanekom drew the link between the members of *Secor Dabar* and Wesley's Methodist circle in Oxford.[105] There were indeed parallels between *Secor Dabar* and Wesley's Holy Club, as had been pointed out earlier by Johannes du Plessis[106] Hanekom agreed, on the one hand, with du Plessis' assessment of *Secor Dabar*'s positive influence on the religious life. On the other hand, he refused to accept du Plessis' following point: 'It would hardly be too much to say that the Murrays, and like-minded South Africans of the *Secor Dabar* circle, were instrumental in saving the Dutch Reformed Church at the Cape from being engulfed by rationalism . . .'[107] This the *Secor Dabarians* did not manage to achieve, according to Hanekom, because by emphasising the religious life, they neglected religious dogma:

> True to the character of the Réveil these student movements shifted the dogma to the background – it was life piety for which they strove. In this the spirit of their time comes to fulfilment: the worth of the dogma is underestimated and the life of faith is ranged on the dangerous side-track of subjectivism, which had since the days of Schleiermacher seemed powerless against liberalism, even preparatory for it.[108]

Despite an acknowledgement of the fact that the Murrays and other participants in the 1860s revivals played a role in counteracting liberalism, for Hanekom as for Vorster, and the soon to be mentioned later twentieth-century *Doppers*, all of this was inadequate, based as it was on unsound foundations. For them, at least in the way the divide was portrayed, it was basically the difference between an emphasis on Calvinistic confessional thinking and a life of piety. *Vroom of Regsinnnig?*, as the South African-Dutch philosopher Vincent Brümmer recently put it.[109] For these confessional thinkers in Afrikanerdom, the real struggle that mattered was the one between *Gereformeerdheid* (Reformed Calvinism) and liberalism. The Scottish influence (aka 'Methodism') presented a problem because the Scots did not seem Calvinist enough in retrospect, relying too little on doctrine in their countering of liberalism. Yet, at least for DRC writers like Vorster and Hanekom at Stellenbosch, the Murrays, especially, could not be so easily attacked. These figures, especially the brothers Andrew and John, had been pillars of authority within their inner circle for many decades. Less influential Scottish ministers were a different matter, however, and a quote attributed to Revd A. McGregor at the opening of a '*Christelijke Conferentie*' on 14 April 1863 is quite telling, especially in the way in which it is appropriated by Hanekom. Hanekom quotes from *De Kerkbode* of 2 May 1863. McGregor opined therein 'that liberalism emerged out of a dead and unsatisfactory orthodoxy and that thus, *the Christian life should be the strongest defence against all heresy*' [my transl./Hanekom's emphasis].[110] That confessional Reformed orthodoxy could be a problem was not conceivable to the theological mainstream in mid-twentieth-century DRC circles. And, in fact, with this statement McGregor had actually betrayed the real problem concerning these 'Christian life' proponents, because his statement came very close indeed to the problematic liberal point of view when looked at through Hanekom's hermeneutical lens. Hanekom illustrates this by quoting as follows from the well-known Cape liberal publication *De Onderzoeker* of 19 January 1863: 'Christianity is no dogma but life; it is a matter of the heart' [my transl.].[111]

Deeper into the twentieth century, it would become possible for writers to denounce Andrew Murray as Methodist without needing to make do with subtle innuendo or by having to resort to the use of pseudonyms, as SRP did towards the end of the previous century. In an academic study commissioned by the Potchefstroom University for Christian Higher Education, an institution affiliated with the Gereformeerde Kerke, this narrative comes especially to the fore in 1975 under the unambiguous title *'Revival' of Reformasie? 'n Studie oor die Metodisme* ('Revival' or Reformation? A Study about Methodism). One of the contributing authors, in a chapter entitled *'Metodistiese Invloede in Suid-Afrika: 'n Histories-kritiese ondersoek'* (Methodist Influences in South Africa: a Historical-critical enquiry), holds Murray as primarily responsible for hybridising Afrikaner reformed Christianity with Methodism.

Relying on du Plessis' biography, which positively compared Murray to Wesley, P. W. Buys used the same testimony to negatively typecast Murray as Methodist, and consequently less than fully reformed. Du Plessis is quoted as follows on Murray, although I translate the quote into English: 'He agreed with Wesley in his practical inclination, tireless activity, and incessant evangelistic journeys. Like Wesley, he delighted in the preaching work, and similarly he preached the simple gospel of repentance and faith, and similarly he believed in present and immediate salvation.'[112] Buys found plenty of ammunition against the Murrays as he described the religious practices of *Secor Dabar* as taken from du Plessis, of which the following sentence is most relevant: 'Once more John Murray led us in prayer, and then we used the bread and wine to fellowship with the body and blood of our Lord, who died for our righteousness's resurrection.'[113]

Buys expressed shock at this portrayal of a student organisation taking Holy Communion. This, in his estimation, made *Secor Dabar* even worse than Wesley, who, although he had started religious societies, still encouraged the society members to take Communion at church.[114]

Buys zoomed in specifically on the detrimental role Andrew Murray supposedly played in terms of weakening Calvinism and strengthening 'Methodism'. He mentioned themes that preoccupied Murray, such as Baptism of the Spirit and faith healing. Buys furthermore called to mind Walter Hollenweger's assessment,[115] according to which Murray subscribed to similar theories as American faith-healing preachers.[116] This line of reasoning is taken further when Buys suggests, again in reference to Hollenweger, that Murray, through his supposed contact with Pieter Le Roux, founding figure in the Apostolic Faith Mission and originally from Wellington, must have had a formative influence on the emergence of Pentecostalism in South Africa, or sectarianism as Buys calls it: 'Is it without reason that Hollenweger, in his discussion of the spiritual drivers in Christianity, mentions Murray, Dowie and the emergence of sectarianism in South Africa in one breath?' [my transl.].[117]

Before explicating the various 'Methodist' influences on Christian societies, in which Murray often played leading roles, such as in the Christian Endeavour Society, Buys moves to the climax of his specific discussion of Murray. This was to compare him, unfavourably of course, with none other than the *Dopper* theologian J. D. du Toit:

> A comparison between the collected works of Murray and those of Totius illustrates a significant difference. With the former there is an ongoing focus on the doctrine of salvation, with the latter a diversity of topics as richly coloured as life itself, and always so that the light of God's Word falls over different areas of life. This difference in approach to life points out exactly the difference between Methodism and Calvinism.[118]

Conclusion

This last quotation provides a helpful point of transition to the final chapter, which will seek to provide a reassessment of the Scottish legacy in Afrikaner reformed Christianity. This comparison between du Toit (Totius) and Murray is a good place to start that analysis. In reference to identity politics in South Africa, Totius had a very clear vision. He saw Calvinism as a life system that differentiated ethnic groups into strictly non-negotiable categories. Hence, Totius could confidently proclaim, when at one stage questioned about which biblical passages supported apartheid, that he did not need to reference any individual passages, because in fact the whole Bible justified apartheid.[119] Strange though it might seem now, this was in fact a completely logical reply for someone who was already committed to Calvinism as a life system while simultaneously taking a differentiated perspective of the creation of humanity as the point of departure. To paraphrase du Toit in reference to the biblical narrative of the Tower of Babel, what God had separated, that is, ethnic-linguistic groups, who might we be to unify that?[120]

In the view of du Toit and the other detractors of the Scottish legacy, 'Methodism' was simply dangerous and untenable because it could not and would not fit in with their vision of Calvinism as a total system of life, which was an ethno-nationalistic vision of remarkable scope and magnitude.

Notes

1. Richard Elphick (2012) *The Equality of Believers: Protestant Missionaries and the Racial Politics of South Africa*. Charlottesville and London: University of Virginia Press, p. 222ff.
2. Brian Stanley (ed.) (2003) *Missions, nationalism, and the end of empire*. Grand Rapids, MI: Eerdmans, p. 6.
3. See Hermann Giliomee (2011) *The Afrikaners: biography of a people*. London: Hurst and Co., p. 218.
4. Ibid., p. 217.
5. Vincent Brümmer describes du Toit growing up in Paarl as a disciple of G. W. A. van der Lingen, the anti-modernist minister mentioned in Chapter 2. When du Toit later studied at the Stellenbosch Seminary, he felt out of place within the context of the prevailing Réveil spirituality. This opposition to the Réveil led to a schism in the DRC in Paarl after his return there when a more hard-line Reformed congregation was formed under his leadership. Brümmer describes it as du Toit's lifelong project to resist the spirituality of the Réveil, as represented by Andrew Murray, the Stellenbosch Seminary, the Huguenot College, revivalist preaching and so forth. He expressed himself particularly in *Di Patriot*, *De Getuige* and, after 1905, in *Stemmen des Tijds*. Between 1897 and 1909 his followers in the Northern Cape and Transvaal formed ten 'Gereformeerde Gemeentes onder die Kruis' (Reformed Congregations under the Cross). After his death in 1911 these congregations joined up with the Gereformeerde Kerke, aka the *Doppers*. See V. Brümmer (2013) *Vroom of Regsinnig?: Teologie in die NG Kerk*. Wellington: Bybel-Media, pp. 168–9.
6. Giliomee, *The Afrikaners*, p. 220.
7. Streng Gereformeerde Patriot (9 February 1893) 'Ds. A. Murray di grootste vyand van ons nasionaliteit', *Di Afrikaanse Patriot*. DRC Archive, Stellenbosch.
8. Ibid.
9. Ibid.
10. Ibid.
11. Ibid.
12. Ibid.
13. Ibid.
14. Streng Gereformeerde Patriot (23 February 1893) 'Ds. A. Murray di grootste vyand van ons gereformeerde leer', *Di Afrikaanse Patriot*.
15. Ibid.
16. Ibid.
17. Ibid.
18. Ibid.
19. *Verslag van Taalkongres en Samenkomst* (1897), gehouden aan de Paarl, op 27 tot 31 Januari, 1897. Paarl: D. F. du Toit and Co., p. 19.
20. Ibid., p. 32.
21. Ibid., p. 32.
22. Ibid., p. 35.
23. Ibid.
24. Ibid., p. 36.
25. For an extensive biography on Malan, see Lindie Koorts (2014) *D. F. Malan and the Rise of Afrikaner Nationalism*. Cape Town: Tafelberg.

26. Elphick, *The Equality of Believers*, pp. 135–8.
27. S. B. Spies (n.d.) 'Malan, Daniel Francois (B)', *Dictionary of African Christian Biography*. https://dacb.org/stories/southafrica/malan-daniel2/
28. See Lala Badenhorst (1981) *Dienskneg*. Koffiefontein: C. L. Badenhorst, p. 15ff.
29. D. F. Malan (1913) *Naar Congoland: Een Reisbeschrijving*. Stellenbosch: Christen-Studenten Vereeniging van Zuid-Afrika.
30. Ibid., p. 9.
31. Ibid., p. 9.
32. Ibid., p. 8.
33. Ibid., p. 12.
34. Ibid., p. 26.
35. Lindie Korf (2007) 'Podium and/or Pulpit? D. F. Malan's role in the politicisation of the Dutch Reformed Church, 1900–1959', *Historia*, 52:2, November, pp. 214–38; Koorts, *D. F. Malan and the Rise of Afrikaner Nationalism*.
36. Malan, *Naar Congoland*, p. 13.
37. Ibid., p. 14.
38. Korf, 'Podium and/or Pulpit?', p. 216.
39. Malan, *Naar Congoland*, p. 28.
40. Ibid., p. 32.
41. Ibid., p. 50.
42. Ibid., p. 51.
43. Ibid., p. 51.
44. Ibid., p. 51.
45. Ibid., p. 52.
46. Ibid., p. 76.
47. Ibid., p. 75.
48. Ibid., p. 76.
49. Ibid., p. 77.
50. Ibid., p. 77.
51. Ibid., p. 78.
52. Ibid., p. 85.
53. Ibid., p. 85.
54. D. F. Malan (13 June 1915) *Doet het al ter Eere Gods. Afscheidsrede van Dr. D. F. Malan te Graaff Reinet*, p. 2.
55. Ibid., p.3.
56. Elphick, *The Equality of Believers*, p. 135 ff.
57. Malan, *Doet het al ter Eere Gods*, p. 3.
58. Ibid., p. 5.
59. Ibid., p. 6.
60. Ibid., p. 6.
61. Ibid., p. 7.
62. A. Murray (14 July 1915) *Godsdienst en Politiek. Oordeel van de Oude Kerkvader, Dr. Andrew Murray*. Wellington, p. 1.
63. Ibid., p. 1.
64. Ibid., p. 2.
65. Ibid., p. 3.
66. Ibid., p. 4.
67. Ibid., p. 1.
68. Charles Bloomberg and Saul Dubow (1990) *Christian-Nationalism and the Rise*

of the Afrikaner Broederbond, in South Africa, 1918–48. London: Macmillan Press, p. 66.
69. Ibid., p. 65.
70. Ibid., p. 66.
71. Andrew Murray, quoted in J. du Plessis, *The life of Andrew Murray of South Africa*. London: Marshall Brothers, p. 178.
72. Giliomee, *The Afrikaners*, p. 215ff.
73. J. D. du Toit (1903) *Het Methodisme*. Amsterdam: Hoveker & Wormser.
74. See J. Kinghorn and C. F. A. Borchardt et al. (1986) *Die NG Kerk en apartheid*. Johannesburg: Macmillan South Africa, pp. 100–1; Elphick, *The Equality of Believers*, pp. 238–57.
75. G. L. Van Heerde (1941) 'Strewersonderwerp: ons sestigjarige bestaan (a) Ons Verlede'. In *Strewerskonferensieboekie. Verslag van die 22ste Algemene Vergadering van die Christelike Strewersunie in verband met die Ned. Geref, Kerke in Suid-Afrika*. Gehou 3–6 Julie 1941 te Riversdal, p. 20. See also G. L. van Heerde (c. 1951) 'Ontstaan en geskiedenis van die C.S.-unie in Suid-Afrika'. In W. de W. Strauss (ed.) *Strewersgedenkboek, 1901–1951*. Kaapstad: Citadel.
76. J. D. du Toit (1905) *De Streversvereeniging beoordeeld van Gereformeerd standpunt*. Potchefstroom: Höveker and Wormser, p. 4.
77. Ibid., p. 5.
78. Ibid., p. 7.
79. '*de Streversvereeniging is een bastaard-Kerk en daarom is ook het Streefwerk een bastaard-ampt. Gods Woord nu eischt, dat wij tusschen echt en onecht onderscheiden . . .*' (Du Toit 1905, p. 35).
80. Ibid., p. 26ff.
81. Ibid., p. 36.
82. Ibid., p. 38.
83. J. D. du Toit (1906) *C.S.V. nog eens*. Antwoord Dr. J. D. du Toit. Potchefstroom, p. iv.
84. J. D. du Toit (1917) *Ds. S.J. du Toit. In Weg en Werk: 'n Periode van Afrikaanse Oplewing*. Paarl: Paarl Drukpers Maatschappij Beperkt.
85. *Het Zoeklicht* (15 October 1932), p. 306.
86. Ibid., p. 312.
87. Elphick, *The Equality of Believers*, pp. 243–5.
88. J. D. Vorster (1941) 'Die Metodistiese Invloed in ons Volkslewe', in H. G. Stoker and J. D. Vorster (eds) *Koers in die Krisis III*. Stellenbosch: Pro Ecclesia, p. 185.
89. Ibid., pp. 185–6.
90. Ibid., p. 187.
91. Ibid., p. 188.
92. Ibid., p. 189.
93. Ibid.
94. Ibid., p. 191.
95. *De Kerkbode* (January 1858), quoted in Vorster, 'Die Metodistiese Invloed in ons Volkslewe', p. 191.
96. Vorster, 'Die Metodistiese Invloed in ons Volkslewe', p. 191.
97. Ibid., pp. 192–3.
98. F. S. Malan (1933) *Ons Kerk en Prof. du Plessis*. Kaapstad: Nasionale Pers.
99. J. du Plessis, *Life of Andrew Murray*.

100. See Retief Müller (2014) 'Afrikaner socio-theological discourse in the early twentieth century: War and mission in J. F. Naudé and J. du Plessis', *Historia*, 59:2, pp. 309–25.
101. Vorster, 'Die Metodistiese Invloed in ons Volkslewe', p. 195.
102. T. N. Hanekom (1951) *Die Liberale Rigting in Suid-Afrika: 'n Kerkhistoriese Studie*. Stellenbosch: Christen-Studentevereeniging-maatskappy van Suid-Afrika, p. 215.
103. Ibid., p. 260.
104. Ibid., p. 280.
105. Ibid., p. 297.
106. J. du Plessis (1920) *Het leven van Andrew Murray*. Kaapstad: Zuid-Afrikaanse Bijbelvereniging, p. 66.
107. Du Plessis, quoted in Hanekom, *Die Liberale Rigting in Suid-Afrika*, p. 297 (my transl.).
108. Hanekom, *Die Liberale Rigting in Suid-Afrika*, pp. 297–8.
109. Brümmer, *Vroom of Regsinnig?*
110. Hanekom, *Die Liberale Rigting in Suid-Afrika*, p. 493–4.
111. Ibid., p. 494.
112. Quoted in P. W. Buys (1975) 'Metodistiese Invloede in Suid-Afrika: 'n Histories-kritiese ondersoek'. In *'Revival' of Reformasie? 'n Studie oor die Metodisme*. Potchefstroomse Universiteit vir C.H.O., pp. 51–2.
113. De Graaff, quoted in du Plessis, *Het leven van Andrew Murray*, p. 78 [transl.].
114. Buys, 'Metodistiese Invloede in Suid-Afrika', p. 52.
115. W. J. Hollenweger (1972) *The Pentecostals: The Charismatic Movement in the Churches*. Minneapolis, MN: Augsburg Pub. House, p. 111ff.
116. Buys, 'Metodistiese Invloede in Suid-Afrika', p. 57.
117. Ibid., p. 58.
118. Ibid.
119. See J. D. du Toit and S. du Toit (1955) *Die Afrikaanse Rassebeleid en die Skrif: Artikels van prof. dr JD du Toit en prof dr du Toit* (2nd edition). Potchefstroom: Pro Rege Bpk., p. 5.
120. See Kinghorn et al., *Die NG Kerk en apartheid*, p. 101.

CHAPTER EIGHT

Conclusion: The Scottish Legacy in Afrikaner Religiosity Reassessed

Although the term 'Scots Afrikaners' is a construct of my invention, it is useful to note that when the *Genootskap van Regte Afrikaners* (Society of True Afrikaners) was in the process of defining its raison d'être at its first meeting in 1875, S. J. du Toit (1847–1911) and his compatriots decided to categorise Afrikaners as follows: Afrikaners with English hearts, Afrikaners with Dutch hearts and Afrikaners with Afrikaans hearts.[1] No doubt du Toit would have classified what I describe as Scots Afrikaners in this book not as Afrikaners with Scots hearts, but rather as part of the more easily denigrated category of Afrikaners with English hearts. Of course, this kind of typecasting of the other within the broader self could only lead to misunderstanding. It is a naming strategy set up for more conclusive stereotyping, for instigating conflict and the purging of impure elements within the hardening identity formation which became Afrikanerdom in the twentieth century. Such internal othering is of course a well-known and often-used strategy within nationalistic discourses generally. Yet such strategies often hide more than they reveal in terms of actual loyalties. Therefore, a brief juxtaposition of S. J. du Toit and Andrew Murray, the representative in chief of the Scots Afrikaners, in terms of their identarian positioning over time, seems like a useful entry point for this chapter. I concluded Chapter 7 with a *Dopper* theologian's comparison of Murray and J. D. du Toit, but S. J. and Andrew are even more comparable as contemporaneously influential nineteenth-century figures in South Africa.

Andrew Murray, S. J. du Toit and their Afrikaner Sympathies

Perhaps the most important issue for S. J. du Toit and his compatriots was the establishment of Afrikaans as a literary language for the 'white' Afrikaner people. This was part of a conscious effort to claim this Dutch dialect as a 'white' language, while it had in fact emerged in an oral setting among illiterate and semi-literate poorer classes, that is, within predominantly 'coloured' communities. For this reason, the first attempt at Afrikaans Bible translation was aimed at this people group.[2] Du Toit, however, had higher, or should we say more exclusivist, ideals for the language: 'The language of a nation expresses the character of that nation. Deprive a nation of the vehicle of its thoughts and you deprive it of the wisdom of its ancestors.'[3] Giliomee further elaborates on du Toit's contribution in this regard:

> The language movement was concentrated in a very small area, Paarl and its immediate surroundings. A single man dominated it as the moving spirit and creative genius ... Du Toit and his associates would publish much in Dutch as well, but to them Afrikaans was the primary language of white Afrikaners. That du Toit would entertain such grand ambitions for Afrikaans as a language, which at that stage was virtually without literature, suggests both his boundless intellectual self-confidence and his nationalist zeal.[4]

Given this portrayal, it is not surprising to note that du Toit authored a heroic history of the white Afrikaner people in Afrikaans.[5] He furthermore decided to try his hand at a political career, and where better for a strident Afrikaner nationalist towards the end of the nineteenth century than in the Zuid-Afrikaansche Republiek (aka the Transvaal), that plucky Boer-controlled state that was showing mounting resistance to the incursions of the British Empire in southern Africa. Du Toit was appointed to head up the education department in Paul Kruger's government in 1882, but it seems that more than idealistic nationalism was required to make a success of a political career, even in the Transvaal Republic. Du Toit and Kruger's collegiality did not last in the long run. When Kruger deputised him to settle a land dispute on the western frontier, du Toit rashly and unsuccessfully attempted to orchestrate the annexation of the territory for the Transvaal. After this episode, du Toit, who had also fallen into financial troubles due to poor investments made in the gold-mining industry, had to vacate his position. Embittered, he disavowed Kruger and the Boer cause, and in a full about face on his earlier leanings he returned to the Cape in 1890 as a supporter of Cecil John Rhodes' imperialist agenda. In the Cape he remained a supporter of the British during the course of the South African War. Giliomee suggests that upon his return to the Cape, du Toit was quite likely wholly financially dependent on Rhodes.[6]

In terms of identarian sentiment and expression and their evolution over time, the contrast with Andrew Murray could not be more striking. I am not going to repeat a narrative already told in the preceding pages but let me briefly recap regarding this theme. In this book I have emphasised a trajectory where Murray and other Scots in the DRC started out as appointees in a colonialist state church under British rulership. Andrew Murray subscribed to the idea of the British Empire as a benevolent presence and he objected, against the majority opinion of his parishioners in Bloemfontein, to the British withdrawal from the Orange River Sovereignty (see Chapter 2). However, the Scots Afrikaners were intentional hybrids, and as British imperial aggression increased towards the end of the nineteenth century, culminating in the South African War, Murray and others, including many of his family members, turned increasingly pro-Boer in their sympathies (see Chapter 5). There was the notable exception of his nephew, Robert Murray, who fought and died on the side of the British (see Chapter 6), but the more general pattern was to side alongside the majority Afrikaner stance in this conflict.

The Twentieth-century Triumph of the du Toits and the Neo-Calvinists

It is quite interesting and perhaps somewhat ironic that despite a growing identification with the plight of the Afrikaner by the Murrays and other Scots-descendant ministers like David Ross (see Chapter 5), it was the tradition established by the du Toit pair of father and son, which, in spite of the former's turbulent relationship with the Transvaal Republic government, became the central stream in Afrikaner Christian nationalism as the twentieth century moved along. Perhaps in line with the legendary narrative of Afrikaner history constructed by S. J. du Toit in *Die geskiedenis van ons land: In die taal van ons volk* (The history of our country: in the language of our people), his son, J. D. du Toit (aka Totius), would contribute to the further mythologising of a heroic Afrikaner discourse centring on victimhood at the hands of the Empire, but followed by triumphant self-actualisation in the years following the South African War. Totius' Afrikaans poetry was a particularly effective and influential vehicle in the construction of Afrikaner nationalism,[7] which together with his anti-'Methodism' and theological justification of apartheid (see Chapter 7), made him a powerful figure with influence across denominational lines in Afrikaner reformed Christianity. As the twentieth century progressed or regressed, depending on one's point of view, Totius and other neo-Calvinist nationalists would steadily supplant and occupy the leading positions in Afrikaner reformed Christian discourse that was formerly occupied by the Scots and other more ecumenically minded evangelicals in the nineteenth century.

The Scots in the DRC as Missionaries

I have suggested that the Scots Afrikaners' identarian positioning should primarily be understood from the point of view of a missionary tradition. Although this missionary identity became particularly actualised towards the end of the nineteenth century via the vehicle of the Ministers' Missionary Union and the birth of the DRC's 'foreign' missionary enterprise (see Chapter 4), it is my contention that this development was a logical consequence of deeply ensconced ideological foundations. In fact, the original Scots ministers in the DRC had come from an evangelical background and they had missionary interests. Quite a few of them were LMS missionaries prior to joining the DRC (see Chapter 2). I have suggested that for them the Dutch Afrikaner was a group to be evangelised and that their ministry within the DRC was perhaps conceived as a missionary labour. A typical missionary strategy would be to seek out points of contact within a local culture, language and religion, which the missionary could then use as conceptual starting points and rhetorical bridges for communicating the gospel message. It is therefore interesting to note that Andrew Murray briefly appeared to consider the budding Paarl-based Afrikaner nationalism in the 1880s within such a missionary framework. This much becomes apparent in a letter he wrote to his wife Emma when he was spending time in the Karoo town of Murraysburg, a town named after his father, while recuperating from a throat infection.[8] In the letter to Emma, dated 12 March 1881, Murray gives the following interesting commentary:

> I have just read a little tract, *Ons Land en Ons Volk*, published at the Paarl. I should not wonder if Mr. J. de Villiers were the writer. It is worth reading to see how strongly the feeling of nationality is asserting itself and mingling with the religious sentiment of the people. One hardly knows what to say of it. That there has been much that is unholy and evil in the anti-English sentiments which helped to stir up this movement is true. And yet there are in it elements of good which must be nourished. A more strongly developed national life in our half-slumbering Dutch population will afford a more vigorous stock for the Christian life to be grafted on. If we cannot influence the movement directly, we must try and put in abundantly the salt which can save it from corruption . . .[9]

This quote is interesting for more than one reason: most obviously because it supports my contention regarding the Afrikaner as a missionary subject for the likes of the Murrays et al., but also for the fact that Murray identified nationalism correctly as a quasi-religious movement, which, optimistically, could be utilised as a point of contact for Christian evangelism. Detractors of Murray and his role in South African reformed Christianity might now easily latch on to this piece of information and argue that this is indicative of how the Scottish evangelical tradition represented by Murray actually served to strengthen this movement of nationalism and thereby contributed to apartheid, and so on. And, of course, Murray's views about nationalism in spite of the caveats he added seem dangerously optimistic in retrospect, but this was the nineteenth century, the height of the modern era, where optimism about human progress was generally at a high point. As indicated previously, Murray was indeed a modern figure, if paradoxically so. It might be somewhat myopic to fault Murray much for the generosity of spirit exhibited towards early Afrikaner nationalism in this passage, especially in light of how he would himself become a larger-than-life target for this very same movement in subsequent decades.

Understanding the Scots Afrikaners as a missionary tradition also helps to explain the easy pragmatism they adopted in what seems in hindsight like a problematic willingness to dispense with their own principles and theological sensibilities in order to accommodate the 'weakness of some' regarding segregated worship and Holy Communion during the 1857 synod. Missionaries knew that they had to pick their battles when evangelising a group of people that might have had only limited understanding of the tenets of Christianity. Hence, among black African groups in southern Africa, missionaries sometimes tolerated what was seen as the unchristian marital practices of polygamy and lobola (the practice of donating and receiving cows as part of a marital agreement between the families involved).[10] By tolerating such practices, missionaries were not typically condoning them. Instead they recognised such practices as deeply entrenched customs integral to the local culture and tradition, and they assumed that over time the leaven of the gospel would internally transform the culture to become more and more 'Christian'.

Let me acknowledge that it might seem a bit controversial to compare Dutch Afrikaner segregationist tendencies to traditional African marital practices, and I beg forgiveness in advance for any undue offence caused. Yet the analogy holds true. From the point of view of a nineteenth-century evangelical missionary mindset, these practices were all equally wrong. The only question was whether they presented insurmountable obstacles to the gospel, or whether they might be taken as cultural practices, which, though undoubtedly heathen, were still accommodatable, if such accommodation might smooth the way for the entrance and spread of the gospel among the people in question. As might be imagined, missionaries positioned themselves on both sides of the equation regarding African marital practices, with some, particularly women missionaries, seeing lobola and polygamy as non-negotiable heathen elements standing in the way of Christian equality. Others, such as the innovative and controversial Bishop of Natal, John William Colenso, were more tolerant of such practices. In the case of segregated worship and communion, the Scots missionaries to the Dutch Afrikaner tended to accede to the accommodationist approach posited by their patriarchal figure, Andrew Murray Sr at the 1857 synod. Insisters on the principle of equality and Christian uniformity in this case were fewer and farther between but not non-existent, as the excellent case of the Dutch missionary/minister P. Huet and his subsequent publication, *Eene Kudde en Een Herder*, illustrates.[11]

It has been the received wisdom in South African church history regarding the 1857 episode that a missionary motive underpinned the 'weakness of some' decision. The consensus understanding has been that by positing the ill-fated motion, Andrew Murray had hoped to remove anti-missionary objections and rather secure the church's broad support for evangelistic ventures among the 'heathen' population, that is, blacks and 'coloureds'. While I have no dispute with that interpretation, what has apparently not really been factored in or even grasped by prior analyses of this episode and its aftermath is that the Dutch Afrikaners in the DRC were themselves representative of a primary mission field from the point of view of the Scots. Accommodating Dutch Afrikaner racism was part of a missionary strategy that optimistically assumed the very racism being accommodated would

Scots Afrikaners as 'Unchristian' Missionaries

be vanquished by the leaven of the gospel over time. This was a missionary miscalculation of magnitude and consequence, as the subsequent history showed.

Fast forward to the 1924 Livingstonia conference and the negotiations regarding the DRC's Nkhoma mission's amalgamation with the two Scots Presbyterian missions of Blantyre and Livingstonia into the unified Church of Central Africa Presbyterian. To eat or not to eat together with the black African delegates was the question for a DRC contingent in which Scots Afrikaner missionaries played leading roles. Discussed in Chapter 6, this episode conveys what might be a sense of shame but also a feeling of unease among the Nkhoma missionaries over the incident. What was reported or not reported seems to have had the home DRC audience in mind to a large extent. A. C. Murray mentioned in his diary specifically asking his fellow representatives not to make much of the incident when writing home (see Chapter 6). J. A. Retief notably did not mention the specific nature of the incident in his book, despite referring to some difficulties, generally, which were overcome by Robert Laws offering a spontaneous prayer. Both A. C. and W. H. Murray seemed to experience mixtures of discomfort, confusion, indignation but also resistance in conversations with Scottish missionaries over the DRC's stance. A. C. Murray clearly indicates the hermeneutical gap between the Scots and the Afrikaners on this issue when he writes that Livingstonia missionary McAlpine expressed surprise when informed about how strongly 'our men' felt about eating together with African ministers at the same table. Then he said that 'our position is unchristian'.[12] In writing about this interchange in his diary, A. C. Murray seemed somewhat perplexed. W. H. Murray, in M. W. Retief's narrative at least, supposedly had a bit of a debate regarding the morality of eating or non-eating together with Africans with Livingstonia missionary Donald Fraser. The issue of Christian inconsistency was reportedly broached, which ended with W. H. Murray issuing the rhetorical trump card of asking whether one could allow the marriage of one's daughter to an African, a notion which Donald Fraser could reportedly also not countenance, thereby exhibiting a similar degree of Christian inconsistency to the DRC missionaries in their communal eating prejudice. This narrative is anecdotally relayed by W. H. Murray in M. W. Retief.[13]

Several interesting deductions could be made from this interchange, supposing it did indeed occur, and more or less in that sequence. Note for example how it affirms the notion of mission as a discourse of difference.[14] Africans are unambiguously othered in Murray's stance, but so are women, specifically daughters, by both Murray and Fraser in this narrative. Daughters could be disallowed to cross the boundary of racial othering, in a rhetorical sequence which of course serves to other and lessen both

Africans and young white women. It is hardly surprising to note that these male missionaries thought of themselves as patriarchal figures. It fits well with general patterns in early twentieth-century Protestantism as well as with typical gender roles in the mission field. I have noted the particularly strict conservatism that was prevalent at the Nkhoma mission and subsequently in the Nkhoma synod, which continues to disallow the ordination of women to the preaching ministry. What still makes this type of attitude ironic is the strong roles that women had played in the foundations of the DRC mission enterprise, including the fact that W. H. Murray's own daughter, Pauline, was an accomplished medical missionary and co-translator working with her father (see Chapter 4).

Whether these Murrays, particularly W. H., were indeed expressing themselves so strongly on the theme of racially integrated eating in reference to their own sentiments or as a kind of smokescreen in order to deflect the possible suspicion of other DRC missionaries from the Free State's *Madzi Moyo* mission and home church representatives such as D. G. Malan, who were all present at the 1924 conference, is indeed an open question. I have indicated in reference to an anecdote told by J. A. Retief that segregated eating might have been rather less commonly practised among Nyasaland missionaries, as evidenced by the surprised reaction of the latter's young son upon witnessing such a situation in South Africa (see Chapter 6).

So perhaps the Nyasaland missionaries insisted on segregated eating as strongly as they did as part of an accommodationist strategy for the benefit of their home church, which at this time in history considered this level of social differentiation far from being some sort of 'weakness', but rather as a Christian national principle to uphold. Whatever their own sentiments might have been, the net result was that not only was the DRC in South Africa sufficiently placated to agree to have its Nkhoma mission join the CCAP, but the Nyasaland missionaries were also able to have their compromised position accommodated by the Scottish missions and the rest of the CCAP, which allowed the Nkhoma synod to become part of the CCAP despite the 'unchristian' persistence of the DRC's missionaries regarding the rejection of integrated eating. Once again we see a situation where themes of mission and church union were at stake and where Scots missionaries accommodated racist 'weakness' in order to smooth the way for the missionary cause to proceed.

To say the least, although historically extremely interesting this is theologically speaking a deeply troubling sequence of events, with none of these parties emerging as admirable vindicators of equality. Instead, pragmatic missionary compromise or accommodation won the day. What is particularly ironic, as I noted in Chapter 6, is that the Scots Afrikaners were now the ones who had to be accommodated in their weakness by other Scots and Africans in Nyasaland, while their ancestor, Andrew Murray Sr, and other Scots in the nineteenth-century DRC were original accommodators of racism of only a slightly different shade.

Hybridity Limited

Hybridity explains a lot, of course. In Chapter 1 I referred to a comment by MacKenzie, the gist of which is well worth repeating here. It concerns the fact that Scots in South Africa tended to stress their affinity with the Afrikaner to such an extent that they contributed to a discourse of race that understood the relationship between so-called white 'races' as the primary relationship of interest. This discourse occurred to the detriment of Africans, whose needs and wishes were sidelined as a result.[15] In line with this, I argue that the Scots Afrikaners were representative of an intentional hybridity, because once points of contact had been established in a missionary discourse, a secondary missionary technique would be to indigenise the gospel. As part of this indigenisation process, missionaries might acculturate themselves as much as possible to the culture of their potential converts. In some cases that might mean 'going native', that is, adopting a full-blown hybridity. This had been successfully achieved in respect to the Scots Afrikaner missionaries discussed in this book – too successfully, it might seem. They had become unadulterated Afrikaners apparently sharing the very same racial prejudices their ancestors had considered unscriptural and which their Scottish colleagues in the mission field considered unchristian.

The above scenario might well serve as added nuance to the idea of mission as a discourse of difference. Scots missionaries to the Dutch Afrikaners, if this reading of them is viable, were able to overcome immediate barriers of difference, although that took a few generations to complete. In the process, other barriers of difference were created as the Scots Afrikaners became missionaries to black Africans. The question now becomes, what happened to hybridity as a factor in this new relationship?

DRC missionaries were indeed interested in potential points of contact in the culture and tradition of the Chewa people in Malawi as a strategy for communicating the gospel. This much is evident from the writings of A. C Murray and J. A. Retief, among others, where quite a bit of attention is given to descriptions of the indigenous religion, but at no point did Afrikaner missionaries apparently consider 'going native' in Malawi or in any of the other places they operated. Intentional hybridity apparently remained precluded as a viable option with respect to black Africans. Even so, one might ask whether there were underlying processes of growing affinity and sympathy emerging in the interaction between DRC missionaries and Africans. Although this is not the theme of this book, centring as it does on Scottish Afrikaner relations and hybridities, this is indeed a pressing question specifically in terms of questions that might be posed regarding the wider relevance of what has been discussed here. Are missionary discourses predetermined to remain discourses of difference, or might the case be made that they could serve to accentuate and strengthen discourses of shared humanity and equality? If one were to take the long view, as Robert Woodberry does, for example, then this latter perspective does indeed become a possibility. In what could be described as a paradigm-shifting study on the legacy of the Protestant missionary movement, Woodberry, in his article 'The Missionary Roots of Liberal Democracy', makes an impressive case for the equalising societal patterns linked to areas where what he describes as 'conversionary Protestantism' was an active force. Based on statistical data, the article makes the case that the normal indicators of modernity, for example, democratic governance, 'religious liberty, mass education, mass printing, newspapers, voluntary organizations, most major colonial reforms, and the codification of legal protection for nonwhites in the nineteenth and early twentieth centuries',[16] were far more likely to be present in parts of the world where conversionary Protestant missionaries operated than in other places. In an argument that is reminiscent of Elphick's thesis in the *Equality of Believers*, that some missionary structures ultimately served to foster forces of equality in South Africa, despite missionaries themselves often trying to limit or contain the radicalness of the message they were proclaiming,[17] Woodberry makes the point that the democratic forces he uncovered also often occurred independently of missionaries' own myopic views and prejudices, including racism.[18]

A Counter-narrative in Afrikaner DRC History?

Perspectives such as those by Woodberry and Elphick are key to understanding the wider narrative and its implications if we look beyond the above-mentioned Scots Afrikaner examples of, firstly, accommodation of racist 'weakness' in 1857 and their own subsequent generation's expression of racist sentiments regarding eating with Africans at the 1924 Livingstonia conference. In the twilight era of apartheid, late South African missiologist David Bosch made an intriguing claim in reference to the work of another South African theologian and anti-apartheid stalwart, Jaap Durand,[19] which amounted to the idea that although evangelicalism among the Afrikaner in South Africa had generally aligned itself with the formation and institutionalising of apartheid, there remained a subsection in this movement that maintained a contrary perspective. Let me quote Bosch directly:

> A third group kept alive the missionary spirit of the eighteenth century awakening. They knew that it was impossible to be concerned with the spiritual needs of Blacks without at the same time getting involved in their very real bodily and social needs. The scores of Dutch Reformed Church missionaries who went to Malawi, Kenya, Nigeria, Zambia, and Zimbabwe, as well as those who worked within the borders of South Africa, virtually all came out of this third group. In the course of time, it was out of this group that the first voices of protest against Afrikaner politics came.[20]

The allusion here primarily relates to people like Beyers Naudé, the quintessential Afrikaner opponent of apartheid, who is known to have been influenced early on by exposure to missionaries and missionary contexts in terms of his early reassessment regarding his position in Afrikanerdom, but Bosch was likely also having in mind his own experience as a missionary in the Transkei.[21] The point of all this is that, sure enough, missionaries typically resisted the allure of hybridity, and less often yet would they consider 'going native'. Still, despite individual intentions and motivations, the foreign missionary experience could open doors of perception for missionaries regarding the life and experiences of their missionary subjects. As a result, it might even change missionaries themselves with respect to their identification with their own sending culture. Implied reference group affiliation might shift, with identarian and even political consequences to follow.

The point made by Bosch in favour of the DRC missionary enterprise is of course too vague to form any kind of basis to argue for the redemption of the Scots Afrikaners and their sphere of influence in terms of racist othering discourses. Their own apologetic complicity regarding the mixed-eating controversy at Livingstonia, as well as their hierarchical missionary views and their generally segregation-ameliorating approaches, firmly place them as complicit in the formation of apartheid, even if their collaboration within this discourse might be partially construed as a pragmatic technique to avert undue attention to the ways that they were in fact mixing with 'liberal' Scots and also to a degree with Africans in Nyasaland.

One might leave the matter at that and go along with the notion that mission as an othering discourse was indelibly implicated in the construction of apartheid, were it not for the fact that this tradition of 'Scottish Methodism' became so vilified by Afrikaner Christian nationalists in the twentieth century. This alerts the observer to the idea that overtly or covertly there was more to the story of the Scots Afrikaners and their missionary and ecumenical engagements.

In fact, subsequent to the Nkhoma mission's tumultuous joining with the CCAP in the mid-1920s, a deep rift had appeared between the ecumenical Scottish Afrikaner missionary tradition, on the one hand, and Christian nationalist missionaries and/or churchmen, on the other. J. A. Retief's public correspondence with J. G. Strydom and Retief's indignation over attacks against the CCAP illustrate this clash between traditions (see Chapter 6). Strydom, as representative in chief of the Afrikaner Christian nationalist missionary tradition, had a specific interest in mind and that concerned the ways in which the DRC's missionary enterprise could be of benefit to the Afrikaner, nationalistically speaking.[1] Clearly, the DRC's Nkhoma mission's participation in the ecumenical Scots-initiated CCAP was a great example of mission circumventing, perhaps even contravening, nationalism. Whatever the case, from Strydom's point of view it was a nationalistically hybrid venture, and doctrinally suspect too. The doctrinal argument was the easier one to make in an ostensibly religious setting such as the DRC, and on this basis the final attack against the CCAP was indeed launched by Strydom's disciple Mentz at the 1945 synod (see Chapter 6). Yet one gets the impression that the real heresy was the cultural heresy of the minimisation or dilution of Afrikaner identity by mixing with Africans and Scots in the CCAP.

By seeking ecclesiastical hybridity between the Livingstonia, Blantyre and Nkhoma synods in Nyasaland, both the Scots and the Scots Afrikaner missionaries and their circle of influence in Nyasaland were exhibiting the well-noted Scottish colonial tendency of pragmatic cultural assimilation. When stumbling blocks arose against this joint missionary product, such stumbling blocks, presenting themselves in the forms of racist 'weakness' or prejudice, were quickly sidestepped and otherwise accommodated. This might have been done under the perhaps misguided optimism that the true scriptural principles would eventually establish themselves through a kind of leavening process. Mission and church unity were the most important factors for the central players. Anything else could be accommodated or even temporarily swept under the carpet. That this was wishful thinking in the short to medium term is a matter of historical record. However, it might appear that once the doors for social mixing had been opened, the potential for even greater hybridity, perhaps across colour lines, had also been created. This seems to be a major aspect underpinning the fear of and aversion to the CCAP project from the likes of Strydom, Kies and others (see Chapter 6). This might also help to explain the neo-Calvinist attacks on Scottish 'Methodism' from the du Toit pair of father and son and their followers in the twentieth century (see Chapter 7). Any kind of mixing, whether social or theological, was abhorred by the neo-Calvinist Afrikaner nationalists. Given the constructed nature of Afrikaner identity formed out of a diversity of ethnic backgrounds, this twentieth-century obsession with 'purity' is of course highly ironic, but the fact is that hybridity was eschewed as dangerously problematic.

Added to the fear of mixing we might dwell on the thought that, typically, nobody really likes to be missionised unless there is some extraneous benefit to be had in relation to that status. An open question related to this might be posed as follows: could the neo-Calvinists' attack on 'Methodism' be partly explained as an unwelcome realisation that the Afrikaner had been missionary subjects for the Scots? And related to that, what would be more unwelcome for a white Christian nationalist than to imagine that you and your people had featured in some other group's scheme of things as being on a par with 'heathen' black Africans? Although it is impossible to prove this, I have a strong suspicion that this is an underlying theme informing much of the vitriol against 'Scots Methodism' from the late nineteenth century onwards. If my suspicion about this is correct, one should not be surprised that the opponents themselves did not level this charge against Andrew Murray and the other Scots. From the opponents' point of view, there would have been great shame in publicly opening up about the implied status of the Afrikaner as a missionary subject. Psychologically far less disturbing for S. J. and J. D. du Toit and the others would have been the route they ultimately took, which was to attack and cast aspersions on the Scots as *Engelsgesind* (English-oriented), anti-nationalist and theologically unorthodox. This course of action could be undertaken from a position of strength within the developing culture of Afrikaner nationalism. Admitting missionary subjecthood, on the other hand, would have opened a can of worms that ideologically speaking might be better left contained. Still, if they were aware of the existence of the proverbial can, unopened or not, it would have been enough to inspire a great deal of racist resentment. What I am suggesting here, if true, is of course a hidden discourse, but it is well worth considering in pursuit of uncovering the various shades of racism informing Afrikaner religious history. Despite being a hidden discourse, this is not a far-fetched suggestion by any stretch of the imagination. I have indicated throughout this book how the Scots in the DRC primarily conceived of themselves as having a missionary identity. The above quote by Andrew Murray clearly suggests that even the blatantly adversarial discourse of Afrikaner nationalism was, at least in its early formation, seen by Murray as a discourse with potential points of contact for the 'Christian life to be grafted on'.

To give a brief recap of how this theme unfolded, one could recall the migrations of Cape Dutch farmers out of the colony from the 1830s, which is popularly known in Afrikaner history as the Great Trek, which was a necessary precursor to the eventual founding of Boer republics to the north. Scots ministers opposed this and portrayed it as an attempt to be free from the godly instituted temporal authority at the Cape, but upon realising the irreversibility of this movement, the likes of Taylor, Reid, Murray and Robertson all endeavoured on what might be described as missionary excursions to evangelise the recalcitrant flock.

Subsequently, after the Empire had extended its own borders northwards, Andrew Murray Jr became the first DRC minister in the Transgariep area known as the Orange River Sovereignty. From here he undertook four tours of a missionary nature to the Transvaal to evangelise the Boers in that area, thus far beyond the control of the British. In effect, these excursions by Murray and his various companions were the first foreign missionary endeavours of the Scots Afrikaners, although unofficially so since they were not named as such. The opposition and threats Murray received on a few occasions during and related to these tours are perhaps indicative of how local Boers were well aware of the fact that they were being missionised and were somewhat less than appreciative of the efforts undertaken on behalf of their eternal salvation.

Another development that received negative attention from the twentieth-century neo-Calvinist opposition was the revivalist movement, which occurred from the 1860s onwards and in which the Scots played a pivotal role (see Chapter 3). The retrospective opposition, which railed against the 'Methodist' nature of these revivals, might be even better understood when one considers these as part of an internally oriented missionary movement within the DRC. Revivalism was a primer for the launch of more focused and programmatic endeavours such as the Huguenot seminary and related schools, as well as the Ministers' Missionary Union, and the official launch of the DRC's foreign missionary enterprises to Nyasaland and elsewhere (see Chapter 4).

A subsequent primer with a similar trajectory to the period of revivalism, that is, an internal missionary movement followed by a wave of outward excursions, might be seen in the ministry of the Christian Endeavour Society (*De Christelijke Streversvereniging*) and its representatives on the POW islands of exile during the South African War (see Chapter 5). This movement, in which Andrew Murray and his family members were central players early on, evangelised Boer POWs and inspired a strong sense of Christian life and responsibility, including missionary responsibility, among its adherents, or converts if you prefer. An influx of personnel and funds into the foreign missionary enterprise of the post-war DRC was a major consequence of this society's work among Boer prisoners in Ceylon, St Helena and elsewhere. As indicated in Chapter 7, the Endeavour Society became a special target for the anti-Methodist ire of J. D. du Toit (Totius) in the early twentieth century. If this society might be identified as principally involved in a missionary campaign among the Boers, then the subsequent Afrikaner nationalist opposition to them becomes a completely rational reaction.

Little wonder it is then, that the Scottish legacy in the DRC became unpopular as the twentieth century moved along, in tandem with hardening apartheid and nationalist discourses underpinning white Afrikaner fears and ideals.

Conclusion

In a country such as South Africa, and among a people group such as the Afrikaner, and within a church such as the DRC, one cannot escape the sordid history of racial oppression and inequality. So, as an insider to all of that, it is perhaps a natural thing to search for rays of light, counter-narratives and the like, anything to prove that we were not all like that. In Christian tradition, even when it is accepted that much of it is a narrative of sinful pride, cowardice and so forth, there is always the potential to find prophets of hope and righteousness in the midst of all the trouble, despair and inequity. This is the case in the biblical narrative, and beyond that in Christian tradition throughout the centuries. This is part of what continues to keep people interested in Christianity. This search for a counter-narrative does not have to derail into the construction of heroic histories, although admittedly it often does. It should be clear to the reader that the preceding narrative of the Scots Afrikaners is no heroic history. It is a narrative of complicity and short-sighted decision making, of compromise to a reigning ideology of racial separation and non-equalisation. So, heroic this story is definitely not. Still, admittedly non-heroic then, it is impossible to engage in this history and not be confronted by the question of whether the narrative of the Scots Afrikaners represents a counter-narrative in Afrikaner and DRC history. This question particularly presents itself in reference to the attacks against the Scots Afrikaners from the side of Afrikaner nationalists and neo-Calvinists. If they were seen as so deviant by these hardliners, would that make them perhaps better than they would otherwise appear?

My basic answer is that as a primarily missionary tradition they had at least two distinguishing characteristics counting in their favour, and also in terms of how we might evaluate them retrospectively. One, like all sincere missionaries, they believed in the possibility of redemption, in the idea of a better tomorrow, however one wants to phrase this concept, which is theologically termed eschatological hope. This is also why, detrimentally, they could forego what they believed to be right in favour of what made diplomatic or pragmatic sense at certain moments. They believed, for example, that things would become better instead of worse in terms of race relations. As I indicated above, the 1857 decision was a miscalculation of some magnitude. However, misplaced hope is still hope. When later generations of Scots Afrikaners exhibited their own shades of racism in the negotiations leading up the Nkhoma mission's amalgamation with the CCAP, the church union still occurred, and once it had occurred the Nkhoma missionaries defended it fervently. Theologically speaking, eschatological hope goes beyond the biases, ideals or individual hopes believers might have. It is actually God's hope for humanity.

Secondly, as a missionary tradition they were willing to engage the other, and they did, however unequally that engagement occurred at times. Again, what makes this a hopeful characteristic is that the willingness to engage and the actual process of engagement often have unplanned and unintended consequences. When Scots Afrikaners in Nyasaland insisted on segregationist eating arrangements, they found themselves challenged by their Scots friends. This occurred in an ecumenical setting, but of course this type of challenge is no anomaly in missionary settings. Missionaries have often been challenged by their potential converts and conversation partners throughout history. Sometimes such challenges resulted in the 'conversion' of the missionary. I am not suggesting anything like this occurred with respect to the Scots Afrikaner missionaries. What I am suggesting is that engaging the other is a good way to open up and expose cracks in ideological armour, especially one's own, if a measure of self-reflectivity is at hand.

There is a level of intentional vulnerability in this tradition, which I find absent in the camp of their ideological opponents in broader Afrikanerdom. Far from being heroic, the Scots Afrikaners represented a flawed tradition, which occasionally, optimistically, took the wrong turn in respect to the broader context of Africa and its inhabitants. As an oft-quoted proverb would have it, the road to hell is paved with good intentions. However, perhaps these very flawed aspects of their actions and interactions are what also humanised the Scots Afrikaners, and this makes them far more interesting to study than were they heroes of the faith.

Notes

1. Hermann Giliomee (2011) *The Afrikaners: biography of a people*. London: Hurst and Co., p. 218.
2. Ibid., p. 216.
3. S. J. du Toit, quoted in Giliomee, *The Afrikaners*, p. 217.
4. Giliomee, *The Afrikaners*, pp. 218–19.
5. S. J. du Toit (1895) *Die geskiedenis van ons land: In die taal van ons volk*. Paarl: D. F. du Toit.
6. Giliomee, *The Afrikaners*, pp. 222–3.
7. See Irving Hexham (1977) '"Just like another Israel" – Calvinism and Afrikanerdom', *Religion*, 7:1, pp. 1–17. DOI: 10.1016/0048-721X(77)90004-5.
8. This throat condition incidentally prevented Andrew Murray from playing an active role at the synod of 1880 as outgoing moderator. See du Plessis, *Life of Andrew Murray*. London: Marshall Brothers, p. 330. This is the synod where the fateful decision was taken to incorporate the 'coloured' congregations into a separate structure, the Dutch Reformed Mission Church (DMRC). The former (1857) understanding that such segregation was unbiblical and wrong, and only allowable if the 'weakness of some' precluded integrated worship, no longer held sway. By 1880 the former weakness had become virtually normative in much of the DRC, with the establishment of the DRMC in 1881 positioning itself as the specially designated church for 'coloureds'. See Chris Loff (1983) 'The history of a Heresy', in John W. de Gruchy and Charles Villa-Vicencio, *Apartheid is a heresy*. Grand Rapids, MI: W. B. Eerdmans Pub. Co., p. 22.
9. Andrew Murray to Emma Murray, 12 March 1881, Murraysburg, quoted in du Plessis, *Life of Andrew Murray*, p. 334.
10. See R. Elphick (2012) *The Equality of Believers: Protestant Missionaries and the Racial Politics of South Africa*. Charlottesville and London: University of Virginia Press, pp. 71–6.
11. P. Huet (1860) *Eéne kudde en één herder: Verhandeling over de toebrenging van heidenen tot de christelijke kerkgemeenschap*. Kaapstad: Marais.
12. A. C. Murray diary, 13 September 1924.
13. M. W. Retief (1948) *Verowerings vir Christus: Die lewe van dr. W.H. Murray van Nyasaland*. Stellenbosch: Christen-Studenten Vereeniging van Zuid-Afrika, p. 234.
14. See E. Cleall (2012) *Missionary Discourses of Difference: Negotiating Otherness in the British Empire, 1840–1900*. Basingstoke: Palgrave Macmillan.
15. See J. M. MacKenzie and N. Dalziel (2007) *The Scots in South Africa: Ethnicity, identity, gender and race, 1772–1914*. Manchester: Manchester University Press, p. 20.
16. Robert D. Woodberry (2012) 'The Missionary Roots of Liberal Democracy', *American Political Science Review*, 106:2, pp. 244–5.
17. Elphick, *The Equality of Believers*, pp. 7–8.
18. Woodberry, 'The Missionary Roots of Liberal Democracy', p. 255.

19. J. J. F. Durand (1985) 'Afrikaner Piety and Dissent', in Charles Villa-Vicencio and John W. de Gruchy (eds) *Resistance and Hope: South African Essays in Honour of Beyers Naudé*. Cape Town and Grand Rapids, MI, pp. 42–5.
20. David J. Bosch (1986) 'The Afrikaner and South Africa', *Theology Today*, 43:2, pp. 208–9.
21. See R. Muller (2013) 'Evangelicalism and Racial Exclusivism in Afrikaner History: An Ambiguous Relationship', *Journal of Reformed Theology*, 7:2, pp. 204–32. DOI: https://doi.org/10.1163/15697312-12341296.

References

Adogame, A. and Lawrence, A. (2014) *Africa in Scotland, Scotland in Africa: Historical Legacies and Contemporary Hybridities*. Leiden: Brill.

Anonymous (1990) 'George Thom (1789–1842): Scottish Pioneer in South Africa', *The Banner of Truth* (https://www.christianstudylibrary.org/article/george-thom-1789-1842-scottish-pioneer-south-africa).

Aschman, G. (1972, 25 June) 'The Gathering of the Murray Clan', *Sunday Times Colour Magazine*.

Askew, T. A. (2000, October) 'The New York 1900 Ecumenical Missionary Conference: A Centennial Reflection', *International Bulletin of Missionary Research*, pp. 146–54, p. 147.

Badenhorst, L. H. (2001) Die Nederduits Gereformeerde Gemeente van Colesberg oor 175 jaar (1826–2001). Unpublished manuscript.

Badenhorst, L. (1981) *Dienskneg*. Koffiefontein: C. L. Badenhorst, p. 15ff.

Balfour, G. (1899) *Presbyterianism in the Colonies with special reference to The Principles and Influence of the Free Church of Scotland*. Edinburgh: Macniven & Wallace.

Bliss, A. (1898) 'Educational growth', in *Annual report of the Huguenot mission society*. Wellington. NGK Archive, Stellenbosch, K-DIV 638.

Bloomberg, C. and Dubow, S. (1990) *Christian-Nationalism and the Rise of the Afrikaner Broederbond, in South Africa, 1918–48*. London: Macmillan Press.

Bolink, P. (1967) *Towards Church union in Zambia: A study of missionary co-operation and church-union efforts in Central-Africa*. Franeker: T. Wever.

Borchardt, C. (1986) 'Die "Swakheid van Sommige" en die Sending', in J. Kinghorn (ed.), *Die NG Kerk en Apartheid*. Johannesburg: Macmillan.

Bosch, D. J. (1986) 'The Afrikaner and South Africa', *Theology Today*, 43:2, pp. 203–16.

Botha, J. G. (1981) *Gedenkuitgawe van die Nederduitse Gereformeerde Sendinggemeente van Malmesbury in die Eeufeesjaar 1981*. Malmesbury: NG Sendingkerkraad.

Boucher, M. (ed.) (1985) *Livingstone Letters, 1843–1872: David Livingstone correspondence in the Brenthurst Library*. Johannesburg (Houghton): The Brenthurst Press.

Brümmer, V. (2013) 'DF Malan en die Hoër Kritiek', *Nederduitse Gereformeerde Teologiese Tydskrif*, 54, pp. 3–4.

Brümmer, V. (2013), *Vroom of Regsinnig?: Teologie in die NG Kerk*. Wellington: Bybel-Media.

Buys, P. W. (1975) 'Metodistiese Invloede in Suid-Afrika: 'n Histories-kritiese ondersoek', in *'Revival' of Reformasie? 'n Studie oor die Metodisme.* Potchefstroomse Universiteit vir C.H.O.
Cachet, F. L. (1875) *Vijftien jaar in Zuid-Afrika: Brieven aan een vriend.* Leeuwarden: H. Bokma.
Cleall, E. (2012) *Missionary Discourses of Difference: Negotiating Otherness in the British Empire, 1840–1900.* London: Palgrave Macmillan.
Coertzen, P. (2011) 'The Huguenots of South Africa in history and religious identity', *Nederduitse Gereformeerde Teologiese Tydskrif,* 52: 1–2, pp. 45–57.
Coetzee, J. M. (1988) *White Writing: On the Culture of Letters in South Africa.* New Haven, CT: Yale University Press.
Comaroff, J. and Comaroff, J. L. (2004) *Christianity, colonialism, and consciousness in South Africa.* Chicago: University of Chicago Press.
Cronjé, G. (1948) *Voogdyskap en apartheid.* Pretoria: J. L. van Schaik.
Christian Express (1906, 1 February), p. 28.
Christian Express (1899, 1 December), p. 179.
Cuthbertson, G. C. (1982) 'James Stewart and the Anglo-Boer War, 1899–1902: a nonconformist missionary perspective', *South African Historical Journal,* 14:1, pp. 68–84.
De Beer, P. (1928, 15 February) 'Helen Murray Retief', *De Kerkbode.*
De Kerkbode (1928, 15 February) 'In Memoriam. Mevr. Ds. J. A. Retief, Mkhoma Nyasaland', and 'Helen Murray Retief'.
De Kerkbode (1899, 30 November) 'Ds. A. Murray, D.D. en Dr James Stewart, over de Transvaalsche kwestie', p. 755.
De Kerkbode (1910, 29 September).
De Kerkbode (1910, 6 October).
De Kerkbode (1927, 30 March).
De Klerk, W. A. (1978) *The Puritans in Africa: a Story of Afrikanerdom.* London: Rex Collings.
De Koningsbode (1911, January).
De Koningsbode (1917, February).
De Koningsbode (1917, November–December).
De Koningsbode (1918, January).
De Koningsbode (1918, February).
De Koningsbode (1918, March).
De Koningsbode (1919, July).
De Koningsbode (1919, September).
De Koningsbode (1921, June) 'Jaarverslag N.G. Kerk, Zending, Nyasaland, 1920'.
De Koningsbode (1921, August).
De Koningsbode (1921, October).
De Koningsbode (1922, March).
De Koningsbode (1922, April).
De Koningsbode (1923, June).
De Koningsbode (1923, October).

De Koningsbode (1924, February).
De Koningsbode (1924, August).
De Koningsbode (1924, September).
De Koningsbode (1924, October).
De Koningsbode (1924, November–December).
Denis, P. (2004) 'The Cape Huguenots and Their Legacy in Apartheid South Africa', in Bertrand Van Ruymbeke and Randy J. Sparks (eds), *Memory and Identity: The Huguenots in France and the Atlantic Diaspora (Carolina Low Country and the Atlantic World)*. Columbia: University of South Carolina Press, pp. 285–309.
De Ondersoeker (1871).
De Strever: voor Christus en de Kerk. Orgaan der C.S.V. onder de Krijgsgevangenen (1901, 19 December) No. 1, Diyatalawa Kamp, Ceylon. NGK Archive.
De Strever (1902, 11 January) No. 4.
De Strever (1902, 18 January) No. 5.
De Vereeniging (1903, 7 October) 'De Kerk en de Bijbel op Commando'.
De Vereeniging (1903, 7 October) 'Onze Kerk en de Scotsche Kerken'.
De Vereeniging (1903, 30 December), p. 6.
Die Gereformeerde Vaandel (1933, June).
Die Kerkbode (1940, 10 July).
Die Kerkbode (1940, 7 August).
Die Kerkbode (1940, 25 September).
Die 43ste Vergadering van die Uitvoerende Raad van die Ned. Geref. Kerk Sending na Midde Afrika, gehou te Mkhoma, vanaf 17 tot 25 September, 1923 (1923). DRC Archive, Stellenbosch.
Die 45ste Vergadering van die Uitvoerende Raad van die Ned. Ger. Kerk Sending na Midde Afrika, gehou te Mkhoma, vanaf 25 Nov. tot 4 Desember, 1925 (1925). DRC Archive, Stellenbosch.
Douglas, W. M. (1957) *Andrew Murray and his message*. Fort Washington: Christian Literature Crusade.
Draper, J. (2003) 'The Trial of Bishop John William Colenso', in J. A. Draper (ed.), *The Eye of the Storm: Bishop John William Colenso and the Crisis of Biblical Inspiration*. Pietermaritzburg: Cluster.
Dreijer, A. (1898) *De Strijd onzer Vaderen tegen het Liberalisme*. Kaapstad: Jacques Dusseau & Co.
Dreyer, A. (1899) *Geschiedenis van de Gemeente Swellendam*. Kaapstad: Taylor en Snashall.
Dreyer, A. (1929) *Die Kaapse kerk en die Groot Trek*. Kaapstad: Van de Sandt de Villiers en Co.
Dreyer, A. (1930) *Gedenkboek van Jansenville, Driekwart-Eeufees, 1855–1930*. Stellenbosch: Pro-Ecclesia.
Duff, S. E. (2005) '"Oh! for a blessing on Africa and America": the Mount Holyoke system and the Huguenot Seminary, 1874–1885', *New Contree*, 50, pp. 95–109.
Duff, S. E. (2006) 'Head, Heart, and Hand: The Huguenot Seminary and

College and the Construction of Middle Class Afrikaner Femininity, 1873–1910', MA thesis (history), Stellenbosch University.
Duff, S. E. (2015) *Changing childhoods in the Cape Colony: Dutch Reformed Church evangelicalism and colonial childhood, 1860–1895*. Basingstoke: Palgrave Macmillan.
Duff, S. E. (2018) 'The Dutch Reformed Church and the Protestant Atlantic: Revivalism and Evangelicalism in the Nineteenth-Century Cape Colony', *South African Historical Journal*, 70:2, pp. 324–47.
Du Plessis, Jean (1988) 'Colonial progress and countryside conservatism: An essay on the legacy of Van der Lingen of Paarl, 1831–1875', MA thesis, University of Stellenbosch.
Du Plessis, Johannes (1917) *De Arme Blanke en de Heiden-Zending*. Kaapstad: Z. A. Bijbel Vereeniging.
Du Plessis, Johannes (1919) *The life of Andrew Murray of South Africa*. London: Marshall Brothers.
Du Plessis, J. (1920) *Het Leven van Andrew Murray*. Kaapstad: Zuid Afrikaanse Bijbelvereniging.
Du Plessis, J. (1924, December) 'Een Eeuw van Zendingarbeid. Haar Onstaan, de Ontwikkeling en de Bloei van ons Zendingwerk', *De Koningsbode*.
Durand, J. J. F. (1985) 'Afrikaner Piety and Dissent', in Charles Villa-Vicencio and John W. de Gruchy (eds), *Resistance and Hope: South African Essays in Honour of Beyers Naudé*. Cape Town and Grand Rapids, MI.
Du Toit, A. (1983) 'No Chosen People: The Myth of the Calvinist Origins of Afrikaner Nationalism and Racial Ideology', *American Historical Review*, 88:4, pp. 920–52.
Du Toit, A. (1987) 'The Cape Afrikaners' Failed Liberal Moment', in Jeffrey Butler, Richard Elphick and David Welsh, *Democratic liberalism in South Africa: its history and prospect*. Middletown, CT: Wesleyan University Press, pp. 49–56.
Du Toit, D. F. & Co. *Verslag van Taalkongres en Samenkomst* (1897), gehouden aan de Paarl, op 27 tot 31 Januari, 1897. Paarl.
Du Toit, J. D. (1903) *Het Methodisme*. Amsterdam: Höveker & Wormser.
Du Toit, J. D. (1905) *De Streversvereeniging beoordeeld van Gereformeerd standpunt*. Potchefstroom: Höveker & Wormser.
Du Toit, J. D. (1906) *C.S.V. nog eens. Antwoord Dr. J.D. du Toit*. Potchefstroom.
Du Toit J. D. (1917) *Ds. S.J. du Toit. In Weg en Werk: 'n Periode van Afrikaanse Oplewing*. Paarl: Paarl Drukpers Maatschappij Beperkt.
Du Toit, J. D. and du Toit, S. (1955) *Die Afrikaanse Rassebeleid en die Skrif: Artikels van prof. dr JD du Toit en prof dr du Toit* (2nd edition). Potchefstroom: Pro Rege Bpk.
Du, Toit, S. J. (1895) *Die geskiedenis van ons land: In die taal van ons volk*. Paarl: D. F. du Toit.
Elmslie, W. A. and White, J. C. (1899) *Among the Wild Ngoni: being some chap-*

ters in the history of the Livingstonia mission in British Central Africa. With an introduction by Lord Overtoun. Edinburgh and London: Oliphant & Co.

Elphick, R. (2012) *The Equality of Believers: Protestant Missionaries and the Racial Politics of South Africa.* Charlottesville: University of Virginia Press.

Elphick, R. and Giliomee, H. (2014) 'The Origins and Entrenchment of European dominance at the Cape, 1652–c. 1840', in *The Shaping of South African Society, 1652–1840* (2nd edition). Middletown, CT: Wesleyan University Press, pp. 521–66.

Faure, D. P. (1868) *De Moderne Theologie. Dertien Toespraken gehouden in de Mutual Hall, Kaapstad.* Cape Town.

Fedorowich, K. (1991) 'Anglicization and the politicization of British immigration to South Africa, 1899–1929', *The Journal of Imperial and Commonwealth History*, 19:2, pp. 222–46. DOI: 10.1080/030865391085 82837, p. 222.

Ferguson, G. P. (1927) *The Builders of Huguenot.* Cape Town: Maskew Miller Limited.

Ferreira, J. (2012) *Boereoorlogstories 2: 32 verhale oor die oorlog van 1899–1902.* Kaapstad: Tafelberg.

Fraser, A. R. (1934) *Donald Fraser of Livingstonia.* London: Hodder & Stoughton.

Fraser, D. (1913, 12 April) 'Boers and Missions', *The Glasgow Herald.*

Gerdener, G. B. A. (1934) *Geskiedenis van die Ned. Geref. Kerke in Natal, Vrystaat en Transvaal.* Kaapstad: S.A. Bybelvereniging.

Gerdener, G. B. A. (1951) *Bouers van Weleer: Lewensketse van enkele groot figure uit die geskiedenis van die N.G. Kerk in Suid-Afrika.* Kaapstad: N.G. Kerk Uitgewers.

Giliomee, H. (2003) '"The Weakness of Some": The Dutch Reformed Church and White Supremacy', *Scriptura*, 83, pp. 212–44.

Giliomee, H. (2011) *The Afrikaners: biography of a people.* London: Hurst & Co.

Goodman, P. (2000). *Of one blood: Abolitionism and the origins of racial equality.* Berkeley: University of California Press.

Grundlingh, A, and Sapire, H. (1989) 'From feverish festival to repetitive ritual? The changing fortunes of Great Trek mythology in an industrializing South Africa, 1938–1988', *South African Historical Journal/Suid-Afrikaanse Historiese Joernaal*, 21, pp. 19–37.

Hanekom, T. N. (1951) *Die Liberale Rigting in Suid-Afrika: 'n Kerkhistoriese Studie.* Stellenbosch: Christen-Studentevereeniging-maatskappy van Suid-Afrika.

Het Zoeklicht (1932, 15 October).

Hexham, I. (1977) '"Just like another Israel" – Calvinism and Afrikanerdom', *Religion*, 7:1, pp. 1–17. DOI: 10.1016/0048-721X(77)90004-5.

Hofmeyr, A. L. (1910) *Het land langs het meer.* Stellenbosch: Christen Studenten Vereniging van Zuid Afrika.

Hofmeyr, G. R. and Murray, C. G. (1906) *Zuid Afrikaansche Jaarboek en Algemeene Gids 1907* (3rd year). Kaapstad: Cape Times.
Hollenweger, W. J. (1972) *The Pentecostals: The Charismatic Movement in the Churches*. Minneapolis, MN: Augsburg Publishing House.
Hopkins, H. C. (1968) *Die Ned. Geref. Kerk Cradock 1818–1968*. Observatory: Pro Ecclesia.
Hopkins, H. C. (1972, 7 June) 'Drie Geslagte Murrays', *Die Kerkbode*.
Huet, P. (1860) *Eéne kudde en één herder: verhandeling over de toebrenging van heidenen tot de christelijke kerkgemeenschap*. Kaapstad: Marais.
Jack, J. W. (1900) *Daybreak in Livingstonia: The Story of the Livingstonia Mission British Central Africa*. New York: Young People's Missionary Movement.
Johns, T. (2013) 'The 1820 Settlement Scheme to South Africa', *BRANCH: Britain, Representation and Nineteenth-Century History*. Ed. Dino Franco Felluga. *Extension of Romanticism and Victorianism on the Net*. Web. Accessed 11 June 2020.
Jubileum-Soewenier van die Ned. Geref. Kerkgebou, Tulbagh (1878–1928).
Katsulukuta, E. E. and Pretorius, J. L. (n.d.) 'The Translation of the Bible into Chichewa, 1900–1923'. DRC Archive, Stellenbosch, PPV 1483.
Kestell, J. D. (1912) *Het leven van Professor N.J. Hofmeyr*. Kaapstad: Hollandsch-Afrikaansche Uitgewers, p. 75.
Kinghorn, J. and Borchardt C. F. A. et al. (1986) *Die NG Kerk en apartheid*. Johannesburg: Macmillan South Africa.
Kipling, R. (1899) 'The white man's burden', *McClure's Magazine*, 12:4.
Kitshoff, M. C. (2010) 'Meesterbouer aan die Teologiese Kweekskool – Ds GWA van der Lingen, 1804–1869', *Nederduitse Gereformeerde Teologiese Tydskrif*, 15:1, pp. 121–2.
Kok, J. W. (1971) *Sonderlinge vrug; die invloed van die Tweede Vryheidsoorlog op die sendingaksie van die Nederduitse Gereformeerde Kerk in Suid-Afrika*. Pretoria: N.G. Kerkboekhandel, p. 33.
Koorts, L. (2014) *D. F. Malan and the Rise of Afrikaner Nationalism*. Cape Town: Tafelberg.
Kriel, C. J. (1963) *Die Geskiedenis van die Nederduitse Gereformeerde Sendingkerk in Suid-Afrika, 1881–1956*. Paarl: Paarlse Drukpers.
Korf, L. (2007) 'Podium and/or Pulpit? D. F. Malan's role in the politicisation of the Dutch Reformed Church, 1900–1959', *Historia*, 52:2, November, pp. 214–38.
Kotzé, D. A. (1981) *Van Roodezand tot Gariep: Die 150-jarige bestaan van die N.G. Gemeente Clanwilliam 1826–1976*. Goodwood: Nasionale Boekdrukkery.
Lamm, J. A. (1994) 'The Early Philosophical Roots of Schleiermacher's Notion of Gefühl, 1788–1794', *The Harvard Theological Review*, 87:1, pp. 67–105.
Laws, R. (1934) *Reminiscences of Livingstonia*. With plates, including a portrait. Edinburgh and London: Oliver & Boyd.
Leacock, S. (1910) 'The Union of South Africa', *American Political Science Review*, 4:4, pp. 498–507.

Lester, A. (2001) *Imperial Networks: Creating Identities in Nineteenth-Century Britain and South Africa*. London: Routledge.

Liebenberg, A. J., in du Plessis, J. (ed.) (1906) *De Kerk en Haar Roeping: het verhaal van het Zendingwerk in Nyasaland, met een beroep op de Ned Ger Kerk van Zuid Afrika*. Kaapstad: Citadel.

Livingstone, W. P. (1921) *Laws of Livingstonia: A Narrative of Missionary Adventure and Achievement*. London: Hodder & Stoughton.

Livingstone, W. P. (1931) *A Prince of Missionaries: The Rev. Alexander Hetherwick C.B.E., D.D., M.A. of Blantyre, Central Africa*. London: James Clarke & Co.

Loff, C. (1983) 'The history of a Heresy', in John W. de Gruchy and Charles Villa-Vicencio, *Apartheid is a heresy*. Grand Rapids, MI: W. B. Eerdmans Publishing Co.

Louw, A. A. (1917) *Dageraad in Banyaland: een verhaal van 25-jarigen arbeid onder de Vakaranga of Banyai in Mashonaland*. Kaapstad: Uitgegeven op last van de Algemeene Zending Commissie door de Publicatie Commissie der Zuid Afrik. Bijbel Vereeniging.

Lowry, D. B. (1951) 'Luther D. Wishard (1854–1925): Pioneer of the Student Christian Movement (1877–1888)'. Princeton University senior thesis (http://arks.princeton.edu/ark:/88435/dsp018910jv758).

MacKenzie, J. M. and Dalziel, N. (2007) *The Scots in South Africa: Ethnicity, identity, gender and race, 1772–1914*. Manchester: Manchester University Press.

Mackinnon, J. (1887) *South African Traits*. Edinburgh: J. Gemmell.

Malan, D. F. (1913) *Naar Congoland: Een Reisbeschrijving*. Stellenbosch: Christen-Studenten Vereeniging van Zuid-Afrika.

Malan, D. F. (1915, Sunday 13 June) *Doet het al ter Eere Gods. Afscheidsrede van Dr. D. F. Malan te Graaff Reinet*, p. 2.

Malan, F. S. (1933) *Ons Kerk en Prof. du Plessis*. Kaapstad: Nasionale Pers.

Manda-Taylor, L. (2006) 'Violence and "othering" in colonial and post-colonial Africa. Case study: Banda's Malawi', *Journal of African Cultural Studies*, 18, pp. 197–213.

Mapala, C. W. (2016) 'Ethnicity and Christianity: A Historical Study of the Border Dispute Between the Livingstonia and Nkhoma Synods of the Church of Central Africa Presbyterian', PhD thesis, University of Kwazulu-Natal, Pietermaritzburg.

McCracken, J. (1977) *Politics and Christianity in Malawi 1875–1940: The Impact of the Livingstonia Mission in the Northern Province*. Cambridge: Cambridge University Press.

Mcintosh, H. (1993) *Robert Laws: Servant of Africa*. Carberry: The Handsel Press Ltd.

Michener, J. A. (2015) *The Covenant: a novel*. New York: The Dial Press.

Moody, D. L. (1902, 29 March) 'Het Voorrecht der Vrijheid', *De Strever*, No. 15.

Mott, J. R. (1900) *The Evangelization of the World in this Generation*, New York: Student Volunteer Movement for Foreign Missions.
Müller, R. (2013) 'Evangelicalism and Racial Exclusivism in Afrikaner History: An Ambiguous Relationship', *Journal of Reformed Theology*, 7:2, pp. 204–32.
Müller, R. (2014) 'War and "racial feeling" in the writings of an Afrikaner missionary', *Studia Historiae Ecclesiasticae*, 40:2, pp. 71–84.
Müller, R. (2014) 'Afrikaner socio-theological discourse in the early twentieth century: War and mission in J. F. Naudé and J. du Plessis', *Historia*, 59:2, pp. 309–25.
Murray, A. (1898), 'The Mount of Sources', *The Huguenot Seminary Annual*, No. 3.
Murray, A. (1899, 5 October) 'An Appeal to the English People on Behalf of Peace', *South African News 5–16*. DRC Archive, PPV 1460/4.
Murray, A. (1899, 13 October) 'A Plea for Peace: Chapter 1', *South African News 5–16*. DRC Archive, PPV 1460/4.
Murray, A. (1899, 16 October) 'A Plea for Peace: Chapter 3', *South African News 5–16*. DRC Archive, PPV 1460/4.
Murray, A. (1899) *In tijd van oorlog: de oorlogsklok: Gods roepstem naar de binnenkamer*. Kaapstad: Townshend, Taylor en Snashall.
Murray, A. (1900) 'Oorlogs Gedachten', *De Kerkbode*, p. 133.
Murray, A. (1901, 19 September) 'De Zegen der Beproeven', *De Kerkbode*, No. 37, Part 18, pp. 523–6.
Murray, A. (1901, September) Personal correspondence to Kitchener. DRC Archive, PPV 1451.
Murray, A. (1915, 14 July) *Godsdienst en Politiek. Oordeel van de Oude Kerkvader, Dr. Andrew Murray*. Wellington.
Murray, A. (1942) *Die Moderne Ongeloof. Dertien Leerredes. Afrikaanse vertaling in deel II van die Versamelde Werke van Andrew Murray*. Stellenbosch.
Murray, Andrew Charles (1897) *Nyasaland en mijne ondervindingen aldaar*. Amsterdam: HAUM.
Murray, A. C. (1924, 12 September) A. C. Murray diary. DRC Archive, Stellenbosch.
Murray, A. C. (1924, 13 September) A. C. Murray diary. DRC Archive, Stellenbosch.
Murray, A. C. (1924, 24 September) A. C. Murray diary. DRC Archive, Stellenbosch.
Murray A. C. (1931) *Ons Nyasa-akker: Geskiedenis van die Nyasa sending van die Nederd. Geref. Kerk in Suid-Afrika*. Stellenbosch: Pro Ecclesia.
Murray, H. (1902, 3 May) Personal correspondence by Haldane Murray to Robert Murray's mother. DRC Archive, Stellenbosch.
Murray, P. (n.d.) Personal commentary on Bible translation. DRC Archive, Stellenbosch, PPV 1483.
Murray, R. (1902, 18 January) Personal correspondence by Robert Murray to his father Willie Murray. DRC Archive, Stellenbosch.

Murray, W. H. (1914) Answers to A. Hetherwick's (n.d.) 'Queries on Native Religious Beliefs'. DRC Archive, Stellenbosch, PPV 1478.

Ned. Geref. Kerk Synod Acta (1924) DRC Archive, Stellenbosch.

Neethling, M. (1909) *Unto children's children: lives and letters of the parents of the home at Graaff Reinet, with short sketches of the life of each of the children, and a register.* London: Printed by T. H. Hopkins.

Nel, O. (2010) *South Africa's forgotten revival: The story of the Cape's Great Awakening in 1860.* Canberra: Olive Twig Books.

Notulen der Commissie voor de Opleiding van Zendeling Arbeiders (1902, 16 September). DRC Archive, Stellenbosch.

Oberholster, J. A. S. (1943) *Gedenkboek van die Ned. Geref. Gemeente Tulbagh: (Roodezand, Waveren) 1743–1943: 'n oorsig van die geskiedenis van die gemeente.*

'Oorsig van die Geskiedenis van die NG Kerk', *Gemeentegeskiedenisargief: 'n oorsig van die geskiedenis van die NG Kerk, sy gemeentes en predikante,* https://www.gemeenteskiedenis.co.za/oorsig-van-die-geskiednis-van-die-ng-kerk/ (accessed 10 June 2020).

Parsons, J. W. (1998) 'Scots and Afrikaners in Central Africa: Andrew Charles Murray and the Dutch Reformed Church Mission in Malawi', *The Society of Malawi Journal,* 51:1.

Pauw C. M. (1980) 'Mission and Church in Malawi: The History of the Nkhoma Synod of the Church of Central Africa, Presbyterian, 1889–1962', DTh thesis, Stellenbosch University.

Philip, J. (1828) *Researches in South Africa.* London: James Duncan.

Phiri, I. A. (2007) *Women, presbyterianism and patriarchy: religious experience of Chewa women in central Malawi.* Zomba, Malawi: Kachere Series.

Reitz, F. W. (1899, 4 October) Personal correspondence to Andrew Murray, Pretoria. DRC Archive, Stellenbosch, PPV 1451.

Retief, B. (2000, 19 April) 'Ds. Kotie Retief, Rebel van Graaff-Reinet se Sneeuberge', *Die Burger.*

Retief, J. A. (1933, 12 August) 'Die Kerk van Midde-Afrika: 'n Skewe Voorstelling', *Die Kerkbode.*

Retief, J. A. (1946, 8 February) Unpublished letter. Kaapstad. DRC Archive, Stellenbosch.

Retief, J. A. (1951) *Ontdekkings in Midde-Afrika.* Stellenbosch: C.S.V. Boekhandel.

Retief, M. W. (1948) *Verowerings Vir Christus.* Stellenbosch: C.S.V. Boekhandel.

Retief, M. W. (1951) *Herlewings in Ons Geskiedenis.* Kaapstad and Pretoria: NGK Uitgewers van Suid-Afrika.

Robert, D. L. (1993) 'Mount Holyoke Women and the Dutch Reformed Missionary Movement, 1874–1904', *Missionalia,* 21:2, pp. 103–23.

Roberts, N. (2012) 'Is conversion a "colonization of consciousness"?', *Anthropological Theory,* 12:3, pp. 271–94. https://doi.org/10.1177/1463499612469583.

Ross, R. J. (1995) 'Abolitionism, the Batavian Republic, the British and the Cape Colony', in Gert Oostindie (ed.), *Fifty years later: Antislavery, capitalism and modernity in the Dutch orbit.* Pittsburgh, PA: University of Pittsburgh Press, pp. 179–92.

Ross, R. (2009) *Status and respectability in the Cape Colony, 1750–1870: a tragedy of manners.* Cambridge: Cambridge University Press, p. 47.

Rothman, M. E. (ed.) (1976) *Oorlogsdagboek van 'n Transvaalse burger te velde.* Cape Town: Tafelberg.

Royer, G. B. (1915) 'William Carey: The Father of Modern Missions', in Galen B. Royer, *Christian Heroism in Heathen Lands.* Elgin, IL: Brethren Publishing House.

Saayman W. A. (2007) *Being missionary, being human: an overview of Dutch Reformed Mission.* Pietermaritzburg: Cluster Publications.

Sass, F. W. (1956) 'The Influence of the Church of Scotland on the Dutch Reformed Church of South Africa', unpublished PhD thesis, University of Edinburgh.

Schapera, I. (1960) 'Livingstone and the Boers', *African Affairs: the Journal of the Royal African Society,* 59:235, pp. 144–56.

Schutte, G. J. (1998/9) 'Between Amsterdam and Batavia: Cape Society and the Calvinist Church under the Dutch East India Company', *Kronos,* 25, pp. 17–49, p. 41.

Serfontein, J. H. P. (1978) *Brotherhood of Power: An Exposé of the Secret Afrikaner Broederbond.* Bloomington and London: Indiana University Press, p. 32.

Singh, M. (2000) 'Basutoland: A Historical Journey into the Environment', *Environment and History,* 6:1, pp. 31–70. Retrieved 21 December 2020, from http://www.jstor.org/stable/20723119.

Smit, A. P. (1967) *Ligbaken aan die Swartkops. Ned. Geref. Kerk Uitenhage 1817–1967.* Uitenhage: Nederduitse Gereformeerde Kerk

Smit, D. (2009) *Essays on Being Reformed: Collected Essays 3.* Stellenbosch: SUN Press.

Smith, E. W. (1952) *The life and times of Daniel Lindley (1801–80): missionary to the Zulus, pastor of the Voortrekkers, Ubebe Omhlope.* New York: Library Publishers.

Spies, S. B. (n.d.) 'Malan, Daniel Francois (B)', *Dictionary of African Christian Biography,* https://dacb.org/stories/southafrica/malan-daniel2/.

Spies, S. B. (1977) *Methods of Barbarism? Roberts and Kitchener and Civilians in the Boer Republics January 1900–May 1902.* Cape Town: Human & Rousseau.

Spoelstra, B. (1961) 'Die stigting van die Gereformeerde Kerk Colesberg', in *Die Gereformeerde Kerk Colesberg gestig 8 Desember 1860 op die plaas Hamelfontein van I. D. du Plessis: Gedenkalbum tydens die Eeufeesviering 27, 28, 29 Oktober 1961.*

Spoelstra, B. (1963) *Die 'Doppers' in Suid-Afrika 1760–1899.* Kaapstad: Nasionale Boekhandel.

Stanley, B. (ed.) (2003) *Missions, nationalism, and the end of empire*. Grand Rapids, MI: Eerdmans, p. 6.

Stanley, B. (2019) 'The Theology of the Scottish Protestant Missionary Movement', in David Fergusson and Mark Elliott (eds), *History of Scottish Theology*. Oxford: Oxford University Press.

Stewart, J. (1899, 1 November), *Mission World*.

Streng Gereformeerde Patriot (1893, 9 February) 'Ds. A. Murray di grootste vyand van ons nasionaliteit', *Di Afrikaanse Patriot*. DRC Archive, Stellenbosch.

Streng Gereformeerde Patriot (1893, 23 February) 'Ds. A. Murray di grootste vyand van ons gereformeerde leer', *Di Afrikaanse Patriot*.

Strewerskonferensieboek: verslag van die 22ste Algemene Vergadering van die Christelike Strewersunie in verband met Die Ned. Geref. Kerke in Suid-Afrika, gehou 3-6 Julie 1941 te Riversdal.

Sturgis, J. (1982) 'Anglicisation at the Cape of good hope in the early nineteenth century', *The Journal of Imperial and Commonwealth History*, 11:1, pp. 5–32. DOI: 10.1080/03086538208582629.

TenZythoff, G. J. (1987) *Sources of secession: The Netherlands Hervormde Kerk on the eve of the Dutch immigration to the Midwest*. Grand Rapids, MI: W. B. Eerdmans Publishing Company.

The Christian Express (1901, 1 June) 'Rev. Dr. Andrew Murray and the Peace Envoys', Vol. 31, No. 369.

The Truth about the Boer and his Church (n.d.) DRC Archive, Stellenbosch, B1250. The letter was signed by J. H. Hofmeyr, A. Moorrees, J. P. van Heerden, A. Murray, J. H. Neethling, N. J. Hofmeyr, J. I. Marais, P. G. J. de Vos and C. F. J. Muller.

Thompson, J. B. (1908) *The Ministers of the North United Free Church, Aberdeen 1843–1908. Some biographical notes*. Aberdeen: W. & W. Lindsay.

Thompson, L. (1995) *History of South Africa*. Revised edition. New Haven, CT: Yale University Press.

Thompson, T. J. (2000) *Touching the heart: Xhosa missionaries to Malawi 1876–1888*. Pretoria: University of South Africa.

Theal, G. M. C. (1898) *Records of the Cape Colony*, Vol. xii. London: Government of the Cape Colony.

Theal, G. M. (1888) *History of the Emigrant Boers in South Africa*. London: S. Sonnenschein, Lowrey.

Unknown Author, likely A. P. Ferguson. *Huguenot Seminary Report and Catalogues* (1874–81). NGK Archive, Stellenbosch, K-DIV 621.

Unknown Author, likely Ferguson (1878) *Records of the Huguenot mission society*. Wellington. NGK Archive, Stellenbosch, K-DIV 638.

Unknown Author (1884) *Records of the Huguenot missionary society: Book 2*. Huguenot Seminary, Wellington. NGK Archive, Stellenbosch, K-DIV 621.

Unknown Author (1890) *Catalogue of the nineteenth year of the Huguenot seminary Wellington SA and branch seminary*. NGK Archive, Stellenbosch.

Van der Walt, I. J. (1960) 'Eiesoortige Kerkvorming as Missiologiese Probleem met Besondere Verwysing na Suid-Afrika'. DTh thesis, Potchefstroom University for Christian Higher Education.

Van der Watt, P. B. (1979) *John Murray 1826–1882: Die Eerste Stellenbosse Professor*. Pretoria: N.H. Kerkboekhandel Transvaal.

Van Heerde, G. L. (1941) 'Strewersonderwerp: ons sestigjarige bestaan (a) Ons Verlede', in *Strewerskonferensieboekie. Verslag van die 22ste Algemene Vergadering van die Christelike Strewersunie in verband met die Ned. Geref, Kerke in Suid-Afrika. Gehou 3-6 Julie 1941 te Riversdal*.

Van Heerde, G. L. (c. 1951) 'Ontstaan en geskiedenis van die C.S.-unie in Suid-Afrika', in W. de W. Strauss (ed.), *Strewersgedenkboek, 1901–1951*. Kaapstad: Citadel.

Verslag van Taalkongres en Samenkomst (1897), *gehouden aan de Paarl, op 27 tot 31 Januari, 1897*. Paarl: D. F. du Toit & Co.

Vorster, J. D. (1941) 'Die Metodistiese Invloed in ons Volkslewe', in H. G. Stoker and J. D. Vorster (eds), *Koers in die Krisis III*. Stellenbosch: Pro Ecclesia.

Vos, A. (1981/2002) 'Inventaris van het archief van het theologisch-litterarisch gezelschap "Secor Dabar" te Utrecht 1844–1969', *Het Utrechts Argief*, hetutrechtsargief.nl/onderzoek.

Waite, C. E. (1900) 'A plea for the mission class', in *Mission Newsletter*. NGK Archive, Stellenbosch.

Woodberry, R. D. (2012) 'The Missionary Roots of Liberal Democracy', *American Political Science Review*, 106:2, pp. 244–5.

https://whc.unesco.org/en/tentativelists/5603/

https://www.executedtoday.com/2017/11/23/1901-willie-louw-boer-commando/

Index

Note: *italic* indicates illustrations; n indicates a note

Aborigines Protection Society, 112
Africans
  DRC membership, 2
  missionaries' attitudes to, 16
  othering of, 193–4
Afrikaans, 118, 138–9, 164, 172, 188–9
Afrikaanse Patriot, Di (journal), 155–8
Afrikaner Broederbond, 117, 170, 171
Afrikaners
  anglicisation of, 4
  British attitude to, 10–11
  and British settlement, 7
  and Calvinism, 3–4
  du Toit's definition of, 188
  and education, 136
  identity formation, 4, 13, 32, 89, 127; *see also* hybridities
  and independence, 43, 44–8
  and migration, 163
  and missionary enterprise, 81–5
  and nationalism, 4, 18, 74, 144, 145, 150, 154, 156, 157, 164, 168, 172, 190, 191, 198, 199
  opposition to ecumenical project, 145–50
  poor whites, 145–6, 158, 162, 165
  and race, 4, 6, 28–9, 40, 41, 98, 145, 146, 195, 199, 201
  Scots, 188, 190–4, 197, 198, 200–2
  and Scots 'missionaries', 8–15, 41
  see also Boers; *Voortrekkers*
Albertyn, Revd J. R., 145–6
Albertyn, P. K., 57, 119
Alston, E. G., 100
Anglican Church, 73–4
Anglican priests, 28
apartheid
  and Afrikaner nationalism, 154
  Dutch Reformed Church and, 148
  ecclesiastical foundation of, 16, 53, 55–60, 77n19, 141, 172
  institutionalisation of, 196, 197
  normalisation of, 144
  opposition to, 1
  theology of, 18, 183
  tradition of, 1, 98

Backhouse, James, 57
Badenhorst, L. H., 28
Bain, Revd, 91
Basotho people, 42
Beaufort West, 25
beer consumption, 142
Bible
  and people's (*volks*) theology, 31–2
  translation of, 100–3, 121, 188
Blake, Robert, 99
Blantyre mission, 90, 101, 131, 134, 148
Bliss, Anna, 82
Bloemfontein, 41
  Grey College, 42, 47
Boer War *see* South African War
Boeren Zending Instituut, 122
Boers
  Commando's Dank Zendingvereeniging (CDZV), 117
  and communion, 58
  and education, 82
  and identity, 12–13, 111–12, 114
  mission consciousness of, 117–19
  and missionaries, 17, 42, 43–4, 199, 200
  propaganda against, 130–1
  and racism, 58, 132
  rebellion of, 25
  Scots' assimilation as, 108
  and slavery, 109, 112
Bolink, P., 98
Borchardt, Carl, 60
Bosch, David, 196
British Empire, 4–7
Brümmer, Vincent, 63, 70, 79n88, 181, 184n5
Burgers, T., 68–9, 70

Burgersdorp, 39–41
Burns, William C., 37
Buys, P. W., 182–3

Cachet. F. L., 68
Calvinism, 3–4, 127, 160–2, 171, 177, 183
  neo-Calvinism, 172, 190, 198
  see also Huguenots
Cape Church
  and apartheid, 55–60
  and Great Trek, 31
  and identity politics, 41, 42
  and ordination of ministers, 45
  and 'Vrije Christelijke School', 180
  see also Dutch Reformed Church
Cape Colony
  British settlement, 4–7, 8–9
  Calvinism, 3–4
  Scots, 7
  see also Bloemfontein; Burgersdorp; Potchefstroom
Cape Dutch, 36, 199
Cape Maclear, 85, 99
Cape Monthly Magazine, 40
Cape of Good Hope Philanthropic Society, 52n122
Cape Town
  Dutch Reformed Church, 2–3
  Free Protestant Church, 69
  Groote Kerk, 69
  Huguenot Seminary, 71
  Roman Catholicism, 31
  St Stephen's Church, 76n17
Carey, William, 121
Chauwa (female rainmaking chief), 93–4
Chewa people, 93–4, 99, 103, 195
children
  baptism of, 43, 142
  in concentration camps, 120
  education of, 101, 121
  at prayer meetings, 64–5
  as slaves, 112
  and Sunday schools, 58
  welfare of, 29
Chiwere, king, 92, 93, 96
'chosen people' discourse, 3–4, 32
Christelijke Vrienden (Christian Friends), 38
Christelike Jongeliedevereniging see Christian Young People Society

Christelike Strewersvereniging see Strewers / Strewers
Christian Endeavour Society (*Christelike Streversvereniging*), 17, 118, 119–21, 122–3, 173–4, 200
Christian Express, The, 115–16
Christian Young People Society (*Christelike Jongeliedevereniging*), 119
Church of Central Africa Presbyterian (CCAP), 18, 135, 146–7, 194, 197–8
  amalgamation with DRC, 140–50
  statement of faith, 149
Church of Scotland, 9; *see also* Blantyre mission
church unification, 134
Clanwilliam, 30
Cleall, Esme, 12, 13
Colenso, John William, Bishop of Natal, 69, 73, 74
colour prejudice, 60; *see also* apartheid; racism
concentration camps, 120
Cradock, 25, 85
Cross, Dr, 91
Cuthbertson, G. C., 110, 111

de Graaff, N. H., 38
de Vries, J. C., 64–5
deism, 79n88
Denis, Philippe, 3
Doppers
  definition, 18
  ecclesiastical apartheid, 59–60
  opposition to hymn singing, 27–8
  opposition to Scottish 'Methodism', 171–4
  origin of term, 49n26
  see also Gereformeerde Kerke van Suid Afrika
Drakenstein (later Paarl)
  Calvinism, 3
  Dutch Reformed Church, 2
  French Huguenots, 4
  see also Paarl
Draper, Jonathan, 73–4
Dreijer, A., 72
Dreyer, A., 59
du Plessis, D. H. C., 171
du Plessis, Johannes
  accusation of heterodoxy, 70
  and Boer independence, 47

du Plessis, Johannes (*cont.*)
  and ecumenical project, 145, 147
  expulsion from Stellenbosch Seminary, 144
  heresy trial, 175, 179
  on Liberal Movement, 69, 72, 74
  and Methodism, 178–9, 180
  on Murray, Andrew Jr, 41, 44–5, 46, 85
  and 'Scottish–Afrikaner hybridity', 154
  on van der Lingen, G. W. A., 54
  on Worcester conference (1860), 61, 63–4
du Toit, André, 3
du Toit, J. D., 18, 71, 155, 160, 172–4, 175, 183, 190, 199
du Toit, S. J., 18, 71, 155, 156, 158, 160–1, 180, 188–9, 190, 199, 200
Duff, S. E., 63, 65, 71, 78n64, 125n56
Durand, Jaap, 196
Dutch East India Company (DEIC), 2–3, 5
Dutch language, 30, 157
Dutch Reformed Church (DRC)
  amalgamation with CCAP, 140–50
  and Anglican Church, 73–4
  anglicisation of, 23, 62
  and anti-imperialism, 74
  and apartheid, 148
  and *Boeren Zending Instituut*, 122
  and church union, 135, 136
  and colonisation of consciousness, 9
  and communal prayer, 40
  Curatorium, 176
  and Dutch East India Company, 2–3
  and education, 132
  as the established church, 9
  and first interdenominational Christian conference, Worcester (1860), 61–4
  and foreign missionaries, 65, 145
  and general mission commission, 144
  and Kasungu mission, 139
  and language, 138–9
  and liberalism, 63, 67–72, 73–4, 75, 148
  and Methodism, 177–8
  and mission, 1, 66–7, 72, 81, 86, 87, 99, 132, 133, 190–1
  Moderamen (church leadership), 108, 111
  and Nkhoma mission, 135, 136
  and Nyasaland mission, 138
  and Presbyterians, 9, 10, 23–5, 72–3
  and prisoners of war camps, 119
  and racially segregated congregations, 16, 55–60, 67–8, 148
  and Reformed principle, 156, 158, 159, 161, 181
  revivalism in, 60–6, 67
  Scottish influence on, 1–2, 8, 15
  Scottish ministers, 9, 10, 16, 30, 99, 160–1, 190
  and South African War, 127–8
  synods
    1618 to 1619 (Synod of Dort), 28
    1824, 2, 16, 33
    1829, 57
    1834, 16–17, 58
    1842, 53
    1852, 46, 73
    1857, 16, 41, 55, 56, 58, 59–60, 68, 77n19
    1862, 67, 79n98
    1870, 70, 72
    1880, 156, 202n8
    1894, 73
    1903, 91
    1924, 144
    1945, 144, 148
  and *Vrouesendingbond* (Women's Missionary Union), 84–5
  'weakness of some' motion, 16, 18, 57, 77n19, 144–5, 191–2
  see also Cape Church

ecumenism, 73, 74, 145–50, 174
Edgar, James, 29
education
  Africans, 166
  children, 101, 102
  and evangelism, 90
  girls, 82–3, 157–8, 159
  and nationalism, 161
  '*volkseie*', 166
  women, 29, 71, 75
  see also Lovedale College; Midland Seminary; Potchefstroom University for Christian Higher Education; schools; Stellenbosch Theological Seminary; Stellenbosch University; Utrecht University
Elmslie, W. A., 91–2, 95, 96
Elphick, Richard, 19n2, 76n19, 140, 154, 162, 172, 196

Index

Eltheto (mission organisation), 39
emigration, 31–2; *see also Voortrekkers*
English language, 8, 9–10, 118, 157
ethnic cleansing, 5
ethnic-linguistic groups, 183
evangelicalism, 74–5
Evans, John, 29

Fairbairn, John, 106n85
Faure, Abraham, 58
Faure, David P., 69
Faure, H. E., 38
Faure, P. E., 32, 74
Ferguson, Abbie Park, 82, 83, 123
First World War, 134–5
Fraser, Agnes, 130–1, 138, 143
Fraser, Colin, 24
Fraser, Donald, 130, 130–3, 138, 140, 143, 193
Frazer, Dr A. J., 46, 47
Free Church of Scotland, 16, 58, 85, 86
    and mission to Nyasaland, 87, 90, 99, 100, 139
French Reformed Church, 46

Gaelic language, 8
gender
    and difference, 12
    and education, 82–3
    and teaching, 28
    see also girls; women
Gerdener, G. B. A., 30
'Gereformeerde Gemeentes onder die Kruis' (Reformed Congregations under the Cross), 184n5
Gereformeerde Kerke van Suid Afrika (GKSA), 18, 27, 39, 171; *see also Doppers*
Giliomee, Hermann, 3, 5, 6, 7, 10, 11, 76n17, 155–6, 189
Gizani, Daniel, 55
Glasgow Herald, 131, 132
Glasgow Missionary Society, 14, 24
Grahamstown Journal, 26
Gray, Bishop Robert, 73–4
Great Lakes Company, 91
Great Trek, 25, 32, 199

Hanekom, Tobie, 174
    Die Liberale Rigting in Suid-Afrika (The Liberal Direction in South Africa), 180–1
Henry, Dr, 90, 99

Hetherwick, Dr Alexander, 100–1, 134, 135
Hofmeyr, A. L.: *Het Land Langs Het Meer*, 92
Hofmeyr, Revd Attie, 133
Hofmeyr, Jan, 158
Hofmeyr, N. J.
    and anti-liberalism, 68
    and colour prejudice, 60
    and prisoners of war, 119
    and revivalist movement, 61, 63
    and Stellenbosch Seminary, 38, 53
    and synod (1857), 55, 57
    and 'third way', 76n17
    and van der Lingen, G. W. A., 54
Holiness movement, 83
Hollenweger, Walter, 182, 183
Hopkins, H. C., 25, 49n26
Huet, Revd J. P. M., 67, 68
    Eene Kudde en Een Herder, 60
Huguenot Mission Society, 84
Huguenots, 3, 158; *see also* Calvinism
hybridities, 8, 10, 11, 13, 15, 33, 150, 154, 182, 195–6; *see also* identity formations
hymn singing, 27–8, 40–1

identity formations
    Afrikaners, 4, 13, 32, 89, 127
    Boers, 12–13, 111–12
    Scots, 127
    see also hybridities
immigrants, 3, 5–6, 7, 8, 9
Innes, James Rose, 24, 33

Jack, James W., 86
Johns, Timothy, 5, 6–7

'Kaffraria', 24, 58
Karoo, 10–11, 25, 34
Kasungu mission, 135–6, 139
Katsulukuta, E. E., 102
Kerkbode, De, 26, 60–1, 108–9, 114, 116, 133, 178, 179, 181
Kgama, King, 163
Khoi people, 6, 22n71
Kies, C. F., 147
Kinghorn, J., 172
Kitshoff, M. C., 75n4
Klance, Miss (American missionary), 84
Klopper, H. J., 171
Koers in die Krisis series, 176
Kok, J. W.: *Sonderlinge Vrug*, 118–19, 120

Kongwe, 96, 99
Koningsbode, De, 100, 101–2, 129, 133, 134–5, 136, 137, 139, 145, 146
Koorts, Lindie, 164
Kotzé, J. J., 68, 69, 70, 71, 79n88
Kriel, C. J., 60
Kruger, Paul
   baptism, 26
   and Boers, 109
   as a *Dopper*, 27
   and du Toit, S. J., 189
   and Murray, Andrew Jr, 66
   respect for, 164
   and *Uitlanders*, 114
Kuyper, Abraham, 167, 172
Kuyper, H. H., 172

language *see* Afrikaans; Dutch language; English language; ethnic-linguistic groups; Gaelic language
Laws, Dr Robert, 91, 92, 93, 96, 100, 134, 135, 136, 140, 142, 143, 193
Le Roux, Pieter, 182–3
Le Vaillant, François: *Voyage dans l'intérieur de l'Afrique*, 6
liberalism, 67–72
   and Methodism, 175–6, 178–9, 180
Liebenberg, A. J., 96–7
Life of Faith, The (religious paper), 108
Lindley, Daniel, 51n89
lions, 96–7
Livingstone, David
   and Boers, 13, 17, 109, 132
   and death of wife, 90
   letters, 34
   lion attack on, 96
   and slave trade, 109
Livingstone, Mary, 90
Livingstone, W. P., 101, 103, 134
Livingstonia mission, 91, 131, 133, 134, 135–7
   conference (1924), 139–42, 143, 149, 193
   Council, 98
Livlezi, 90, 99
Loedolff of Malmesbury (elder), 67, 68
London Missionary Society (LMS), 12, 14, 25, 42
Louw, A. F., 17, 119, 120, 122, 128
Louw, Andrew A., 18, 85–6, 119, 128, 131, 163
Louw, Francina 'Cinie', 131
Louw, Willie, 115, 128
Lovedale College, 14
Lovedale mission, 58
Lyon, Mary, 82

McAlpine (missionary), 141, 193
McCracken, John, 136
McGregor, Revd A., 181–2
MacKenzie, John M.: *The Scots in South Africa*, 2, 7, 8, 10, 14, 15, 108, 127, 195
McKidd, Alexander, 16, 63, 65, 67
McKidd, Hessie, 65, 67
Mackinnon, James, 55
Macmillan, W. M., 10
Malan, Cinie, 18
Malan, D. F., 18, 70, 154, 162–9, 170–1
Malan, D. G., 194
Malawi, 93, 102, 103; *see also* Nyasaland
Mapala, C. W., 136
Marchand, Revd D. J. le R., 174
marriage practices, 163–4
Mashonaland, 85, 128; *see also* Morgenstêr mission
Mazangera, chief, 94
Mentz, Revd J. F., 149, 198
Merriman, John X., 158
Methodism
   and Calvinism, 179–80
   and Dutch Reformed Church, 177–8
   and liberalism, 175–6, 178–9, 180
   Scottish, 171–3, 197, 198
Midland Seminary, 84
Ministers' Missionary Union (MMU), 16, 85–7, 98–9, 190
missionaries
   American, 81, 84
   attitude to Africans, 16
   conferences, 120
   and difference, 12
   and ecology, 16
   recruitment, 66
   Scots, 8–15
   tradition, 1
   training, 82–5
   World Missionary Conference (Edinburgh, 1910), 174
   see also names of individual missionaries
Moffat, Robert, 14
Morgan, C. S., 29, 55
Morgan, George, 24, 29
Morgenstêr mission, 165–6

Morrees, Revd J. C. Le Febres, 67–8
Mott, John R., 120
Mount Holyoke Seminary (Massachusetts), 82, 85
Mshawashi (wife of king Chiwere), 93
Murray, Andrew Jr
  Afrikaanse Patriot's attacks on, 155–60
  and Boer independence, 44–8
  and Calvinism, 171
  and Christian Endeavour Society, 118, 173, 200
  on church and politics, 169–70
  and colour prejudice, 60
  and ecumenicity, 73, 74
  education of, 36, 37–8
  educational ventures, 47, 71, 82
  and England, 113
  and Holiness movement, 83
  and hybridity, 11, 34–5, 112–13, 154
  and liberalism, 16, 67–72, 181
  and Malan, D. F., 162
  marriage to Emma Rutherfoord, 47
  and Methodism, 183
  as a missionary minister, 41, 42–4, 199
  and missions committee, 57
  and nationalism, 191, 199
  and Nyasaland mission, 86–7
  and predestination, 70
  and prisoners of war, 119
  and revivalist movement, 36–7, 61–2, 63, 64, 65, 66
  and Rutherfoord family, 48
  and Salvation Army, 159
  on Scots' allegiances, 27
  and *Secor Dabar*, 39
  and slavery, 71
  and South African War, 17, 108–9, 111, 112–17, 189–90
  Truth about the Boer and his Church, The, 111–12
Murray, Andrew Sr, 24–5
  and apartheid, 55–6, 60
  and emigrants, 113
  as patriarch, 33–6
  and Stellenbosch Seminary, 54–5
Murray, Andrew Charles
  at Bandawe, 98–100
  and Bible translation, 101, 121
  and church unity, 18
  on Hetherwick, Alexander, 132
  at Kasungu, 136, 139
  leopard attack on, 100, 139
  at Livingstonia conference, 139
  as a missionary minister, 127–8, 132
  and modernism, 142–3
  and Mvera conference, 129–30, 131–2
  and Nyasaland mission, 16, 86, 87, 88–93, 95–6, 137
  and one blood doctrine, 97–8
  Ons Nyasa-Akker, 92
  and protectorate, 135
  and racial prejudice, 89, 141, 193
  and South African War, 129
Murray, Catherine Margaret, 83–4
Murray, Charles, 35, 118
Murray, Emma, 47
Murray, George, 17, 119–20
Murray, Helen 'Ella', 84, 94, 118, 123
Murray, John, 16, 33, 34–5, 183
  and anti-liberalism, 68, 181
  education, 37–8
  as a missionary minister, 39–41
  and revivalist movement, 36–7, 61, 63
  and Stellenbosch Seminary, 47, 54
Murray, John Neethling, 112, 115
Murray, Maria Susanna Magdalena, 33
Murray, Martha, 99
Murray, Mary, 84
Murray, Pauline, 102, 194
Murray, Robert, 128, 190
Murray, William, 35
Murray, William Hoppe
  and Bible translation, 100–3
  and church unity, 18, 135
  and Nyasaland mission, 99, 137, 143–4, 145, 147
  and racial segregation, 140–1, 193
  and South African War, 128
Mvera (Nyasaland), 99, 100, 103
  ecumenical missionary conference (1910), 129–30

Napier, Revd Robert H., 100, 102, 135
National Party, 140, 147, 162
nationalism
  Afrikaners, 4, 18, 74, 144, 145, 150, 154, 156, 157, 164, 168, 172, 190, 191, 198, 199
  Christian, 168, 176, 190, 197
  and racism, 155
Naudé, Beyers, 117, 196–7
Naudé, Jozua, 117
Naudé, S. P., 68

Neethling, J. H.
  on Murray, Andrew Jr, 44
  in Potchefstroom, 43
  and prisoners of war, 119
  and revivalist movement, 61
  and synod (1857), 55, 57
Neethling, Maria: *Unto Children's Children*, 33–5, 84
Nel, Olea, 66, 67
Ngoni people, 92, 95
Nkhoma mission, 135, 136, 141, 142, 143–4, 149, 193, 194, 197, 201
'noble savage' myth, 6
Nyasaland
  Chilembwe rising (1915), 134
  ecclesiastical hybridity, 198
  ecumenicity, 138, 148
  Kasungu controversy, 129
  post-First World War, 145
  segregated eating, 194, 201
  see also Kasungu mission; Kongwe; Livingstonia mission; Livlezi; Nkhoma mission; Tamanda mission

Onderzoeker, De, 182
one blood doctrine, 14, 97–8
Ons Land en Ons Volk (tract), 191
Oorlogsklok, De (pamphlet), 114–15
Orange Free State, 18, 47, 146–7
Orange River Sovereignty (later Orange Free State)
  and independence, 43, 46, 47, 155, 156–7
  and missionaries, 41–2
Ordinance 49, 22n71
Ordinance 50, 22n71, 41–2
organ playing, 28
otherness, 23, 76n18, 97–8, 188, 193; *see also* apartheid

Paarl (formerly Drakenstein)
  conferences (1897), 160
  Gymnasium, 75n4
  see also Drakenstein
Paris Evangelical Mission Society (PEMS), 4, 42
Parsons, Janet Wagner, 88, 99, 101, 102
Patriot, Di (journal), 175
Pauw, Martin, 104n34, 141, 144, 146, 147

Philip, John
  and abolition, 25
  and Boers, 13
  and Murray, Andrew Jr, 48
  and Ordinance 50, 41–2
  radical evangelicalism, 14, 22n71
  Researches in South Africa, 42, 22n71
Phiri, Isabel Apawo, 93
Portuguese: and race, 140
Potchefstroom, 43, 45
Potchefstroom University for Christian Higher Education, 182
Predikanten Zendingvereniging see Ministers' Missionary Union (MMU)
Prentice, Dr, 100
Presbyterians
  and Dutch Reformed Church, 9, 10, 23–5, 72–3
  and liberalism, 144
  and modernism, 142
  Nyasaland, 87
  see also Church of Central Africa Presbyterian (CCAP)
Pretorius, Andries, 44–5
Pretorius, Johan L., 102
Pringle, Thomas, 7
  The Emigrant's Cabin, 5–6
prisoner of war camps, 116–17, 118–19
  Christian Endeavour Society and, 119–21
prisoners of war, 17, 119, 122

race
  and difference, 12
  and violence, 12, 13
race equality, 90; *see also* one blood doctrine
race relations, 138, 140; *see also* apartheid
racial domination, 11
racial prejudice, 133, 195
racial segregation, 28, 140–1, 164–5, 176, 193, 194, 201
  Dutch Reformed Church and, 16, 67–8
  see also apartheid
racism
  Afrikaners and, 145, 146, 199, 201
  Boers and, 58, 132
  Cape Colony, 4
  and democracy, 196

and nationalism, 155
Stellenbosch Seminary, 55
rainmaking, 94–6
rationalist theology, 23
Rees, William, 167
Reformed Congregations under the Cross *see* 'Gereformeerde Gemeentes onder die Kruis'
Reid, Thomas, 25, 27–9
Reitz, F. W., 114
Retief, J. A., 93–4, 122–3
  and Chauwa (rain goddess), 118
  and church unification, 137
  and Fraser, Donald, 130
  and Livingstonia conference, 140–1, 142, 143, 144, 193
  and social mixing, 147–9
Retief, M. W., 62–3, 134, 140–1
Réveil movement, 38, 180, 181, 184n5
revivalism, 15–16, 36–7, 53, 60, 117, 181, 199–200
Rhodes, Cecil John, 189
Rhodesia
  marriage practices, 163–4
  missionaries, 146, 147
Robert, Dana L., 71, 81, 83, 84, 86
Robertson, William, 16, 29–32, 46–7
  and British sovereignty of the Transvaal, 42
  and ecumenicity, 74
  and racial segregation, 59
  and revivalist movement, 62–3, 64
  and Stellenbosch Seminary, 55
Roman Catholicism, 31, 89
Ross, Revd David, 108
Ross, Robert, 4, 52n122
Rothman, M. E., 11
Roux, Revd P. H., 133
Rutherfoord, Howson Edward, 47–8

Saayman, Willem, 76n16
Salvation Army, 159
Sand River Convention (1852), 45
Sass, Frederick William: 'The Influence of the Church of Scotland on the Dutch Reformed Church of South Africa', 23, 24, 26, 56, 58, 59
Schleiermacher, Friedrich, 38
schools, 136, 157, 180
  Sunday schools, 58
Schreiner, Olive, 10–11
Schutte, Gerrit J., 2, 4

Scots
  Afrikaner, 188, 190–4, 197, 198, 200–2
  and Afrikaners, 13
  as Boers, 108
  Cape Colony, 7
  identity, 8, 127, 150
  migration, 7
  as missionaries, 8–15
Scott, Revd, of Blantyre, 90
Secor Dabar (student organisation), 38–9, 54, 57, 61, 180–1, 182
Shand, Revd Robert, 15–16, 29, 55–6, 62
Shand, Samuel, 64
Shepherd, R. H. W., 14
slave trade, 93, 109
slavery
  abolition of, 32, 34, 48, 113
  anti-slavery societies, 48, 52n122
  Boers and, 109, 112
slaves: church membership, 2, 56, 58, 132
Smith, Alexander, 24, 29, 58
Smith, Sir Harry, 41
Smuts, General Jan, 138, 145
Somerset, Lord Charles, 9, 23, 24
South African Evangelical Alliance *see* '*Zuid-Afrikaansch Evangelisch Verbond*'
South African War (Boer War) (1899–1902), 13, 17, 108–23
  Britain and, 110, 111, 113
  concentration camps, 120
  effect on English–Afrikaans relations, 74
  and identity formation, 127
  missionary tensions, 128
  prisoner of war camps, 116–21
  propaganda, 130–1
Spoelstra, B., 29, 40, 42–3, 46–7, 59–60
Stanley, Brian, 90, 155
Stellenbosch, 10
  Dutch Reformed Church, 2, 4, 59
  revivalist movement, 61
  Student Mission Society, 87
Stellenbosch Theological Seminary, 16, 38, 53–5, 72, 83, 158–9
Stellenbosch University, 24
Stephen, John, 87–8
Stewart, James, of Lovedale, 14
  and Boers, 17, 108, 109, 110
  and Kruger administration, 110–11

Stewart, James, of Lovedale (*cont.*)
  and Livingstone, David and Mary, 90
  and mission to Nyasaland, 87
  and Murray, Andrew Jr compared, 127
  and South African War, 110
Steyn, M. T., 165
Stockenstrom, 57–8
Strever, de: voor Christus en de Kerk (journal), 119–20, 121
Strevers / Strewers see Christian Endeavour Society
Strydom, J. G., 146, 147, 148, 162–3, 197
Sunday Times, 34
Sutherland, Henry, 24, 29
Sutherland Fencibles, 24
Swellendam, 11, 46–7

Tamanda mission, 136, 137
Taylor, Antonia Francina, 25, *26*
Taylor, Henry Vicars, 66
Taylor, John, 25–7, *26*
Theal, George, 111–12
Thom, George, 23–4, 33, 36
Thom, Dr H.B., 24
Thomson, William Ritchie, 24, 29, 57
Transvaal Republic
  Murray, Andrew Jr in, 43, 199
  resistance to British, 189
  slavery, 112
  South African War, 114

Uitlanders (foreigners), 114
  Uitlander 'franchise', 113
Universities' Mission (Likoma island), 139–40
Universities' Mission to Central Africa (UMCA), 90–1
Utrecht University, 37

van Arckel, Ds Joannes, 2
van der Hoff, Revd Dirk, 45
van der Lingen, G. W. A., 53–4, 55, 60, 61, 157

van der Walt, I. J., 76n15
van der Watt, P. B., 37, 38, 40–1
Vereeniging, De (newspaper), 117, 127
Vlok, Bessie, 99–100
Vlok, T. C. B., 86, 91, 92, 95–6, 99
Volksblad, Het, 66
volkskerk (people's church), 18, 167–8
Voortrekkers, 15, 26, 29, 43
Vorster, J. D. (Koot), 174, 176–9
Vos, Revd M. C., 25
Vrouesendingbond (Women's Missionary Union), 84–5

Waite, C. E., 83
Wellington
  Huguenot Seminary, 82–5
  Missionary Institute, 147
Welsh, Alexander, 29
Wesley, John, 182
Wishart, Luther, 130
women
  concentration camps, 120
  education, 29, 71, 75, 159
  emancipation from slavery, 52n122
  missionary impetus, 81, 83–5, 86, 93–4, 99–100, 121
  othering of, 193–4
Women's Missionary Union *see Vrouesendingbond*
Woodberry, Robert, 195–6

Young South Africa (later *Afrikaner Broederbond*), 171; *see also* Afrikaner Broederbond

Zoeklicht, Het (journal), 175, 179
Zondagh, Miss (missionary teacher), 121
Zuid-Afrikaan, De, 7, 9–10, 26–7
'*Zuid-Afrikaansch Evangelisch Verbond*' (South African Evangelical Alliance), 178
Zuid-Afrikaansche Republiek *see* Transvaal Republic

EU representative:
Easy Access System Europe
Mustamäe tee 50, 10621 Tallinn, Estonia
Gpsr.requests@easproject.com

www.ingramcontent.com/pod-product-compliance
Lightning Source LLC
Chambersburg PA
CBHW070350240426
43671CB00013BA/2457